Accelerated
NetWare 5 CNA
Study Guide

Dorothy Cady

McGraw-Hill
New York • San Francisco • Washington, D.C. • Auckland • Bogotá
Caracas • Lisbon • London • Madrid • Mexico City • Milan • Montreal
New Delhi • San Juan • Singapore • Sydney • Tokyo • Toronto

McGraw-Hill

A Division of The *McGraw·Hill* Companies

The views expressed in this book are solely those of the author, and do not represent the views of any other party or parties.

2 3 4 5 6 7 8 9 0   AGM/AGM   9 0 3 2 1 0 9

ISBN 0-07-134532-9

The sponsoring editor for this book was Judy Brief and the production supervisor was Clare Stanley. It was set in Dante by Patricia Wallenburg.

Printed and bound by Quebecor/Martinsburg.

McGraw-Hill books are available at special quantity discounts to use as premiums and sales promotions, or for use in corporate training programs. For more information, please write to the Director of Special Sales, McGraw-Hill, 11 West 19th Street, New York, NY 10011. Or contact your local bookstore.

 This book is printed on recycled, acid-free paper containing a minimum of 50% recycled, de-inked fiber.

Acknowledgments

Many people contribute to the creation of a book, from those who inspired it to those who made sure every aspect of its layout and printing as well as its distribution was successfully completed. For the latter, McGraw-Hill's staff gets the credit. For the former, Judy Brief at McGraw-Hill gets the credit. As for everything in between, well, my family (Raymond, Shana, and Ray) gets credit for their patience and understanding, and my friend Nancy Cadjan gets the credit for ensuring I didn't stray too far from the intent of the book, or leave out anything of importance.

To each of these people, as well as to all of those who helped me to finish this book on time, I give my thanks and appreciation.

Contents

Introduction   **xi**

  Who Should Read This Book   xii
  What This Book Covers   xii
  What This Book Does Not Cover   xv
  For More Information   xv

**1 Understanding NetWare 5 Networks
   and Their Components**   **1**

  Understanding the Function of a Network   2
    NetWare 5's NOS   3
    NetWare 5 Network Resources and Services 3
  Working with a Network's Hardware Components   4
  Taking Advantage of a Network's Software Components 6
    The Novell Client   6
    The Workstation's Operating System   7
    Communications Protocols   8
    How the Client and Server Communicate   8
  Understanding a Network Administrator's
    Responsibilities and Tasks   12
    Designing and Setting Up the Network   12
    Managing the Network   12
    Protecting and Backing Up the Network   13
    Documenting the Network   13
  Understanding NetWare's Basic Resources and Services 14
    NDS   15
    File Management   15
    Printing (NDPS)   17
    Application Access   17
    Security   17
    Storage Management Services   17
  Learning About NetWare 5 and What's New in It   18
  Chapter Summary   21
  Practice Test Questions   23
    Answers to Practice Test Questions   27

**2   Understanding NetWare Directory Services
and the Directory Tree**   **29**

Learning About NDS and the Directory Tree   29
Understanding NDS Objects   30
    The Directory's Structure   30
    The Role and Benefits of NDS   32
Understanding NDS Objects   32
    The [Root] Object   33
    Container Objects   33
    Leaf Objects   34
Understanding NDS Properties and Values   37
Managing NDS Trees, Objects, and Properties   37
Chapter Summary   40
Practice Test Questions   41
    Answers to Practice Questions   43

3   Setting Up a NetWare 5 Network   **45**

Installing NetWare 5   46
    A Brief Overview of NetWare 5   46
    NetWare 5 Components   47
    Prerequisites to Installing NetWare 5   50
    Install NetWare 5   52
Designing and Organizing Network Resources   58
    Effects of the NDS Tree's Design on the Network   59
    Accessing Objects Regardless of their Location   64
    Setting Up Shortcuts to Resources   64
    Guidelines for Designing and Organizing
        Resources on the Network   66
Setting Up User Accounts   68
    Function of the User Object   69
    Using NetWare Administrator to Create User Objects   69
    Using UIMPORT to Create User Objects   70
Controlling Access to Network Resources   71
Chapter Summary   72
Practice Test Questions   74
    Answers to Practice Test Questions   79

4   Establishing Security on a NetWare 5 Network   **81**

Understanding File System Security   82
    Function of the File System   82
    Components of the File System   83

Understanding NDS Security   84
Understanding Rights   85
   NDS Rights   85
   File System Rights   88
Implementing NDS Security   93
Managing Network Security   95
   Login Security   96
   Server Security   100
   Network Printing Security   100
Chapter Summary   101
Practice Review Questions   104
   Answers to Practice Review Questions   107

5 Making Print Services Available   109

Understanding NDPS   109
NDPS Manager   112
   Printer Agents   113
   Gateways   114
   NDPS Broker   115
Setting Up Print Services   116
   Meeting Minimum Requirements   117
   Installing the NDPS Software   117
   Creating and Running the NDPS Manager   118
   Creating Printer Agent and Printer Objects   119
Managing Network Printing   123
   Convert a Public Access Printer to a
      Controlled Access Printer   123
   Set Up Printer Access for Client Workstations   124
   Manage Printer Access and Print Jobs   124
Chapter Summary   127
Practice Test Questions   131
   Answers to Practice Test Questions   134

**6 Setting Up and Customizing Network
     Access for Users   135**

Installing the Novell Client   135
Managing NetWare User Licenses   137
   Assign Objects to License Certificates   139
Install Additional Licenses   140
Understanding the Login Process   141
Understanding Login Scripts   142

Creating and Modifying Login Scripts | 143
Exploring the Network | 147
    Taking Advantage of Windows to Explore the Network | 148
    Using Browsers to Explore the Network | 148
Chapter Summary | 149
Practice Test Questions | 152
    Answers to Practice Test Questions | 154

7 Using Application Launcher   155

Learning About Application Launcher | 156
    How to Set Up Application Launcher on Your Network | 158
    How to Use SnAppShot to Capture a
      Workstation's Pre-Installation Configuration | 159
Creating and Working with Application Objects | 163
    How to Create an Application Object in the NDS Tree | 164
    Associating the Application Object with Other Objects | 166
Distributing and Managing Network Applications | 169
    Specifying Where the Icon Displays | 170
    Distributing the Application Launcher | 171
Chapter Summary | 173
Practice Test Questions | 175
    Answers to Practice Test Questions | 178

8 Using Other Z.E.N.works Features   179

Understanding Z.E.N.works | 182
    Minimum Requirements for Using Z.E.N.works | 182
    Setting Up Policy Packages in Z.E.N.works | 183
    NDS Issues and Z.E.N.works | 183
    Registering and Importing Workstations | 185
    Understanding What You Can Do with Policies | 185
    Understanding Remote Control | 186
    Understanding the Help Requester | 187
Managing Network Workstations Using
  Policy Packages and Policies | 188
    Create Policy Package Objects and Enable Policies | 188
    Associating Objects with Policy Packages | 192
Customizing the User's Desktop and Printing Environments | 193
    Configure the User's Desktop Environment
      by Configuring Control Panel Options | 193
    Establish Printing Policies for Users | 195
Chapter Summary | 195

Practice Test Questions   196
    Answers to Practice Test Questions   199

9   Taking Full Advantage of Z.E.N.works   201

Making NDS Aware of Network Workstations   202
    Create a User Policy Package   202
    Enable, Modify, and Associate a Workstation
        Import Policy   203
    Register and Import Workstations   204
    View Information Associated with Each
        Workstation Object   207
Setting Up and Using Remote Control   208
    Setting Up Remote Control   209
    Establish a Remote Control Connection
        to the Workstation   212
    Ending a Remote Control Session   214
Setting Up and Using the Help Requester   214
    Load Help Requester on the User's Workstation   214
    Make Sure Users Have Sufficient Rights
        to Run Help Requester   215
    Meet Minimum Software Requirements for
        Running Help Requester   215
    Enable and Configure a Help Desk Policy   215
    Distribute the Help Desk Application to Workstations   217
    Use the Help Requester   217
Chapter Summary   218
Practice Test Questions   219
    Answers to Practice Test Questions   221

10 Administering a NetWare 5 Network   223

Configuring NetWare Administrator   223
    Change the Appearance of the Toolbar and Status Bar   224
    Filter How Objects Are Displayed   225
    View and Change Object Information   226
Using NetWare Administrator to Perform Basic Tasks   227
    Enhancements to NetWare Administrator   229
Maintaining the Network's File System   229
    Manage the File System with the Filer Utility   230
    Manage the File System with the NetWare
        Administrator Utility   231
    Manage the File System Using Windows   236

Distributing the Workload with Role-based Administration   237
   Allow a Container's Object and Property
      Rights to Be Inherited   237
   Create and Implement Organizational Role Objects   238
Chapter Summary   242
Practice Test Questions   244
   Answers to Practice Test Questions   246

Index   **247**

Introduction

In today's fast-paced, highly-competitive world of technology, you must either keep up or be passed by. That is just as true for individuals as it is for companies. That is why companies readily upgrade their software to the latest release, and why individuals such as yourself also must upgrade your knowledge to include that information as soon as possible.

Because technologies today, especially networking technologies, are so complex, companies cannot afford to turn over their information systems, including networks, to just anyone. Companies need some assurance that the individual who is managing their network is qualified to do so. For companies running Novell NetWare-based networks and the employees who keep the networks running, that assurance is a Novell certification.

Novell offers several certifications, but the *CNA* (Certified Novell Administrator) and *CNE* (Certified Novell Engineer) are the two most widely-held certifications. As of April 1, 1998, Novell reports that there are 135,000 people currently holding a CNE, and a total of 600,000 people working towards a Novell certification of one type or another.

If you are one of those who presently holds a Novell certification, it is likely that your certification is either a NetWare 3.x or NetWare 4.x certification. With Novell's release of NetWare 5, it may be necessary to upgrade that certification. If you have limited time with which to obtain that knowledge and certification, then this book is for you.

If you presently do not hold a Novell NetWare certification, but want to get into the field and be ready for network administration tasks on a Novell NetWare 5 network as quickly as possible, then this book is also for you.

It is the goal of this book to help you learn the basics about NetWare 5. Its contents cover that information which you must know in order to pass the official Novell authorized NetWare 5 Certified Novell Administrator (CNA) test, number 050-413. This book covers the same basic information that you would learn if you took Novell's authorized NetWare 5 Administration course. Unlike the course, which costs several hundred dollars more than this book, however, this book's goal is to help you prepare yourself as quickly, easily, and inexpensively as possible. This book is also designed to help you reach your goal of becoming a NetWare 5 CNA in as short a period of time as possible. And, if you are interested in obtaining the NetWare 5 CNE (Certified Novell Engineer) certification, this book's companion, the *Accelerated NetWare 5 CNE Study Guide*, in combination with this *Accelerated NetWare 5 CNA Study Guide*, will help make it possible for you to reach that goal in a relatively short period of time, using the bits and pieces and snatches of time that a busy professional such as yourself has available.

Who Should Read This Book

As a busy professional in a highly-competitive environment, or as an individual just starting out in the Novell NetWare world, the ability to learn about NetWare 5 and become certified in a short period of time can be crucial to maintaining your current job as well as to obtaining a new one. The average development time for a new software product is only two to three years. That means that as a NetWare 5 CNA/CNE candidate, you cannot afford to wait to obtain your certification. You must get it as soon after the release of NetWare 5 as possible, in order to avoid the fate of obsolescence.

To learn the needed information and pass the required tests for certification, you may find it necessary to study whenever snatches of time are available. That means that you need learning tools which are portable, small, and to the point. Thus, this *Accelerated NetWare 5 CNA Study Guide* was designed to meet those requirements.

What This Book Covers

This book covers the information you need to know to pass the NetWare 5 CNA test in ten chapters. Each chapter concentrates on an area of

NetWare 5 such as print services, or on a major task such as setting up a NetWare 5 network.

Chapter 1: *Understanding NetWare 5 Networks and Their Components* provides an overview of what a NetWare 5 network is, including the components that make up a NetWare 5 network. For example, it discusses such topics as the function of a network, a network's hardware and software components, a network administrator's responsibilities, and the basic resources and services of a network in general, and of a NetWare 5 network specifically.

Chapter 2: *Understanding NDS and the Directory Tree* discusses NDS, the heart of NetWare 5. It provides information about objects which are part of the directory tree, the properties and values associated with objects, and how to manage the directory tree as well as its objects and properties. You will need to know this in order to plan your directory tree. However, training and experience in planning your directory tree is not a requirement for the CNA certification, and is not covered in the Novell authorized NetWare 5 Administration course. It is also not covered in this book.

Chapter 3: *Setting up a NetWare 5 Network* delves into the process of installing a NetWare 5 network. It also gives you information on how to design and organize resources on your network, and particularly concentrates on setting up user accounts. It also discusses how to control access to network resources.

Chapter 4: *Establishing Security on a NetWare 5 Network* concentrates on the issue of network security. In a NetWare 5 network, the administrator needs to be concerned not only with securing physical access to network servers, but also with securing NDS and the network's file system. This chapter identifies the difference between NDS and file system security, helping you to understand such things as how to implement NDS and file system security, and how to manage network security.

Chapter 5: *Making Print Services Available* shows you how to ensure your users can access and print to printers on the network. It explains how to set print services in NDS, as well as how to manage network printing.

Chapter 6: *Setting Up and Customizing Network Access for Users* gets into the details of installing the Novell Client on computers so that users can access the network, discusses how to manage user licenses, and provides an overview of how the login process works. It also discusses relevant information such as login scripts and how to create and modify them, as well as how to explore and browse the network from a workstation.

Chapter 7: *Using Application Launcher* explains what Application Launcher is and how it is of benefit to you, your users, and your network. It also explains how to create and work with the Application objects which are so integral to taking advantage of Application Launcher. In addition, it explains how to distribute and manage network applications using the features of Application Launcher.

Chapter 8: *Using Other Z.E.N.works Features* explains how you can take advantage of Z.E.N.works' other features (besides Application Launcher) to manage network workstations, and customize the environment for network users. In addition, it explains how to use remote control to remotely access workstations, and how to set up the Help Requester, a feature which lets users report problems directly to you through the network.

Chapter 9: *Taking Full Advantage of Z.E.N.works* discusses how to create user policy packages and how to make the best use of the workstation import, remote control, and help requester features of Z.E.N.works.

Chapter 10: *Administering a NetWare 5 Network* covers a few other basic things a NetWare 5 network administrator needs to know such as how to configure the NetWare Administrator utility and use it to perform basic network administration tasks. It also discusses how to maintain the network's file system and how to distribute some of your administration workload to others using role-based administration.

Each chapter in this book contains a Practice Test Questions section. Going through these questions is designed to help further your knowledge of NetWare 5. In addition, the questions are designed to help you become comfortable with answering test questions so that you will be more relaxed and thus do better on the actual certification test than you might otherwise have done.

Novell's certification tests are presented in electronic format at a certified testing center. Each question is chosen from a database of test questions which have themselves been tested for validity and in many instances, for level of difficulty. Although most test questions are multiple-choice, more than one correct answer may be possible. Where more than one correct answer is possible, you are told to choose more than one answer.

For example, a test question may include instructions which tell you to choose the two best answers. In this case, you must provide the two correct choices, or you will not receive any credit for answering the question. (Sorry, but the test is not designed to give you partial credit if you get part of the answer right.)

To help ensure you are properly prepared for answering questions on the Novell certification exam, the practice test questions follow a format most like that of official certification test questions that Novell commonly uses. However, these test questions are for practice purposes only, and in no way should be construed as being the actual test questions contained within the Novell authorized database of test questions for the NetWare 5 CNA or CNE certification exams.

To ensure you understand which concept each of the sample test questions were designed for, the correct answers for the practice test follows the practice test questions. Use the answers to help you see what concept or detail you may need to study further.

What This Book Does Not Cover

This book concentrates on teaching you the basics of Novell's NetWare 5 network operating system and accompanying utilities and features. It assumes that you have a basic understanding of computers, as well as a basic understanding of and some experience with operating systems such as DOS, Windows 95, and Windows NT. Thus, it does not cover hardware or software associated with computers, except where that information is relevant to using a computer as a network workstation or file server.

This book also assumes that you have at least some limited knowledge of or experience with computer networks. If not, you should at least pick up and read an introductory book on networks and networking technologies to accompany this *Accelerated NetWare 5 CNA Study Guide.*

For More Information

Although this book is designed to help you pass the Novell NetWare 5 CNA test without additional assistance, you may find that there are certain aspects of NetWare 5 about which you would like more information. As previously noted, you may also want to pick up and read McGraw-Hill's *Accelerated NetWare 5 CNE Study Guide,* also by this author (particularly if you want to get your CNE, not just your CNA). Along with this *Accelerated NetWare 5 CNA Study Guide,* this author's *Accelerated NetWare 5 CNE Study Guide* will help prepare you to take the NetWare 5 Advanced Administration test which you must take and pass if you want to become a NetWare 5 CNE.

If you want to get your CNE or just learn more about networking technologies and NetWare, you may also want to pick up one of McGraw-Hill's other excellent books such as *The CNA/CNE Study Guide IntranetWare Edition* by Mueller and Williams. The Mueller and Williams book covers NetWare 4 rather than NetWare 5, but is an excellent reference for learning about those features of NetWare 5 which existed in NetWare 4. In addition, it covers the information contained in several of the other courses whose certification exams you must pass in order to obtain your CNE. The Mueller and Williams book contains 900 pages of information. It is designed to aid new CNE candidates with obtaining their certification, so it provides information the candidate needs in order to pass other certification tests required of a new CNE candidate. (Unfortunately, just passing the NetWare 5 Administration and NetWare 5 Advanced Administration tests is not all you need to do to get a CNE.) Thus, for the individual who is just beginning their CNE program, this Mueller and Williams book also will be a valuable resource.

While the Mueller and Williams book is based on Novell's NetWare 4 operating system software, many of the concepts and basic features of NetWare 4 (such as NDS, security, and so on) are the same for NetWare 5.

Once you have access to a NetWare 5 network, you can also take a look at Novell's online documentation for more information about NetWare 5. Their online documentation is presented in HTML format and shipped with the Netscape browser for viewing. While you can read it using almost any Internet browser software, the included Netscape browser software has a powerful search engine and printing capabilities not available with other browsers.

No inexperienced individual can become a NetWare network administrator overnight. But if you have experience with a previous version of NetWare, particularly NetWare 4, or you've been working in the field for some time, you will find that this *Accelerated NetWare 5 CNA Study Guide* will help you to learn what you need to know as quickly as possible in order to pass Novell's authorized CNA certification test, and to obtain your NetWare 5 CNA certification. It's designed to let you learn in short snatches of time, and to let you test your knowledge using the Practice Test Questions section provided in each chapter. So take this book with you wherever you go so that you can make the best possible use of your time.

Good luck, and welcome to the *Accelerated NetWare 5 CNA Study Guide*.

CHAPTER 1

Understanding NetWare 5 Networks and Their Components

I f you are new to networking, the first three sections of this chapter give you a brief overview of networking. Their purpose is to help you understand what a network is by explaining:

- the function of a network
- the network's hardware components
- the network's software components

If you are already familiar with networks, you can briefly skim the first three sections, and concentrate on the three remaining sections which discuss:

- a network administrator's responsibilities and tasks
- NetWare's basic resources and services
- NetWare 5 and what's new in it

Once you have covered these sections, answer the questions in the Practice Test Questions section. Remember, whether or not you are familiar with networking, the sections in this and other chapters contain information for potential NetWare 5 Administration test questions, so you will still want to know the data they contain. Answering the practice test questions is a good indicator of how well you know the material contained in each chapter.

Understanding the Function of a Network

The Glossary in Novell's NetWare 5 online (HTML) documentation set defines a network as "a system of interconnected, individually controlled computers and peripherals, and the hardware and software used to connect them." Thus, a network is a combination of hardware (equipment) and software (programs) which allow individuals (network users) to share various resources such as application programs, data files, and printers.

KEY CONCEPT

The most common type of network is the client/server network in which one or more computers function as the host or server, and other computers function as clients. NetWare 5 is a client/server network.

A *server* is any sufficiently powerful computer with appropriate server operating system software running on it which provides clients with the services and resources they request. A *client* is any device which requests services or resources from the server. Servers provide access for users via *workstations* (a computer functioning as a network client) to the network services or resources they need. Workstations are connected to and communicate with servers on the network using network cables and network boards.

KEY CONCEPT

Examples of network clients include:

- computer systems (workstations) used to access the network
- peripheral devices such as printers and modems
- software such as word processing applications

Novell's NetWare 5 network operating system (NOS) software is the software that turns a powerful computer into a NetWare file server. While a sufficiently powerful computer is needed to run the NetWare 5 NOS, NetWare 5's client software allows companies to use other various and potentially less-powerful types of computer equipment running most types of workstation operating systems (Windows 95, Windows NT, DOS, etc.) as network clients. A variety of computers running different operating systems can be used on a NetWare 5 network, because Novell's client software is designed around a specific set of guidelines referred to as open systems architecture (OSA). The following operating systems are supported by Novell's client software on your NetWare 5 network:

- Windows 95

- Windows NT
- Windows 3.1x
- DOS
- Macintosh
- UNIX

NetWare 5's NOS

NetWare 5's networking operating system (NOS) software, along with its client software and various networking hardware, is what makes it possible to create small, medium, or large networks. The NOS and client software are also what make it possible for these networks to communicate with each other, with other networks around the world, and with the Internet.

NetWare 5's NOS accomplishes all of this because it has a strong *kernel* (core or heart of the NOS) which can run on servers with only a single microprocessor, as well as on servers with multiple microprocessors. The kernel is that part of the network operating system that provides basic networking services such as scheduling processor time and handling input/output (I/O) interrupts.

The NetWare 5 kernel's ability to accomplish these tasks makes it possible for the NetWare 5 NOS to provide many networking services, and grant access for users to various network resources.

NetWare 5 Network Resources and Services

The network provides both resources and services to clients (any device such as a printer or a user on a workstation which requests services or resources from the network).

KEY CONCEPT

A *resource* is anything you may need to use that is provided through the network. For example, a printer is a network resource, as is a file server's hard disk (although the actual resource is the volume on the hard disk which contains the data or programs that you may need). Communication devices such as network modems are also resources. A *service* is the method or approach the NOS follows in order to provide network resources when needed.

NetWare 5 provides several basic network services including:

- NDS (NetWare Directory Services)
- File system

- Printing (through NDPS—Novell Distributed Print Services)
- Access to applications
- NDS and file system security
- SMS (Storage Management Services)

Internet access can also be considered a network service. NetWare 5 supports Internet access because in addition to its support of various networking protocols (set of rules which define how networks communicate) such as IPX, SPX, and IP, NetWare 5 supports TCP/IP—the core protocol of the Internet, as well as of many heterogeneous networks and intranets. NetWare 5 also supports Java, a programming language developed by Sun Microsystems, Inc., in an ongoing effort to make Java the language of the Internet.

KEY CONCEPT

The function of a network is to ensure that all clients have access to and the ability to share the resources and services available on the network. In NetWare 5, that access is provided through NDS (discussed in Chapter 2).

Working with a Network's Hardware Components

A network's primary hardware components consist of at least one computer with the network operating system software loaded on it—the server, and at least one computer functioning as a workstation. A workstation is a computer such as a PC that contains the other necessary pieces of hardware which allow it to access the services provided by the network.

Both the server and the workstations must have a network board in them. A *network board* is an electronic circuit board which acts as the interface between the software running on the computer and the hardware. Its function is to ensure that communication between servers and clients can be successfully completed. The network board's primary function is that of ensuring the workstation has a means or path by which it can communicate successfully with the rest of the network. Success depends on data not being lost or corrupted during transit. Thus, the network board is also responsible for verifying the quality of data it sends and receives.

Network boards (also referred to as NICs, Network Interface Cards, boards, or cards in hardware manufacturer's and other documentation) must be connected to each other in order to communicate. Most communications media is physical—using a network cable—but it does not necessarily have to be. For example, some networks are connected by radio waves.

Physical connections consist of some type of connector, depending on the type of board and cabling system used, and the actual cabling, of which the two most common types are co-axial (similar to that used for your cable TV) and twisted-pair (similar to that used for your telephone).

Beyond two computers and two network boards connected by a cabling system or other type of communications media, additional hardware is not needed to define a network. Additional hardware is often included, however. Figure 1-1 shows some of the hardware that is found on a network.

Other hardware which can be added to the network includes printers, modems, and additional computers acting either as servers or clients. Just about any piece of hardware you can connect to the network can be a network client. That event includes such hardware as a Jet Direct box (Jet Direct box allows you to connect a printer directly to the network cabling system instead of to a workstation or server).

Once all the pieces are connected, these devices make up the hardware components of a network. The hardware is mostly useless for networking, however, if no software exists to control and ensure communication between as well as within devices.

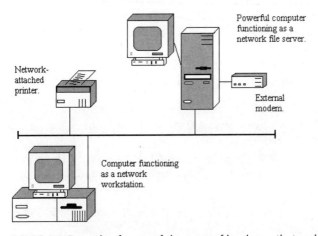

Powerful computer functioning as a network file server.

Network-attached printer.

External modem.

Computer functioning as a network workstation.

FIGURE 1-1 Example of some of the types of hardware that make up a network. While the network board and communications media along with at least one server and one workstation are mandatory to create a network, other hardware is optional.

Taking Advantage of a Network's Software Components

KEY CONCEPT

There are two basic elements of networking software. One has already been mentioned and described: the server or network operating system (NOS). Its primary task is resource management. Just as it is the responsibility of a PC's operating system in a stand-alone computer to manage the resources of that computer, it is the NOS' job to manage the resources related to the network.

The NOS is the heart and soul of a network. Without it, resource sharing, even simple communication with clients and other servers across the network would not be possible.

The second basic element of networking software is the Novell Client software. Every computer that is to access the network requires some type of networking client software. The Novell Client software that ships with NetWare 5 provides this for computers using DOS, Windows 3.1x, Windows 95, or Windows NT as their operating system.

The Novell Client

The network-related software on computers that is vital to networking is the network client software. In Novell's networking products, this is commonly referred to as the *Novell Client*. The Novell Client consists of software which makes it possible for the workstation to access the network and to communicate with it.

The Novell Client software has three primary responsibilities. First, like the workstation's operating system software, the Novell Client:

- helps ensure that only authorized users access the network
- manages the flow of data to and from the workstation, ensuring it is in the proper format
- enables the user through the workstation to have access to network services, such as printers, file storage and retrieval, and shared applications.

Once the Novell Client is installed, and if you are using a workstation running Microsoft Windows 95, Windows NT, or Windows 3.1x, you can then access the network using the GUI (Graphical User Interface) login window. The Windows 95 GUI login window is shown in Figure 1-2.

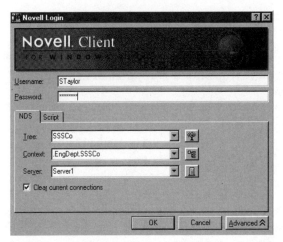

FIGURE 1-2 The login window you see when you run the Windows 95 GUI login with the Novell Client installed.

The NOS and the Novell Client are the two basic elements of a network. However, there are other software components: the workstation's operating system software, and applications such as WordPerfect, which users access to accomplish various job-related tasks.

The Workstation's Operating System

The workstation's operating system (OS) can be one of several different types, but NetWare 5 ships with support for DOS and Microsoft's Windows 3.1x, Windows 95, and NT workstation operating system software. In addition, Windows 98 support is included. The workstation's OS is responsible for:

- ensuring that the user has access to files stored either on the workstation's hard disk or on the network
- displaying the data contained in the files stored on the hard disk as well as on the network (a responsibility shared with the Novell Client)
- printing documents to local (attached to the workstation) printers or to network printers
- processing the format of the data sent between the workstation and the network

Since the client/server network is designed to allow processing to take place at each network workstation rather than only on the server, the workstation's operating system is an important part of the network's software. In addition to allowing for processing at the workstation, the workstation software must also take responsibility for:

- preparing the content of requests being sent from as well as received by the workstation
- allowing access to the network by only those users who are authorized to access the network
- formatting the data to be transmitted on the network in a form all network devices can understand
- controlling a workstation's data flow between application software and workstation users

The NOS and the Novell Client software communicate with each other to provide the network services and resources that the user needs. For communication to occur, however, both the server and the client must be using the same language, just as you and I must speak the same language (English, French, etc.) if we are to successfully understand each other.

Thus, to fully understand the network's software components and how they communicate, you must also understand what communications protocols are, and how the client and server communicate.

Communications Protocols

A communications protocol is a set of rules by which computers and related hardware successfully communicate between two points. There are several different communications protocols, some common ones of which include Transmission Control Protocol/Internet Protocol (TCP/IP), Internetwork Packet Exchange (IPX), and Internet Protocol (IP).

A protocol defines not only the format the network follows in order to transmit between two points, but also the timing of the data transmitted, and the order or sequence in which it is transmitted.

How the Client and Server Communicate

Using a workstation, a network user can communicate with a NetWare file server on the network. The communication process can be described in simple terms, although it sometimes takes a rather complex process to actually succeed at network communications. The communication process involves three primary tasks:

- establishing a connection
- processing the request

- sending and receiving network data

A workstation sends a request for services or data to a NetWare file server through the software and hardware by which it connects to the network. To send a request, the workstation creates the information or request that it wants to send, addresses that information or request, and then sends it out across the network.

A workstation also listens to the network to see if anything on the network is addressed to it, much like you might listen for your telephone to ring as an indication that someone wants to talk to you (or more likely, to your teenage child). You may hear other telephones ringing in your neighborhood, but you don't try to answer them because you know they are not intended for you or for members of your household.

The workstation's and file server's hardware (network cable and network board), along with the software they are running (the Novell Client, the workstation operating system, and the network operating system) ensure that network communication takes place. For example, in order to speak with you on the telephone, I must have the hardware (the phone connected to the cable system), and I must have the software (your telephone number and the telephone company's computer and switching systems which see to it that my call is routed to your telephone when I dial your phone number).

Once you answer the telephone, we know how to communicate with each other because we both know the rules of the language we speak. The hardware and software in a workstation must also communicate, and they do so by following a set of software-implemented rules developed to ensure communication. Those rules are defined not by a long list of dos and dont's like our own written and spoken language, but through something called the communications model. To best understand how hardware/software communication takes place, you need to understand the communications model.

The communications model contains several component layers. The lowest layer of the model encompasses the workstation's hardware components, including the network board and cabling. The middle layer encompasses software components, such as the Novell Client and the workstation's operating system (Windows 95, Windows NT, DOS, etc.), which are responsible for processing network data to ensure the data is both usable and secure. The top layer of this model encompasses applications such as WordPerfect and GroupWise, which are run on the workstation. Figure 1-3 shows this model.

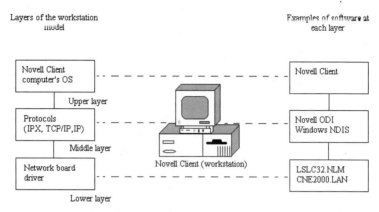

FIGURE 1-3 Diagram of the communications model showing the software responsible for successfully connecting the workstation to the network.

For communication to take place, several steps must occur. A physical connection must be made, and the software (driver) for the network board must accept the incoming data from the network and send it to the OS and Novell Client software, where it is processed and then sent to the appropriate software program for which it was intended.

For example, if you run your word processing software and request a copy of a particular word processing file from the network, that file is sent to your workstation. The network cabling system transmits that word processing file to the network board installed in your workstation, which in turn sends it to the operating system software and Novell Client software. The word processing file is then forwarded to the application from which you requested the file. The word processing program receives the file and then opens it for you to view, as requested.

When you send data out from your workstation, the reverse of this process is performed. For example, if you make changes to the word processing file, then tell the application to save the revised version to the file on the network of the same name and path, the application program hands the file to the Novell Client and workstation operating system software, which in turn hands it to the network board driver software. The network board driver software then causes the network board to transmit that saved file out across the network cabling to its final destination.

In Figure 1-4, you can see the general process involved in transmitting data or a file across the network. The numbered steps (1 through 5) show the process involved when a user requests a data file from a NetWare file server. The alphabetical steps (A through E) show the process involved when the user sends a changed data file back to the file server to be stored.

Ensuring that the network is set up and running properly—so that communication can take place and the user can get the resources and services that are needed—is part of the job a network administrator performs. There are several responsibilities and tasks associated with ensuring that the network is set up and running properly.

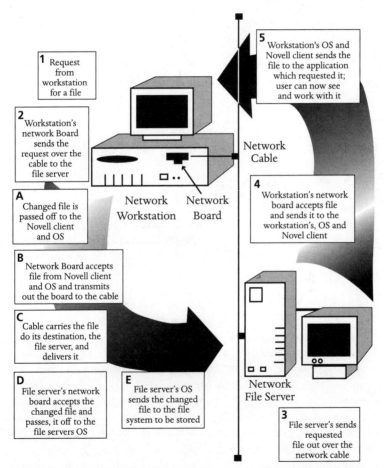

1 Request from workstation for a file

2 Workstation's network Board sends the request over the cable to the file server

A Changed file is passed off to the Novell client and OS

B Network Board accepts file from Novell client and OS and transmits out the board to the cable

C Cable carries the file do its destination, the file server, and delivers it

D File server's network board accepts the changed file and passes, it off to the file servers OS

E File server's OS sends the changed file to the file system to be stored

5 Workstation's OS and Novell client sends the file to the application which requested it; user can now see and work with it

Network Cable

4 Workstation's network board accepts file and sends it to the workstation's, OS and Novel client

Network Workstation   Network Board

Network File Server

3 File server's sends requested file out over the network cable

FIGURE 1-4 How communication between a workstation and the network occurs.

Understanding a Network Administrator's Responsibilities and Tasks

The network administrator has two primary responsibilities: setting up network services, and organizing and configuring network resources. Within those two responsibilities are several tasks that can be broken down into four categories:

- designing and setting up the network
- managing the network
- protecting and backing up the network
- documenting the network

Designing and Setting Up the Network

Designing and setting up the network primarily involves:

- setting up servers, workstations, and related networking hardware
- ensuring users have access to shared and personal directories on the network for storing their data
- ensuring workstations automatically connect to the network to make a user's access to the network as easy as possible

Designing the network can also includes such tasks as determining how the tree should be structured before you begin creating objects in that tree. Setting up the network includes such tasks as installing the client software on each user's workstation. If you wanted to build a house, for example, you would first need to at least sketch out a rough picture of what the house should look like, both from the inside (floor plan) and the outside (elevations). You wouldn't simply cut down a few trees and start nailing them together. Just as designing a house before starting construction is important to being a successful house builder, so too is designing the network before setting it up if you are to be a successful network administrator.

Once you have designed your network, you must set it up just as a builder must build the house once it has been designed. The builder must concentrate on tasks associated with building the house, while the network administrator must concentrate on tasks associated with setting up the network.

Managing the Network

Managing the network has two primary tasks associated with it: managing and maintaining both network security and printing.

Managing the network can also include such tasks as ensuring that users have sufficient network storage space on which to save their files, and can access all of the applications they need to and should have access to.

If you are a doctor with several patients to care for, you would have to successfully manage their appointments to see you, the medications they are taking, any surgery or hospital stays that are necessary, and so on in order to be successful at treating and caring for that patient. As a network administrator, you need to manage the network to ensure that it runs smoothly, is always available when needed, gives each user what they want and need without giving them what they are not authorized to have, and so on.

Protecting and Backing Up the Network

Protecting and backing up the network means that you are responsible for:

- ensuring that network data integrity is maintained
- protecting network data from both deliberate and inadvertent damage
- developing and implementing a method for regularly backing up data, and for restoring it if needed

This responsibility can include such tasks as determining what hardware and software you will use to make copies of the important data and configuration of your network, how often backups will be done, where you can physically locate the file servers to protect them from unauthorized access, and so on.

You perform various protection and backup functions in your daily life, even if you don't necessarily recognize them as such. For example, you protect your car from theft by always locking the doors when you leave it, never leaving the windows down so far that someone could reach in and open the door, never leaving the keys in the car, and looking for lighted or well-traveled areas in which to park your car. You may even backup your transportation alternatives by buying a second car or getting a bus pass. Providing for protection and backup of yourself, your family, and your possessions is part of living, just as providing protection and backup for the network is part of being a network administrator.

Documenting the Network

Documenting the network means that somehow you keep information about the directory tree (its design and content), what rights and accesses users have to network resources and data, and what approaches or decisions were made regarding network security.

Troubleshooting problems on the network is also an important network administrator function, and is accomplished by taking steps both before and after a problem occurs. Before any problem occurs, you should take the time to document your network's current hardware, software, and configuration. You should know, for example, how the cabling is designed and where it runs (in the ceiling, under the floor, which rooms it runs through and where, etc.). That design should be documented. Then if a cabling problem occurs, you won't have to remove half of the room's flooring or ceiling to find it.

Other things could go wrong on your network as well. For example, a user may suddenly be unable to log in because they accidentally made a configuration change. This problem can also be easily fixed if you documented what the configuration was suppose to be before the problem occurred. That way, when you research the problem, determine what it was, and how to fix it, you can easily implement the fix. To ensure ease of troubleshooting and repairing of similar problems in the future, your documentation should also include an overview of the problem, symptoms it presented, and what you did to correct the problem. Keeping this kind of documentation will eventually cause a pattern to show itself if one exists. In addition, you'll have an idea of what the problem might be for someone else if their symptoms are similar, and you'll know how to fix the problem without having to start over. You'll also leave behind (when you get promoted for your efficiency and effectiveness as a network administrator, of course) the information the next network administrator needs to successfully carry on.

Thus, to successfully document the network, consider what you might need to know if you have to later troubleshoot any problem or security breech on your network.

Understanding a network administrator's responsibilities and tasks (see Fig. 1-5) should also help you understand what resources and services a network provides.

Understanding NetWare's Basic Resources and Services

NetWare's basic resources and services can be divided into six main areas:

- NDS
- File management
- Printing (NDPS)
- Application access

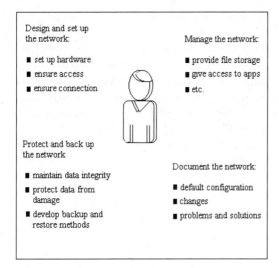

Design and set up
the network:

■ set up hardware
■ ensure access
■ ensure connection

Manage the network:

■ provide file storage
■ give access to apps
■ etc.

Protect and back up
the network

■ maintain data integrity
■ protect data from
  damage
■ develop backup and
  restore methods

Document the network:

■ default configuration
■ changes
■ problems and solutions

FIGURE 1-5 A network administrator's common responsibilities and their associated tasks.

■ Security
■ Storage Management Services (SMS)

NDS

Networks—and thus NetWare—make communication among various computers and users possible. That communication is fundamental to networking. One of the most fundamental network services that NetWare provides, in addition to network communication, is NDS.

NDS (the official name for what was previously called NetWare Directory Services) is responsible for maintaining a database of all network *resources* (anything a network client may need to use) in a directory. NDS is also responsible for processing and responding to requests for resources or services which a client may make. Both resources and services are provided by NetWare file servers, and can be accessed simultaneously by multiple clients.

File Management

File management is also a primary function of NetWare. File management's primary responsibility is that of controlling access by users from workstations to the information contained on the disk drives attached to NetWare servers.

File systems store, share, and allow the use of data files. The file system also stores and lets clients share various application programs.

While NDS is a database that stores information related to the entire network, the file system is a collection of files—including data files, application programs, and so on—that are stored on the network. The NDS database contains information such as which users exist on the network and what rights they have to the network, while the file system contains copies of user's data files and various program files.

While the NDS database and the NetWare file system are two separate entities, there are two things they have in common:

- they both consist of files which are stored on the hard disks of NetWare servers throughout the network
- they both have security systems of their own

KEY CONCEPT

NDS security controls which network resources and network services you can access. File system security controls which data and programs you can access.

For example, to log in to the network so that you can access files and programs on NetWare file servers, your login request goes to NDS. NDS then reviews your login request and must approve it. Once your login request is approved by NDS, NDS applies the appropriate NDS rights to your User object in order to restrict what network resources and services you can access, while also ensuring that you can get to all network resources and services you are *supposed* to be able to get to. Then, once you are logged in to the network, if you want to run a program such as WordPerfect which is stored on the network in the file system of a NetWare server, the file system security checks to ensure you have file system rights to access the related program files before you can actually run that program.

NOTE

There is some overlap between NDS security and file system security, because NetWare file servers (and thus the file system they contain) are represented in the Directory tree. The design of this aspect of the Directory tree allows for rights to the NetWare file server which have been set in NDS to flow into the directory structure of the NetWare file server's file system. You will learn more about this and other aspects of NDS and file system security in Chapter 4: *Establishing Security on a NetWare 5 Network*.

Printing (NDPS)

NDPS (Novell Distributed Print Services) is responsible for ensuring that clients can print to any network printer to which they have been authorized to print. NDPS makes it possible to print to a network printer, whether it is physically connected to a workstation that is connected to the network, to a file server that is connected to the network, or directly connected to the network cable (which is possible with printing devices such as the Jet Direct box, and with printers that are NDPS-aware). Chapter 5, *Making Print Services Available*, covers NDPS printing in detail. It explains how to set up NDPS printing, as well as how to manage network printing.

Application Access

Administrators install and configure applications on the network so that users can access them. The Z.E.N.works Starter Pack included with NetWare 5 provides the Application Launcher (also sometimes referred to as NAL or Novell Application Launcher). The Application Launcher feature of Z.E.N.works lets you install, distribute, run, or repair network applications from a single workstation.

The Application Launcher feature of Z.E.N.works is covered in some detail in Chapter 8, *Using Application Launcher*. In addition, Chapter 9, *Using Other Z.E.N.works Features*, discusses other useful components of Z.E.N.works.

Security

Many network services help you regulate access to network resources, and protect the network from both intentional and inadvertent damage. For example, User objects in NDS, and their associated properties and values, are used to regulate network access.

Chapter 4, *Establishing Security on a NetWare 5 Network*, discusses security associated with both NDS and the file system.

Storage Management Services

SMS (Storage Management Services) assists in ensuring the integrity and reliability of network data. It accomplishes this by providing a method for backing up and restoring network data.

Although ensuring network data integrity and reliability is an important network administrator and SMS responsibility, it is not discussed in the authorized Novell NetWare Administration course cur-
riculum or the related certification test. SMS is covered in a different Novell authorized course, thus it is not discussed in any detail in
this book.

As you can see if you have any experience with using or administering a
NetWare 4 network, many of the basic resources and services provided
in a NetWare 5 network are also provided in a NetWare 4 network.
There is much that is new and different in NetWare 5, however, and as it
is important to your success as a network administrator to understand
these differences and new features, the next section discusses the new
features of NetWare 5.

Learning About NetWare 5 and What's New in It

NetWare 5 has kept the best and most reliable aspects of NetWare 4,
including NDS (NetWare Directory Services). To give you an introduction, this section discusses those features of NetWare 5 which are new or
significantly changed. Even if you aren't already familiar with NetWare
4, you will benefit from learning about the new features of NetWare 5.
More information about the NetWare 5 features with which you will
have the most interaction, and of which you need specific knowledge
both to administer a NetWare 5 network and to pass the certification
test, is provided throughout the other chapters of this book. Consider
this to be just a brief overview and introduction.

NetWare 5 with NDS is designed to help you easily manage and control your company's entire network. NetWare 5 supports multiple protocols, including IP and IPX. It also supports multiple operating systems,
including NT Server, and various applications.

NetWare 5 also supports Java by including a JVM (Java Virtual Machine)
embedded within the NetWare 5 kernel. In NetWare 5, Java support
includes Java-based utilities, and a GUI network management utility called
ConsoleOne. ConsoleOne's functions in the first release of NetWare 5 are
limited, including only two Java-based utilities which can be plugged into
ConsoleOne. Those utilities are an X-Windows-based GUI install program
written in Java, and a utility for managing DNS (Domain Name System)
servers and DHCP (Dynamic Host Configuration Protocol).

NetWare 5 also includes the OSA (Open Systems Architecture) SDK
(Software Developer's Kit), which makes it possible for other companies

to develop snap-in tools to ConsoleOne. ConsoleOne's ability to have Novell-developed and third-party developed tools snapped into it will soon make ConsoleOne an even more valuable piece of NetWare 5.

The heart of the NetWare 5 NOS—the kernel itself—has also been improved. Sufficient file server memory for running both the NOS and all of the applications a company may want to run can severely strain the memory capabilities of a server. Improvements to the NetWare 5 kernel are aimed at optimizing the kernel to support the user's running of applications on servers. Those improvements include enhanced memory protection, virtual memory capabilities, and prioritization of applications. In addition, NetWare 5's enhanced kernel supports not only uniprocessor servers, but also multiprocessors on network servers. The improved kernel in NetWare 5 overall makes for a more stable and reliable NOS.

NetWare 5 also supports the open standards of the Internet, which is one reason why NetWare 5 is considered by many to be the best strategic platform on which to develop and deploy distributed Internet/intranet applications. In addition, NetWare 5 supports another industry-standard Internet protocol: Service Location Protocol (SLP). The SLP protocol was developed to provide a scalable framework for locating and choosing network services so that computers accessing the Internet would no longer have to be configured to such demanding and rigid specifications.

NetWare 5 also provides a new storage access system called NSS (Novell Storage Services). NSS is a high-performance storage and retrieval system, making the storage of data on the network and access to data on the network much quicker. In addition, NSS is backwards-compatible with the storage system used in earlier versions of NetWare, so access to data on those NetWare servers will not be interrupted.

NetWare 5 also ships with an enhanced print service as its default: NDPS (Novell Distributed Print Services). NDPS makes it possible to install, setup, configure, and manage all of your network printers from one central location. It even automates the installation of print drivers for network printers.

In addition, with so many companies accessing the Internet, network security has become even more important than before. NetWare 5 recognizes that and provides a variety of new security system features, including public-key cryptography and SAS (Secure Authentication Services). Public key cryptography provides two mathematically-related security keys—one public key and one private key—which are used to ensure network security. The public key is easily accessible, but the private key is stored in a key database file on the user's computer. The private key is stored in secret on the user's computer. To ensure network security, the mathematical calculation based on the information in both the public and private key must be accurate before network services or data can be accessed. Public key cryptography is supported by PKIS (Public Key Infrastructure Services), which is also included in NetWare 5.

Although NetWare 5 still includes support for IPX/SPX, it also supports TCP/IP. Thus, network systems which run on TCP/IP alone, as well as those which use IPX/SPX or a blend of these protocols, can take full advantage of NetWare 5.

When running earlier versions of NetWare, many companies chose to purchase and run one of many backup utilities provided by third-party developers, even though NetWare included a backup utility. NetWare 5 also provides a backup utility, but this new utility is protocol-independent, easier to use than the previous utilities because it has a friendly GUI (Graphical User Interface), is fully integrated with NDS, and lets you manage network backup activities from a single, central location.

In addition to all of the enhancements and additions previously noted, NetWare 5 also includes:

- Compatibility mode which lets older IPX applications run on an IP-only network, thus giving you some flexibility when migrating your network from IPX/SPX to TCP/IP
- I_2O support, which provides support for this emerging technology that enhances a system's input/output and overall performance
- A five-user version of Oracle8 for NetWare, which lets you use NDS to control access to your database
- Netscape FastTrack Server for NetWare, which lets you create and post web pages and develop and deploy web applications in a cross-platform environment
- Zero Effort Networks (Z.E.N.works) Starter Pack, which simplifies distribution and updating of applications and workstations on your network
- Catalog services, which provides a flat-file catalog of the NDS database so you can use and write applications that search the NDS database
- Contextless login, which makes it easy for users to log in to the network from wherever they happen to be at the time
- Support for LDAP (Lightweight Directory Access Protocol), which makes it easy for users to access X.500-based directories such as NDS
- WAN Traffic Manager NLM (NetWare Loadable Module) and snap-in module for Novell's NetWare Administrator utility, which lets you control the traffic generated by replication
- Auditing services, which let you monitor and record users' access to your network

As you can probably tell, there is a lot to NetWare 5. Many of NetWare 5's features and capabilities happen within NetWare itself and thus are not obvious to users (or to most administrators, for that matter). What administrators and users will notice, however, is how much adding NetWare 5 to their network will help them realize their work goals.

As a CNA or CNE candidate, you need to understand basics about NetWare 5, and how to administer a NetWare 5 network. This book is designed to help you accomplish that task. In addition, the practice test questions which follow are designed to help you learn what you need to know, as well as to be prepared to take and pass the NetWare 5 Administration certification test.

Although there are many aspects of NetWare 5 that differ from NetWare 4, you only need to know about those aspects which affect your job as a network administrator. This chapter has introduced you to the primary features of NetWare 5, but the remaining chapters in this book cover in sufficient detail only those features and functions you need to know in order to administer a NetWare 5 network and to pass the NetWare 5 Administration certification exam.

Chapter Summary

The function of a network is to allow network users to share various resources, such as application programs, data files, and printers. NetWare 5 is a network operating system designed to allow users to share network resources, including NDS, application access, file system access, storage management services, printing, and security.

A network's hardware components include computers with the NOS loaded and which therefore function as servers. In a NetWare 5 network, a server must contain at least a 486 or Pentium processor and the Novell NetWare 5 operating system software.

For a user to access a NetWare 5 network, the user must have a computer running the Novell Client software. The computer must also have either a DOS or Windows NT, Windows 95/98, or Windows 3.1x or above operating system software, or an optional OS for which additional network client software has been purchased. (Macintosh and UNIX clients are available on the Web.)

Each server and workstation on the network must contain a network board (NIC), and be connected to the network using the appropriate communications media. Two popular communications media types are co-axial cable, and twisted-pair cable.

Networks also contain peripheral devices. Printers and modems are two common peripheral devices included in networks.

Networked computers running the Novell Client software and servers on the network (computers running the Novell NetWare 5 NOS software) must be able to communicate with each other in order to share resources. The language network devices use to communicate is defined by the communications protocol (the set of rules by which computers and related hardware successfully communicate between two points). Three common communication protocols are TCP/IP, IPX, and IP.

The client and server successfully communicate due to a combination of hardware referred to as the communications media (network boards and cabling), and software, including the network board driver (found at the bottom of the workstation model), the Novell Client and workstation operating system software (found at the middle of the workstation model), and the applications on the workstation (found at the top of the workstation model).

The actual communication process is simple in design. Incoming data from the network cabling is intercepted by the network board and then sent by the network board's driver software to the Novell Client and the workstation's operating system. From there, the data is forwarded to the application software which needs it.

For outgoing data, the process is reversed. The data goes from the application software to the Novell Client and workstation operating system, to the network board driver software, and finally through the network board itself and out over the network cable.

The network is managed by a network administrator whose primary responsibilities include:

■ designing and setting up the network
■ managing the network
■ protecting and backing up data
■ documenting the network

The network operating system software, which runs on a computer thus creating a file server, is NetWare 5. NetWare 5 provides a broad range of networking resources and services, including NDS, file management, printing, application access, security, and storage management services. NetWare 5 is feature-rich, containing several new features not found in previous versions of the Novell NOS. These features and the access to the network that Novell's NetWare 5 provides makes NetWare 5 the leading network operating system software.

Practice Test Questions

1. Which one of the following is *not* part of a network?
   A. Stand-alone computer
   B. Computer with a network board installed and connected
   C. Jet Direct box
   D. Powerful computer with NetWare's NOS installed
   E. Novell Client

2. When a powerful computer has network operating system software loaded on it, it functions as a:
   A. Client
   B. Workstation
   C. Service
   D. Server
   E. Resource

3. Any device which requests services from a server is called a:
   A. Client
   B. Workstation
   C. Service
   D. Server
   E. Resource

4. Printers, modems, and computers can all be network
   A. Software
   B. Workstations
   C. Servers
   D. Clients

5. Any of the following can run on a computer functioning as a network workstation except
   A. DOS
   B. Macintosh
   C. Jet Direct
   D. Windows 95
   E. UNIX

6. Which of the following does not apply to NetWare 5?
   A. It can run on servers with multiple microprocessors
   B. The kernel schedules processing time
   C. Services are provided by network clients
   D. Any network client can request services from NetWare

7. Anything a network client requests is called a
   A. Server
   B. NOS
   C. Workstation
   D. Kernel
   E. Resource

8. Three services that NetWare 5 provides are
   A. NDS
   B. NDPS
   C. NOS
   D. SMS

9. The primary function of a network is to
   A. ensure all clients can access resources and services
   B. make networks function equally well with intranets and Internets
   C. provide access to applications
   D. establish communication between computers

10. The responsibility of ensuring that the workstation has a path by which it can communicate with the rest of the network belongs to:
    A. Cable system
    B. Network board
    C. NOS
    D. Server
    E. Client

11. The two basic elements of networking software are
    A. Novell Client
    B. Communications media
    C. NOS
    D. Workstation OS

12. Networking software which makes it possible for a workstation to communicate with the network is
    A. Novell Client
    B. Communications media
    C. NOS
    D. Workstation OS

13. Which three are responsibilities of the Novell Client?
    A. Help ensure only authorized users access the network
    B. Manage data flow and ensure it is properly formatted
    C. Boot the computer so it can access the network
    D. Enable users via workstations to access network services

14. Communication to ensure network resources and services that are provided to the user succeed when which two communicate with each other?
    A. NOS
    B. Cable
    C. Workstation OS
    D. Novell Client software
    E. Communications protocols

15. The rules which govern how computers and related hardware communicate is known as
    A. NOS
    B. Cable
    C. Workstation OS
    D. Novell Client software
    E. Communications protocols

16. Which three tasks are part of the communication process?
    A. Establish a connection
    B. Identify a communications protocol
    C. Backup network data
    D. Process requests
    E. Send and receive network data

17. The workstation's network board is part of which layer of the communications model?
    A. Lowest
    B. Middle
    C. Upper
    D. Not part of the communications model
    E. Combination of the lowest and middle layers

18. Which two are primary responsibilities of a network administrator?
    A. Set up the network
    B. Purchase networking software
    C. Organize and configure network resources
    D. Install operating system software on each workstation

19. Which one of the following is not a network design and setup task?
    A. Ensure users have access to network directories
    B. Ensure workstations can automatically connect to the network
    C. Setup workstations
    D. Setup networking hardware
    E. Ensure data integrity is maintained

20. If you can easily find a break in a network cable, you have probably done a good job of
    A. Backing up the network
    B. Installing the NOS
    C. Connecting workstations
    D. Documenting the network
    E. None of the above

21. Which of the following is responsible for maintaining a database of all network resources?
    A. NOS
    B. NDS
    C. Security
    D. NDPS
    E. File system

22. The basic NetWare resource or service responsible for ensuring a user can print to a network printer is
    A. NOS
    B. NDPS
    C. Z.E.N.works
    D. SMS
    E. Security

23. The basic NetWare resource or service responsible for ensuring that network resources are accessed only by authorized users is
    A. NOS
    B. NDPS
    C. Z.E.N.works
    D. SMS
    E. Security

24. The ability to repair network applications from a single workstation is provided by
    A. NOS
    B. NDPS
    C. Z.E.N.works
    D. SMS
    E. Security

25. Which of the following is not a new feature of NetWare 5?
    A. NSS
    B. NDPS
    C. Z.E.N.works
    D. NLMs

Answers to Practice Test Questions

1. A	8. A,B,D	15. E	22. B
2. D	9. A	16. A,D,E	23. E
3. A	10. B	17. A	24. C
4. D	11. A,C	18. A,C	25. D
5. C	12. A	19. E	
6. C	13. A,B,D	20. D	
7. E	14. A,D	21. B	

CHAPTER 2

Understanding NetWare Directory Services and the Directory Tree

An important aspect of network management is the network manager's ability to manage and administer the Directory. This chapter provides you with an overview of NDS and the Directory tree—an important prerequisite to planning, implementing, and maintaining NDS. It explains what NDS is, what the Directory is, and how information is classified, organized, and stored in the Directory (objects, properties, and values). It also explains how the network administrator manages the Directory.

Learning About NDS and the Directory Tree

NDS, like security and printing services, is a network service. Its primary function is that of ensuring appropriately secured access to all other network resources, such as applications, and to services, such as printing.

KEY CONCEPT

To provide access to network resources and services, NDS maintains information about these services and resources in the NetWare Directory, commonly called just the *Directory*. So that resources and services can be easily located, added, and so on, the logical resources contained within the Directory are displayed in a hierarchical design referred to as the *Directory tree*.

While many networks have only a single NDS tree, some networks have more than one tree. The benefits of a single NDS tree design are:

- all users log in only once to the tree, giving them access to all resources and services to which they have been given rights
- the tree contains a single Directory which can be *partitioned* (divided into logical sections which then reduces the dependence on a single file server for all Directory information)
- the tree contains a single Directory which can be *replicated* (copied across one or more servers to provide quicker access to the Directory and greater protection of the Directory itself)

NDS is also referred to as a naming service. It is a database of all information and resources. Managing NDS is a key role of the network administrator.

KEY CONCEPT

Understanding NDS objects

In order for the Directory to store information about the network's resources, the manner in which those resources are to be identified and displayed needs to be established. The Directory itself must contain a defined structure into which those resources can be logically organized if anyone is to be able to use them.

The Directory's Structure

The NDS Directory structure resembles something most of us are familiar with: a tree (maple, oak, etc.). Like any tree, the Directory tree has branches, leaves, and roots, although they do not exactly use the same terminology. Unlike a maple or oak tree, the Directory tree is upside down, with the roots at the top and the leaves at the bottom.

The Directory tree does have branches, but they are called container objects. The Directory tree also has leaves, but they are called leaf objects. And, the Directory tree has only a single root, not multiple roots. That single root which identifies the top of the Directory tree is called the [Root] object.

If you were to compare the structure of the Directory to the structure of a database file, each object in the Directory would be the same as a record or row in a database file. Each object in the Directory contains specific information, with a record or row in a database file.

NOTE

KEY
CONCEPT

An object is any entity defined in the NDS database. There are three general categories of objects in the NDS database:

- container objects
- leaf objects
- [Root] object

Objects can represent abstract or physical network resources. For example, container objects represent abstract entities because they generally act as place holders so that other objects can be logically organized and contained within them. Leaf objects generally represent physical entities such as users on the network, or a printer.

The structure of the Directory tree then consists of both container and leaf objects, as well as the [Root] object which represents the top of the Directory tree. Figure 2-1 shows how the Directory tree's hierarchical structure is represented. You will commonly use the NetWare Administrator utility in NetWare 5 to see this type of Directory tree display.

KEY
CONCEPT

Every single resource on the network must be represented in the Directory if users (via their network workstations) or other network clients are to be able to access them. In NDS, resources are represented by objects. You will learn more about objects in a later section of this chapter titled "Understanding NDS Objects."

FIGURE 2-1 The graphical display of a sample Directory tree structure as you would view it using the NetWare Administrator utility.

The Role and Benefits of NDS

Just as every child in a family has a specific name so that one child can be identified from another, every object in the Directory has a name. That name is called the *NDS object name*, and it must be unique in order for NDS to store it in the database to begin with, and to retrieve it when it is needed.

It is NDS's role to locate any object in the Directory that a user may request, verify that the user has the appropriate rights to access that object, and then connect the user with the requested resource that the object represents. NDS locates requested resources in the Directory by their NDS object name.

Because NDS uses a database which contains objects with unique NDS object names, there are several benefits to having NDS:

- the database can be global, and although it may encompass objects whose physical location can be anywhere around the world, management of the network's resources is centralized
- only one standard method is used to store or access network resources
- organization of the database can be logical instead of physical
- access to resources can be made as the result of dynamic instead of static mapping

Easy administration, central organization, and dynamic access to network resources are all results obtained because of the design of NDS and its directory structure.

Understanding NDS Objects

KEY CONCEPT

There are three different classes of objects in the Directory tree: [Root], Container, and Leaf. The objects within these classes represent one of two different types of network resources: physical or logical. A *physical resource* is any network resource which physically exists, such as a computer functioning as a network workstation. This specific type of physical resource is represented in the Directory as a Workstation object. A *logical resource* is any resource that does not have a physical counterpart, but which is used primarily to organize the Directory and the objects it contains. A logical grouping of all users in the accounting department is an example of a logical object which would be represented in the Directory by a Group object.

The [Root] Object

The first class of object in the Directory tree structure is the [Root] object. It represents the top of the Directory tree. It is rather unique from the other objects in the tree because:

- only one [Root] object can exist in the Directory tree
- it is always and only located at the very top of the tree
- it contains no information
- only the Organization, Country, and Alias objects are beneath it
- it and [Public] are the only objects whose names include and require the use of square brackets

Container Objects

There are three types of container objects: Country, Organization, and Organizational Unit. Only Organization and Organizational Unit objects are generally used, however. The Country object was designed to represent the geographic or political branch of the Directory tree, but it is optional and only required for connection to certain X.500 global directories. Most companies create their Directory without including the Country object, since it often just adds an unnecessary level to the tree.

The container object's sole purpose is to provide a place holder within the Directory tree. It provides a method for implementing a logical organization within the Directory tree's structure. Because you have to have at least one Organization container object below the [Root] of the tree, your Directory tree structure will have at least one container object in it.

NOTE

You can place only Country or Organization container objects, or Alias leaf objects directly beneath the [Root] in the Directory tree.

The Organization object was initially designed to represent the equivalent of a company within the Directory tree. For example, for the SunShoeShine Company, the Organization object would be used to represent the company.

For companies such as Fortune 500 corporations whose corporate physical structure contains many different companies, multiple Organization objects—one for each separate company—may be created in the tree.

Using Organizational Unit objects lets you further subdivide your Directory tree to make management and administration easier.

Organizational Unit objects can be placed within Organization objects or within other Organizational Unit objects.

NOTE With a Directory tree structure containing several Organizational Units, you can give different network administrators the responsibility for managing one or more of those individual Organizational Units. This is easy to do using the Organizational Role object. You simply create the Organizational Role object, assign it the appropriate rights needed to manage one or more Organizational Unit objects, then assign individuals to the Organizational Role object. Chapter 5, *Establishing Security on a NetWare 5 Network* , provides you with information about assigning rights and other security-related issues.

Leaf Objects

Like Container objects, there are different types of Leaf objects. However, unlike Container objects, there are many types of Leaf objects and Leaf objects are not designed to hold additional objects below their level in the tree. Except for some Leaf objects such as the Alias and Directory Map objects, most leaf objects represent physical network resources, such as NetWare Server and Printer objects.

The most common Leaf objects with which you should be familiar are shown in the following list. All objects except [Root], but including leaf objects, are represented in the Directory tree by an *icon* (a small graphic designed to give the viewer an idea of what the associated text represents). The icon associated with each type of object listed below shows what the icon looks like for each of the represented objects when you view the Directory tree using the Novell NetWare Administrator utility.

Alias. Points to another object in the tree. For example, you can create an Alias object in one container to point to a printer in another container. This makes it easier for users in the container where the Alias is contained to access the Printer object, which currently exists in another container.

Application. Refers to an application program from which the user can launch that program if they have the right to do so.

Directory Map. Represents a path on a volume allowing users to map a drive to a resource without first having to know where on the network that resource is actually located.

Group. Represents multiple users who have something in common, such as the same network resource or service needs. Use of the Group object makes it easy to manage users.

 NetWare Server. Represents a NetWare file server on the network. Various other objects use the NetWare Server object to gain access to specific network services.

 Organizational Role. Allows the network manager to assign divided network management responsibilities and thus rights to other individuals, so that the workload associated with managing and administering the network can be divided among other users, such as managers or administrative assistants.

 Print Queue. Represents a print queue, which is a defined storage area on a server where print jobs can be held until the printer is available for output.

 Print Server (Non-NDPS). Identifies physical network devices known as print servers: devices responsible for getting print jobs from print queues and directing them to network printers.

 Printer (Non-NDPS). Identifies physical network printing devices. Those devices can be standard printers, such as LaserJet printers, but they can also be printing type devices, such as plotters.

 Profile. Provides to users through the use of a login script a defined set of resource needs, some of which are the same as other users, even though the users may be in different containers. If used, the profile login script associated with the Profile object runs after the container login script for the container in which the User Object exists, but before the User login script, if that user has a User login script.

 User. Represents a network user (person who accesses resources on the network and for whom a User object exists). Anyone who wants to access the network and its resources must have a User object.

 Volume. Represents a physical volume on a server. When a file server is added to the network, Volume objects are created for each of its volumes.

 Workstation. Represents and contains information about a computer connected to the network and set up to access network resources and services.

When designing your Directory tree, it is important that you are aware of which types of objects can be placed where, and what they can contain. Table 2-1 gives you a quick overview of those important relationships.

Table 2-1 shows the types of objects in the Directory tree, tells where they can be placed in the Directory tree structure, and shows you what other objects (if any) can be placed within that object type.

TABLE 2-1 Displays Directory object types and provides a quick summary of where they can be placed within the Directory tree structure as well as what they can contain, when applicable.

Object Class	Object Type	Can Contain	Can Be In
[Root]	[Root]	Country Organization	Only at the top of the tree, and only one can exist per tree
Container	Country	Organization Alias	[Root]
	Organization	Organizational Unit All Leaf objects	[Root] Country
	Organizational Unit	Organizational Unit All Leaf objects	Organization Organizational Unit
Leaf	There are many. The most commonly used ones are: Alias Application Directory Map Group NetWare Server Organizational Role Print Queue Print Server Printer Profile User Volume Workstation	(Cannot contain other objects)	Organization Organizational Unit Note: The Alias leaf object can be placed in a Country object in addition to being in an Organization and Organizational Unit object.

Understanding NDS Properties and Values

All Objects except the [Root] Object in the Directory Tree have properties, and those properties in turn have values.

KEY CONCEPT

A *property* identifies specific information about an object. For example, a property associated with a user would be that user's telephone number. You can compare the property of an object to that of a single item of information in a record in a database. Just as a person's telephone number can be an item of information in database record, so too can it be a property of an object in the Directory.

However, the fact that a User object has the property of telephone number associated with it does not necessarily mean that there must be a telephone number actually contained within the Directory for that property.

KEY CONCEPT

A *value* is associated with a property, and it represents the actual information for a specific object that is part of the property. In the case of a user's telephone number property, the value is that user's actual telephone number.

Objects in the Directory have properties associated with them, and properties have values. The ability to add a telephone number to a User object and thus the ability to store a telephone number in the database is the object's property, and the actual telephone number is the value of that property.

KEY CONCEPT

Many properties, such as the Name property of a User object, have only one value associated with them. Some properties, such as the Telephone property, can have multiple values.

Figure 2-2 graphically shows the associations between objects, properties, and values.

Managing NDS Trees, Objects, and Properties

To successfully manage a company's NDS tree, you must be able to manage the objects within that tree, as well as the properties (and thus the values of those properties) associated with those objects. To let you do that, NetWare provides an administration utility called *NetWare Administrator.*

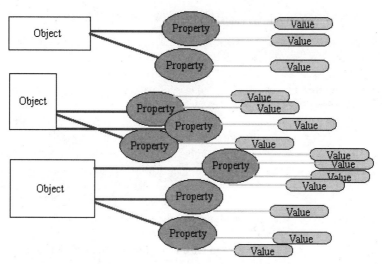

FIGURE 2-2 A graphical representation of how properties are associated with objects, and of how values are associated with properties.

Using NetWare Administrator, you can view the tree, add objects to the tree, move objects from one container to another within the tree, and provide values for different properties associated with objects within the tree. Many of the tasks you need to perform as a network administrator are done with the NetWare Administrator utility. It is helpful to have a basic understanding of this utility and how to use it.

When you start the program, a view of your existing Directory tree structure is displayed. How much of the tree structure and whether or not the very top of the tree ([Root]) is shown, depends on where in the Directory structure your User object exists. As a rule, that part of the Directory tree structure (the container) where your User object resides and containers within that container will be available for you to view. To see other parts of the Directory tree structure, you must have sufficient rights (discussed in Chapter 4, *Establishing Security on a NetWare 5 Network*). For now, simply work within the current Directory structure to familiarize yourself with it as viewed and modified using the NetWare Administrator utility.

Figure 2-3 shows a view of the NetWare Administrator utility. Notice how each object in the tree is displayed with an icon which helps identify the type of object. For example, a User object is identified by a single artistic bust-style icon, while a Group object is identified by a grouping of three of these bust-style icons.

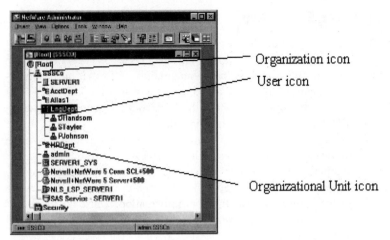

Organization icon

User icon

Organizational Unit icon

FIGURE 2-3 An initial view of a directory tree seen when you start the NetWare Administrator utility.

When using the NetWare Administrator utility, you should be aware that you can:

- use the scroll bars to move the portion of the Directory tree that you can see up or down the screen
- use all of the mouse operations in the NetWare Administrator that you can use in other Windows-based applications (single-click, double-click, shift-click, and drag-and-drop)
- use the Control menu button or the **Close** button to close the NetWare Administrator utility
- get online help by either pressing the **F1** key, or by choosing the **Help** menu option

NOTE

You can also use another utility provided by NetWare Administrator called the *CX utility*. It is a DOS-based command line utility; you use it by typing **CX** at the DOS prompt or in a DOS box. It displays the official name of the location in the Directory tree where your User object is currently located, or where you are currently directed to by default in the Directory tree (your *current context*). You learn more about moving through the Directory tree, your current context, and other related information as you go through the different chapters in this book, as the information you need to know is presented when you need it.

Chapter Summary

NDS, a naming service, is one of NetWare's network services. Its primary function is that of ensuring appropriately secured access to all other network resources, which it does by maintaining information about services and resources in a database commonly called the Directory. The logical resources contained within the Directory are displayed in a hierarchical design referred to as the Directory tree.

NDS and its design benefits network users in three ways. First, a single login to the directory tree gives each user access to all resources and services within the NDS tree for which they have been given rights. Second, the Directory can be partitioned, reducing or eliminating the dependence on a single file server for all Directory information. Third, the Directory can be replicated to provide greater protection of the Directory itself, and thus of the network.

Every resource is represented in the directory by an object. An object is any entity defined in the NDS database. These objects and the Directory's structure can be viewed and managed using the NetWare Administrator utility. To manage the Directory tree, you must understand its structure.

The Directory's structure resembles an upside-down tree in nature. The Directory has branches like a tree. The branches of the Directory tree are called container objects. The Directory tree also has leafs, called leaf objects. The Directory tree has a single root which identifies the top of the Directory tree, and which is called the [Root] object.

Only one [Root] object can exist in the Directory tree. The [Root] object is always and only located at the very top of the tree, contains no information, and can contain within it only the Organization, Country, and Alias objects.

The Country object represents the geographic or political branch of the Directory tree, but is optional and only required for connection to certain X.500 global directories. Most companies do not use the Country object.

The Container object's sole purpose is to provide a placeholder or container for other objects within the Directory tree. It lets you and NDS provide a logical organization to the Directory tree's structure.

The Organization object is used to subdivide the Directory tree. It was initially designed to represent the equivalent of a company within the Directory tree.

Organizational Unit objects let you further subdivide your Directory tree so as to make management and administration easier. Organizational Unit objects can be placed within Organization objects, or within other Organizational Unit objects.

Most leaf objects represent physical network resources, such as NetWare Server and Printer objects. There are many leaf objects, but the ones with which you should be most familiar are: Alias, Application, Directory Map, Group, NetWare Server, Organizational Role, Print Queue, Print Server, Printer, Profile, User, Volume, and Workstation.

Objects in the Directory have properties associated with them, and properties have values. A property is a single item of information about an object. A property's value is that information which is actually associated with the property. For example, a User object can have a Telephone property associated with it. The value of the Telephone property would be the actual telephone number that it contains. Many properties, such as the Name property of a User object, have only one value associated with them. Some properties, such as the Telephone property, can have multiple values.

Many of the tasks you need to perform as a network administrator are performed using the NetWare Administrator utility. To run the NetWare Administrator utility, you launch it from the desktop just as you do any other software—by double-clicking the icon. When you start the NetWare Administrator utility, a view of your existing Directory tree structure is displayed. As you progress through this *NetWare 5 CNA Accelerated Study Guide*, you learn how to view and manage your network and its Directory using NetWare Administrator.

Practice Test Questions

1. NDS is a/an:
    A. Object
    B. Service
    C. Property
    D. Value

2. The primary function of NDS is:
    A. Ensuring appropriately secured access to all other network resources
    B. Classifying resources on the network
    C. Administering network services
    D. Replicating network services

3. Any entity defined in the NDS database is called a/an:
   A. Object
   B. Container
   C. Leaf
   D. [Root]

4. Which of the following is *not* part of the NDS tree structure?
   A. Leaf
   B. Container
   C. [Root]
   D. Tree

5. An object in the Directory tree which exists primarily to help organize the tree structure is a/an:
   A. Physical resource
   B. Unique entity
   C. Logical resource
   D. Object without leaf objects

6. Which three statements regarding the [Root] object are true?
   A. It is found only at the top of the tree
   B. There can be multiple [Root] objects in one tree so that a [Root] object exists for each tree in a multi-tree network
   C. Network administrators can add only Organization, Country, and Alias objects directly below it in the tree
   D. It contains no information

7. Which of the following is *not* a container object?
   A. Country
   B. Organization
   C. Computer
   D. Organizational Unit

8. The object which was designed primarily to distribute the network administrator's workload is the:
   A. Organizational Unit
   B. Organizational Role
   C. User
   D. Group

9. You can quickly grant access to resources for multiple users by creating a:
   A. Leaf object
   B. Organizational Role object
   C. User object
   D. Group object

10. That which identifies specific information about an objects is known as a/an:
    A. Property
    B. Resource
    C. Identity
    D. Object

11. That which represents the actual information contained within the property of an object, such as a user's actual telephone number, is known as a/an:
    A. Resource
    B. Identity
    C. Value
    D. Property

12. Which two can you use to view your current context?
    A. NetWare Administrator utility
    B. COMMAND.COM
    C. Control menu
    D. CX

Answers to Practice Questions

1. B	7. C
2. A	8. B
3. A	9. D
4. D	10. A
5. C	11. C
6. A,C,D	12. A,D

CHAPTER 3

Setting Up a NetWare 5 Network

etting up a NetWare 5 network involves a variety of tasks. Planning the NDS tree, deciding on the names of the containers, deciding on rights for users, and so on are all part of setting up a NetWare 5 network. The ideal approach to setting up a NetWare 5 network requires that all planning and decisions be made first, that the organization of the NDS tree be designed, and that all things be ready before you begin setting up the network. That isn't always possible or necessarily realistic, however. Thus, this chapter is organized based on what is reasonably realistic. Decisions are sometimes made at the moment they need to be made, rather than in advance of their actual implementation.

This chapter discusses four aspects of network setup which are commonly done, often in the order in which this chapter is arranged. These four network setup tasks are:

- installing NetWare 5
- designing and organizing network resources
- setting up user accounts
- controlling access to network resources

Even though designing and organizing resources should normally come before installing NetWare 5, some administrators find it useful to install their first NetWare 5 file server and begin the set up of the NDS tree before they complete these other three tasks. Having access to a NetWare 5 server can be useful in planning how to organize the rest of the network's resources. That is why this chapter starts with information about and the procedure to follow when installing the first NetWare 5 file server into the NDS tree. Be aware, however, that it's best to design the Directory tree first.

The balance of this chapter covers several other setup tasks which a network administrator must do. However, not every setup task is discussed in this chapter. For example, setting up print services is covered in Chapter 5, *Making Print Services Available*. As a general rule, however, you can perform the setup tasks discussed in this chapter without having to understand all of the subtleties associated with a NetWare 5 network. Those tasks that require considerably more knowledge or are considerably complex are covered in separate chapters.

Installing NetWare 5

NetWare 5 is a high-performance, versatile, and fully functional network operating system with associated networking software which makes it possible for computers in diverse geographical locations to communicate with each other. Various resources attached to or provided by NetWare 5 file servers, and critical (as well as limited importance) information contained within these NetWare 5 servers make it possible to provide all the information contained in NetWare 5 servers.

Resource sharing cannot occur until the hardware is in place and the actual network has been set up. For the setup to occur, at least one NetWare 5 file server has to be installed. Before installing the first NetWare 5 file server, you will find it useful to have some understanding of NetWare 5's components, prerequisites to installing NetWare 5, and a variety of other information.

A Brief Overview of NetWare 5

NetWare 5 is the software which, when run on a powerful computer, provides services and resources to network clients. As a network administrator, you manage the resources and services that NetWare 5 provides to network clients. Those resources and the NetWare 5 server can be managed either from a workstation (usually from the network administrator's workstation), or directly at the file server's *console* (the combination of the monitor and keyboard directly connected to the NetWare file server).

Like the DOS command prompt, the file server console gives you a command prompt. The default DOS prompt is identified by a drive letter followed by a colon (:) and a greater than sign (>). For example, the default DOS prompt may be displayed as **C:>**. The NetWare 5 prompt is identified only as a colon (:). You manage the file server from the prompt using either console commands, which are similar in nature to DOS commands, or by loading utility or management *NLMs* (NetWare Loadable Modules) such as the **MONITOR.NLM**.

NetWare 5 Components

As you might imagine, NetWare 5 is not just a simple set of software programs, but is instead a combination of important and functional components. The NetWare 5 operating system is modular in its design and implementation.

KEY CONCEPT

NetWare 5 consists of two major components: the NetWare (core) operating system (the NOS), and NLMs (NetWare Loadable Modules). Console commands are part of the operating system, while NLMs are separate programs which must be *loaded* (placed into the file server's memory) before they become a functional part of the NetWare file server.

NetWare 5 Operating System

The NetWare 5 operating system was discussed in much detail in Chapter 1, *Understanding NetWare 5 Networks and Their Components*. While the NOS will be talked about to some extent in this chapter as part of discussing the setup of a NetWare 5 network, basic NOS information is not repeated in this chapter.

NetWare Loadable Modules

NLMs are an important part of a NetWare server. They provide valuable services to network clients—and to the network administrator, who is trying to install, set up, manage, maintain, or troubleshoot a NetWare network.

KEY CONCEPT

NLMs are software programs which are not part of the core NetWare operating system. They are loaded into memory on the file server after the core NOS has been loaded. NLMs link various software components to the NOS so that communication and interaction is possible. NLMs provide various network services, depending on which type of NLM they are.

There are four different types of NLMs:

■ Name space

- *LAN* (Local Area Network) drivers
- Utilities
- Disk drivers

KEY CONCEPT

To help you remember the different types of NLMs, remember this: Besides remembering that NLM is an acronym for NetWare Loadable Module, remember that NLM can also stand for Never Lay in mUD: Never (Name space) Lay (LAN) in mUD (Utilities and Disk drivers).

Name Space Modules

Name Space NLMs are responsible for ensuring the NetWare file server can understand and thus support different types of name spacing other than the DOS eight-dot-three (xxxxxxxx.xxx) naming convention, and long names, which NetWare supports by default. For example, the IBM OS/2 naming convention and the Apple Computers Macintosh naming convention follow different rules than those of DOS.

For the NetWare file server to understand these other naming rules and thus be able to store and retrieve files which follow these other rules, Name Space NLMs must be loaded on the NetWare file server. **OS2.NAM**, which supports IBM's OS/2 file naming conventions, and **MAC.NAM**, which supports Apple Computer's Macintosh file naming conventions, are examples of Name Space NLMs.

NOTE

Did you notice that Name Space NLMs do not end with **.NLM**, but instead end with **.NAM**? Keep this fact in mind because even though Name Space NLMs end with **.NAM**, they are still called NLMs, and they function as NLMs.

LAN Driver Modules

LAN (Local Area Network) driver NLMs have two responsibilities. First, they are responsible for establishing communication between the network board and the network board (LAN) driver. Once loaded, LAN driver NLMs are then responsible for facilitating communication between the file server and network clients. **NE2000.NLM** is an example of a LAN driver NLM. It supports NE2000 network boards.

Utility Modules

Utility NLMs are responsible for providing other network services, such as management utilities. **MONITOR.NLM** and **NWCONFIG.NLM**, both of which ship with NetWare 5, are examples of Utility NLMs.

Many NLMs are available for performing such tasks as setting up and configuring network file servers and the services they provide. Those tasks are performed through the interface (menu or command-line access) which the NLM also provides.

Disk Driver Modules

Disk driver NLMs are responsible for enabling communication between the NOS and the hard disk controller on the file server's computer. Because there are different types of disk controllers, there are different types of disk driver NLMs.

NetWare 5's Modular Design

NetWare 5 was designed to be modular. There are several reasons for and benefits associated with using a modular design supported by NLMs. In particular, modular design:

- reduces memory usage
- allows modules to be easily loaded or unloaded when appropriate
- lets other companies provide modules to enhance the benefits of NetWare

First, NetWare 5 uses NLMs to assist in its modular design because they can help control and reduce the amount of file server memory in use at any particular time. NLMs themselves are designed to provide one or more specific services to networks and to the users who access their services and resources. When the services or resources the NLM provides are not currently needed, the NLM can be unloaded from the server, or simply never loaded to begin with. This ability frees up file server memory (RAM) for use by other services and processes. When an NLM is needed, it can be loaded into file server memory and provide the needed service. It can then be unloaded from file server memory.

For example, when it is time to back up the data stored on a particular server, you can load the NLM which handles backup services, run the backup, then unload the NLM. That way, it does not take up memory needed by other NLMs, such as those providing printing or communication services.

Second, NLMs (which have been tested and approved by Novell) can be loaded into or unloaded from file server memory while the NOS is running without causing problems or abending the server. A server abend is an unexpected interruption of server processes which makes the services provided by the NOS and NLMs unavailable to network clients. A server *abend* requires that the server be restarted before its services and resources are once again available to network clients.

NOTE Novell has an extensive program of cooperation with third parties (companies other than Novell) in the development of networking software. This cooperation between Novell and third-party NLM developers helps to ensure that the NLMs they create and market function safely and effectively with the NetWare 5 product.

Finally, NLMs make the NetWare 5 NOS more valuable to companies because they make it possible—even relatively easy—for other companies to design and develop services other than those designed into the NetWare 5 product. For example, Novell provides NLMs which:

- load disk drivers
- load LAN drivers
- ensure successful migration of network data from one server to another
- provide printing services
- provide backup and restore services
- provide *UPS* (Uninterruptible Power Supply) services
- provide server monitoring services

Other companies develop and market NLMs that provide some of these same services as well. For example, other companies market NLMs that provide an alternative to the backup and restore capabilities of NetWare's *SMS* (Storage Management Services).

Other companies also develop and market NLMs that enhance or compliment the services already provided by NetWare 5 NLMs. Novell also develops and markets NLMs that enhance the basic services provided through the NLMs and core OS shipped with NetWare 5. For example, enhanced network management functionality is provided through Novell's ManageWise™ product.

Prerequisites to Installing NetWare 5

There are two basic prerequisites to Installing NetWare 5:

- meeting minimum hardware and software requirements
- planning and gathering needed information

MEETING MINIMUM HARDWARE AND SOFTWARE REQUIREMENTS

The "System Requirements" section of "Installing a Novell Server" in the online documentation describes the minimum NetWare 5 file server hardware requirements as:

- A PC with a 486/66, Pentium, or higher processor
- VGA or higher resolution monitor (SVGA recommended)
- 250 MB available disk space
- 32 MB of RAM (48 MB suggested)
- One or more network boards
- Serial or PS/2 mouse (optional)
- A CD-ROM drive that can read ISO 9660 formatted CD
- CD-ROM disk (for local installations)

In addition to meeting these minimum hardware requirements, you must also meet certain minimum software requirements. For example, you must have a licensed version of the NetWare 5 product. In addition, your license must be for a sufficient number of users to meet your peak networking demand, in order to ensure you do not inadvertently violate software copyright laws.

If you are not familiar with what these hardware or software requirements mean, you will find it useful to read Chapter 1, *Understanding NetWare 5 Networks and Their Components*, before

NOTE   you continue with the installation of NetWare 5.

Planning and Gathering Needed Information

During the installation of NetWare 5, you will be prompted to provide needed information. Some of the information requires that you first at least have decided what you will name the Directory tree, as well as what you will name the first container in that tree. That is why, if you have not already done so, you will want to read and understand the information in this book's Chapter 2, *Understanding NDS and the Directory Tree*, before you continue with the installation of NetWare 5.

Other information you may need to gather and provide during the installation of NetWare 5 includes:

- whether you are running a new installation or upgrading from another NetWare operating system
- the driver software for the network board installed in the computer, if it is not one of the Novell approved boards for which driver software is included in the Novell NetWare 5 product
- the settings that have been made on the network and hard disk boards in the event that these settings cannot be auto-detected (automatically read, identified, and provided to the install program) during the installation process

- the protocol your network uses: IP (Internet Protocol), IPX (Internet Packet Exchange), or both
- whether you will install this NetWare 5 file server into a new NDS tree, or into an existing NDS tree
- the name of the existing NDS tree if you are installing this NetWare 5 server into an existing NDS tree, the name for the new NDS tree otherwise
- what the container name is or will be for the container within the NDS tree into which you will be adding the NetWare Server object during install
- the password you will assign to the Admin User object, or the password for the existing Admin User object
- the name you will assign to this NetWare 5 file server
- the time zone (such as Mountain Standard Time) this file server is being installed into, and whether Daylight Savings Time applies
- whether there are additional products or services (such as Novell Distributed Print Services—NDPS) you want to install onto this file server once the installation of the file server has been accomplished
- whether you want to further customize the installation using the Custom Hallway provided with NetWare 5

To ensure that the hardware prerequisites are met, make an effort to use hardware (specifically network boards and disk drivers) supported by Novell and for which the drivers are included in NetWare 5, and to determine and gather the needed information before beginning the install. If this is done, the installation of NetWare 5 should go very smoothly.

Install NetWare 5

Although some time is required to install a NetWare 5 server, the majority of the work is actually done by the install program itself. The install program handles copying files, setting up the Directory tree if it doesn't already exist, and other basic installation tasks. As the individual who is conducting the install, you must:

- physically set up the file server hardware before you can begin the install
- create and format a DOS partition on the hard drive of the computer on which you will be installing the NetWare 5 server software (if needed)
- choose whether to use the CD-ROM or network install process
- insert into the CD-ROM drive the CD-ROM containing the installation and related software, and any other CD-ROMs for which you may be prompted (if you are doing a CD-ROM installation)

- provide any information for which you are prompted during the install, such as the network protocol to be used and whether the file server will be installed into an existing or a new NDS tree
- follow the procedures to further customize the install or add other products to the file server if you choose to do so

Even though it may sound from this list as though your tasks are far greater than that of the installation software's tasks, the installation software handles the vast majority of the actual installation process.

RUN A BASIC NETWARE 5 INSTALLATION FROM CD-ROM

You can install a NetWare 5 server from the CD-ROM or across the network when another NetWare 5 server already exists on your network. The NetWare 5 install has been designed to be as easy as possible, considering the complexity of the product being installed. To make it easier to install NetWare 5, the installation itself is GUI based, except for the first few screens which must be run before the GUI-based installation interface can be loaded and run. Once you are past the few text-based screen, the remainder of the install is even easier to complete.

To install a NetWare 5 file server from CD-ROM, complete the following steps:

1. Install the CD-ROM into the drive, change to the drive letter for the computer's CD-ROM drive, type **INSTALL**, and press **Enter**.

   If you prefer to run a text-based install instead of the default GUI-based install, type **INSTALL /T** instead of **INSTALL**.

2. Choose either **New Server** or **Upgrade** from the Type of Installation menu (see Figure 3-1). Choose **New Server** if this is the first time that a network file server has been installed on this computer.

3. When prompted, choose the appropriate settings for country, code page, and keyboard (see Figure 3-2).

4. After the install software auto-detects the computer's storage devices, network boards, and Platform Support Module, continue with the next step. If the install software cannot auto-detect these components, however, you will have to modify the list of Devices by choosing the correct device and providing the appropriate device driver. Then you can continue with the next step.

5. Choose to **Create a NetWare Partition**. The actual task of creating the NetWare partition is performed by the installation process by default. The install program also creates the SYS: volume on the NetWare partition, and creates and loads the Java virtual machine. This is required for the GUI portion of the install program.

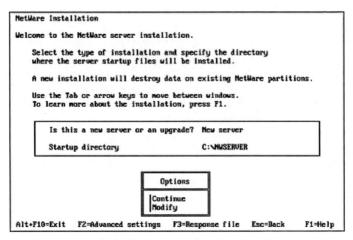

FIGURE 3-1 Type of Installation menu for choosing either a New Server install or an Upgrade.

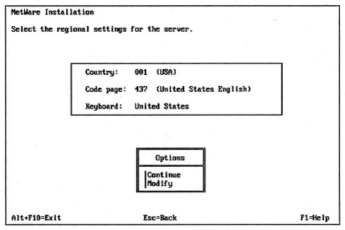

FIGURE 3-2 Menu from which you choose country, code page, and keyboard settings.

6. With the Java virtual machine loaded and the Server Properties window open (see Figure 3-3), type the name you chose for this file server, then click Next. While you provide a server name, the install software automatically provides an ID number for the server.

7. Click **IP**, **IPX**, or both in the Protocols window to bind the protocol(s) to the network board. Then, if applicable, provide the:

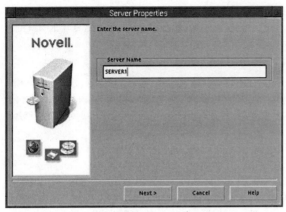

FIGURE 3-3 Server properties window through which you provide a name for this server.

- **IP address.** A number consisting of a 4-byte network number, a 6-byte node number, and a 2-byte socket number which uniquely identifies this server on the network
- **Subnet mask.** A bit mask which selects bits from an Internet address to create a subnet.
- **Router address.** A number which identifies this server as a network router so that it can successfully transmit packets across the network.

8. Choose the time zone in which this server physically resides, then specify whether Daylight Saving Time applies.

9. When prompted for the NDS Installation type, click the appropriate option depending on whether you want to install this server into a new tree (which you must do if this is the first file server in the network), or to add this server to an existing NDS tree.

10. When prompted, provide the name of the existing tree, or a name for the new tree; the container name into which the Server object is to be placed; and the Admin password, then click **Next**. (If creating a new NDS tree, you will have to enter the Admin's password twice to verify its spelling.) Be sure to document the information you provided in these fields.

   If you choose to create a new NDS tree, the install program verifies that its name is unique, then sets the time zone to that which you chose, initializes NDS, and creates NDS schema extensions.

11. Provide the license file path and name when the Licenses window opens, then click **Next**.

12. Check the box next to any of the additional products or services you want to install on the Other Products and Services window, then click **Next**. The needed files are copied and the Summary window opens, showing what products will be installed.

At this point, the main installation is almost finished. You can cause the installation to complete by clicking **Finish**. However, you can customize the installation by clicking the **Customize** button instead of the **Finish** button.

CUSTOMIZE THE NETWARE 5 INSTALLATION

From the Summary screen which opens when you are almost finished with the basic installation of a NetWare 5 server, you can choose to customize the NetWare 5 installation. This customization option lets you customize:

- the NetWare 5 OS
- the file system
- installed protocols
- NDS

Procedure for Customizing the NetWare 5 Installation

To customize any of these NetWare 5 services or resources during the installation, click the **Customize** button. This opens the Custom Hallway. From there, complete the following steps to customize the server install:

1. To modify information related to the NetWare 5 operating system, click **Operating System**, then click **Properties**.
2. As needed, make changes to the following:
   - the server's ID number, if you have a specific one you need to use because you are filtering or registering server numbers in your network
   - the server language or the Admin language
3. Click the **Close** button.
4. To modify information related to the file system, click **File System**, click **Properties**, then make any of the necessary changes as follows:
   - As needed, delete or make changes to existing volumes or partitions. To delete or modify volumes or partitions, select to highlight either the volume or partition you want to delete or modify, then click **Delete** to delete it, or **Edit** to modify it. Follow the prompts to complete the delete or modify process

See the Additional Information About Creating and Modifying Volumes section following this procedure.

NOTE

- As needed, create a new volume or partition by selecting **Free Space**, then clicking **New**. Follow the prompts to continue the create process, making choices and providing additional information as needed.

5. To modify protocols, click **Protocols**, then click **Properties**. As needed, modify any of the following:
   - the protocol type
   - the DNS (Domain Name Service) entry
   - SNMP (Simple Network Management Protocol) trap targets
   - Bindery gateway

The default frame types for NetWare 5 are Ethernet_II for TCP/IP, and Ethernet 802.2 for IPX/SPX. *Compatibility mode*, the ability to use both IP and IPX protocols, is provided in NetWare 5 by default.

KEY
CONCEPT

6. To customize Directory Services, click **Directory Services**, then click **Properties**.

   You can then modify properties associated with the Time Zone including:
   - time zone region
   - abbreviation
   - offset from Greenwich Mean Time
   - allowance for daylight saving time

   You can also specify which type of server is to be the *Time Server* (file server functioning as a source of time for other servers or workstations on the network). The default for the first server installed into the tree is *Single Reference* (a server which functions as the sole source of time on the network, providing time to secondary time servers and to client workstations), and *Secondary* (a server that gets its time from another time server, and provides time to workstations) for each additional server installed into the Directory tree.

7. When you have finished making changes to customize the server install, click **Finish**, then click **Close**. The server must now be rebooted.

Additional Information About Creating and Customizing Volumes

To minimize memory and disk space requirements on a NetWare 5 server, the default block sizes which are set during installation should be used. You can change them if you need to, increasing them in size for example if you choose to enable *block suballocation* (the ability to divide remaining space in partially-used disk blocks into 512-byte sizes so that the last portions of multiple files can share a single block).

KEY
CONCEPT

The default block size is determined by the volume size and is set during installation as follows:

- if the volume is 0 to 31 MB in size, the default block size can be 4 or 8 KB
- if the volume is 32 to 149 MB in size, the block size is 16 KB
- if the volume is 150 to 499 MB in size, the block size is 32 KB
- if the volume is 500 MB or larger, the block size is 64 KB

When you choose to create or modify volumes during install, you can change default options associated with volumes, including:

- enabling volumes to automatically mount (become available for access and use) when they are created
- enabling block suballocation
- enabling file compression (the automatic reducing in size of files not used for a period of time so as to save disk space)
- enabling data migration (enable the storage of seldom-used files on an external storage system which NetWare views as though the files were still on the NetWare volume)

KEY
CONCEPT

Enabling options such as file compression and data migration help you make better use of the file server's available storage space. Be aware, however, that if you enable file compression and the **SYS:** volume becomes full, NetWare will not be able to automatically uncompress any compressed files on the **SYS** volume, which could cause substantial NetWare server problems.

Designing and Organizing Network Resources

Most of the time, you will want to put as much time and energy as possible into designing your network's structure and the resources it provides before you perform the detailed tasks associated with installing and setting up your network, including installing your first NetWare file server. The simplest way to do that is to plan it on paper. Erasing a container name or two from a structure drawn on paper is much easier than moving a container within the actual Directory tree.

It is possible, however, to simply begin installing your network file server without having a diagram of the proposed network already drawn on paper. This is especially true if you are setting up a network for a company with only a few users and other objects. Thus, the instructions for installing the first NetWare server into the NDS tree were given first in this chapter. However, if you have a network of any noticeable size, you should design and organize your network resources, in your head at least if not on paper, before you install the first file server. This section provides design and resource organization suggestions and guidelines to help you be better prepared to design and organize your NetWare 5 network's resources.

When designing and organizing the network's resources, consider the following:

- how the design of the NDS tree affects the network
- how objects in the NDS tree can be accessed
- what shortcuts you can set up to simplify resource access and management
- which guidelines are available to help you effectively design and organize the network's resources

Effects of the NDS Tree's Design on the Network

There are three main ways in which the design of the NDS tree affects the network. The design of the NDS tree can affect the network when:

- planning NDS
- setting up resources
- accessing resources

DESIGN CONSIDERATIONS FOR PLANNING NDS

Although a company's actual structure is geographic in nature and the structure of the Directory tree can be geographic, a logical tree structure is often more useful. A logical structure must be carefully conceived and implemented if it is to be useful. A well-planned, well-designed Directory tree can make locating resources easier for the user, make managing the network easier for the network administrator, decrease traffic on the network, and provide some fault tolerance for the NDS database by ensuring sufficient distribution and duplication of the database across multiple network servers.

Design Considerations for Setting Up Resources

NDS planning by itself is not enough to ensure that the design of the Directory tree makes resource access as simple as possible. You must also consider where various objects are located within the Directory tree, the location of User objects being one of the more important considerations.

In order for users to have access to needed network resources such as printers, access to the objects associated with those resources must be given to each user's User object. By placing User objects into the same network container as the resources the user needs, you simplify user access to those resources. By default, network users whose User objects reside in the same container as the resources they want to access are given access to those resources without requiring additional setup by the network administrator.

KEY CONCEPT

Besides placing different resource objects such as Printer and Directory Map objects in the same container as the network user's User object, you simplify a network user's access to resources by automatically setting the user's current context for them before they login. The *current context* is the location within the Directory tree to which the workstation is currently pointed. The current context is displayed as a path of containers, listed in order from the current container to the [Root] of the Directory tree.

There are two specific places where you can automatically set the user's current context:

- in the Novell NetWare Client Properties page of a Windows 95 or Windows NT workstation
- in a login script (a list of commands that run when a user logs in to the network; sets up access to network resources and defines the user's networking environment)

In the Novell NetWare Client Properties page of a Windows 95 or Windows NT workstation (see Figure 3-4), provide the name of the *Preferred server* (the name of the file server you want the network to access when logging this user into the network). Also specify the name of the NDS tree in which the Preferred server is located. Then, specify the name context which leads from the container where the user's User object is located, up the Directory tree structure to [Root]. (You do not specify [Root] itself when specifying a name context.)

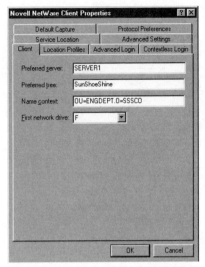

FIGURE 3-4 Example of the Novell NetWare Client Properties page used to set the user's current context.

KEY CONCEPT

When specifying a name context, you separate the name of each object with a period. This is similar to the way you specify a path in a file system. When specifying a file system path, however, directory names and the final file name in the file naming convention are separated by slashes (\), and the path goes from the highest level in the directory structure to the lowest level. When specifying a name context in the NDS Directory, container names are separated by periods (.), and the path goes from the lowest level in the Directory tree to the highest level.

For example, in the Directory tree and file system structures shown in Figure 3-5, the path to the file called **letter.txt** would be written as **c:\files\wp\letter.txt**. The name context for the User object called **STaylor** would be written as: **STaylor.EngDept.SSSCo**.

When using a login script to set the workstation's current context for the user, you use the **CONTEXT** command. You place this command either in the login script associated with the container in which the user's User object is located, or in the login script associated with the specific user's User object login script.

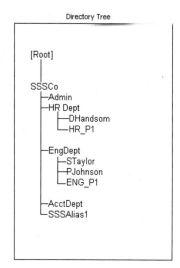

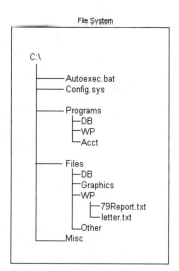

FIGURE 3-5 File system naming versus NDS name context.

NOTE

Setting the workstation's current context in the container login script is generally preferable to setting it in a user's User object login script. The single **CONTEXT** command within a container login script sets the current context for all users whose User object is in that container. Using a User object's login script to set the current context for multiple users within the same container would mean that you would have to place this command in the login script associated with every user whose User object resides in the container.

KEY
CONCEPT

When setting the workstation's current context in a login script, you follow the **CONTEXT** command with the User object's distinguished name. A *distinguished name* is the object's name and complete path, running from the container in which the object is located to the top of the Directory tree.

There are two kinds of distinguished name: typeless distinguished name, and typeful distinguished name. A *typeless distinguished name* lists the path from the object to the [Root] of the Directory tree without specifying the associated identifier. When using a typeless distinguished name, you use periods between each container and object name. An example of a typeless distinguished name would be: **.STaylor.EngDept.SSSCo**.

When you use a *typeful distinguished name*, you still specify the path from the object to the [Root] of the Directory tree, and you still use a period between each container and object name. However, you must also use the identifier for the type of object being specified, and follow that identifier with an equal sign (=). No space can exist between the identifier and the equal sign. The same example just given for a type-less distinguished name if shown using a typeful distinguished name would look like this: **.CN=STaylor.OU=EngDept.O=SSSCo**.

NOTE

When specifying a name context, you do not include [Root].

There are three identifiers used in most typeful distinguished names:

- **O**—Used to specify that the container is an Organization
- **OU**—Used to specify that the container is an Organizational Unit
- **CN**—Used to specify that the object being named is a Common Name (the name assigned to the object when it was created, such as the name of a User object)

KEY
CONCEPT

A common name is also known as a *relative distinguished name* because it identifies the object relative to its current location in the Directory tree, but does not specify the context of the object. Because objects in different containers on the network can have the same common name, they can only be uniquely identified by using a *distinguished name* (sometimes referred to as a *full distinguished name*). When specifying a distinguished name, you specify the common name of the object as well as the entire path from the object to [Root]. In addition to the use of a period between each object in the path, the path also must start with a period so that NDS knows you are specifying the complete, unique name for a specific object within the Directory tree.

For example, to specify the distinguished name as a typeless distinguished name for the **STaylor** User object shown in Figure 3-5, you must type the following: **.STaylor.EngDept.SSSCo**

To specify the full distinguished name as a typeful distinguished name for the **STaylor** User object shown in Figure 3-5, you must type the following: **.CN=STaylor.OU=EngDept.O=SSSCo**

To set the current context for the **STaylor** User object shown in Figure 3-5, using the **CONTEXT** command in a login script, you put the following command into the login script: **CONTEXT .STaylor.EngDept.SSSCo**

DESIGN CONSIDERATIONS FOR ACCESSING RESOURCES

Understanding name context and how to specify it, as well as what type of name context to specify, will help you set up and manage access to objects in the Directory tree. This is particularly important when you want to provide access to an object that is not in the same container as your network user's User object.

Accessing Objects Regardless of their Location

Once a user has logged in to the network, their current context has been set. The workstation is, by default, pointed to the container in which the user's User object resides. Whenever that user wants to access a network resource (object), the user can do so by specifying the object's common name. For example, the user can access a printer or network directory using the common name for the associated Printer or Application object, if the object resides in the same container as the user's current context. When a user accesses a network resource using its common name, NDS searches the current context for that object. If it does not find the object, it does not search any other containers. Consequently, a user can only use an object's common name to access an object if that object is in the same container as the user's (workstation's) current context. If the object is in another container, the user must specify the object's distinguished name.

When designing the network tree, consider whether the user will have to specify the name context for a resource (object) they want to access. If the user has to specify the name context, you may want to determine whether putting that object into the same container as the user would be simpler for the user.

Sometimes it isn't practical to place all of the objects a user may need to access in the same container as the user's User object. This is especially true if even just one of those users needs access to other objects which have been placed in other containers for ease of access by that container's users. When this happens, you can set up some shortcuts to help your users access the needed resources, and make managing those resources easier for you as the network administrator.

Setting Up Shortcuts to Resources

There are four types of objects you can create that were designed specifically to help simplify management of and access to network resources:

- Alias
- Application

- Directory Map
- Group

An *Alias* object refers to an object in another container. Commonly, you create Alias objects so that users in different containers can easily access the referred object. For example, a Printer object in one container can easily be accessed by users in other containers if you put into each of the other containers an Alias object that refers to the single Printer object.

An *Application* object points to an application on a volume in another container. By placing an application object in each container where User objects reside, and pointing that Application object to a single network application on the file server, all users on the network will have easy access to that application.

A *Directory Map* object refers to a directory on a volume in another container. Using a Directory Map object in a container lets users in that container easily access the directory to which the Directory Map object points. For example, you can create a Directory Map object to point to a directory on the file server where users can share common files.

A *Group* object is used to simplify the assignment of the same rights to network resources for multiple users whose User object exists in different containers throughout the network. Using a Group object makes the establishment of access to the same objects for multiple users a simple task. By creating a Group object, assigning User objects as members of that Group object, and giving the Group object the access to resources its members are to have, quick access to network resources is given simultaneously to all users whose User object is a member of that Group object.

To create any new object—particularly Alias, Application, Directory Map, and Group objects—start the NetWare Administrator utility, then follow these steps:

1. As needed, expand containers in the directory tree until you locate the container where you want the Alias, Application, Directory Map, or Group object to reside.
2. Right-click the container in which you want the object to reside, and then choose **Create**. You can also select the container and then choose **File > Create** from the File menu.
3. From the list of available objects (Class of New Objects), choose either **Alias**, **Application**, **Directory Map**, or **Group** to create the associated object.
4. Fill in the required information. The window that opens (see Figure 3-6) and the information it requests depends on the type of object you are creating. For example, if creating an Alias object, you must

give it an Alias name and a distinguished name which represents the Aliased object.
5. Click **Create**.

Although these steps were written to show you how to create a specific type of object using the NetWare Administrator utility, follow these same basic steps to create any type of object. Before using NetWare Administrator to create objects in the Directory tree—whether you are creating User, Alias, or any other type of object—make sure you have first selected the container into which you want to put the new object. Once you choose to create a specific type of object by clicking the object's type in the Class of New Objects window, you then provide information about that object. Some of the information you provide is required, such as the name of the object. Some information is optional, such as the telephone number of the user associated with a User object. Regardless of the type (class) of object you are creating, the NetWare Administrator will not create it in the Directory tree until you have provided all the required information. If you did not fill in all required fields, NetWare Administrator prompts you for any missing required information when you click **Create**.

Guidelines for Designing and Organizing Resources on the Network

When designing the Directory tree, determining where its available resources (objects) are to be placed, and defining access to those resources, there are some basic guidelines you should follow. Those guidelines fall into four categories:

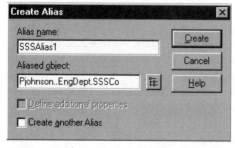

FIGURE 3-6 Example of the window that opens and the information you provide when creating an Alias object.

- NDS and NDS security
- file system and file system security
- printing
- user accounts and login security

The guidelines associated with all but the last of these categories are discussed here. Guidelines associated with user accounts and login security are discussed at the beginning of the next section in this chapter: ("Setting Up User Accounts").

NDS AND NDS SECURITY GUIDELINES

Chapter 4, *Establishing Security on a NetWare 5 Network*, discusses both NDS and file system security. By the time you reach Chapter 4, however, you should have planned how your network is to be set up and how security will be implemented. The guidelines in this and the following section: ("File System and File System Security Guidelines"), are here to help you in the planning of NDS and file system security.

When planning NDS security, consider the following:

- You don't have to do it all yourself. NetWare 5 is designed to let you split the responsibility for network management between multiple local network administrators. This ability is particularly useful when your network spans a large geographical area. When considering whether you will divide some of the network management responsibility, decide whether you will grant the local network administrators the Supervisor object right, or more limited object rights such as Create, Delete, and Rename. (Object rights and how to grant them are covered in detail in Chapter 4, *Establishing Security on a NetWare 5 Network*.)
- As much as possible, use default rights assignments. Each time you modify the rights which have been assigned to an object by default, you add a level of complexity to your management tasks. When you create an object in the Directory tree, NetWare 5 is designed to provide, by default, the rights that each class of object needs. Consider modifying those default rights only as the exception to the rule, rather than as the rule, and your administration tasks will be fewer.

FILE SYSTEM AND FILE SYSTEM SECURITY GUIDELINES

When planning the network's file system, consider the following guidelines for establishing file system security:

- When practical to do so, grant rights to access the file system to global network objects instead of individual network objects. Global objects are objects such as container (Organization and Organizational Unit), Group, [Root], and [Public] (an object created by the installation program designed to let users see the entire Directory tree as appropriate).

- Give an object specific rights to a volume by making that User's object a *trustee* (any object with assigned rights to another object in the Directory tree) of the volume. Then give that User object the appropriate rights. As with granting NDS security rights, certain default rights are established when you make the User object a trustee of the volume. If possible, use the default rights without modification to simplify your network administration tasks—including troubleshooting, which you may need to do on your network at some point in the future.
- Create Directory Map or Alias objects to give users access to network resources in containers other than that in which their User object resides. Creating these two objects makes it much easier to map a drive (set up a file system path for access to a specific directory or volume on a file server, and assign a drive letter to that directory or volume path).

PRINTING GUIDELINES

When planning and setting up network printing, consider the following guidelines:

- If possible, use a single print manager to manage printers in multiple contexts. Doing so simplifies management of network printers as you only have one print manager to work with.
- Unless you have printers on your network to which only a very limited number of users should have access (such as a printer that is always and only set up to print checks), grant public access to network printers.
- Assign the user role for a printer in one container to objects in another container which need to access and print to that specific printer.

Setting Up User Accounts

After planning user access to the network, setting up User Accounts begins with creating User objects in their appropriate containers. As with other objects in the Directory tree, each user object must have a name. Before you begin creating User objects, decide on a naming convention. For example, you may decide to use the person's first initial and last name, up to a maximum of eight characters, as the name for the associated User object. Because many first names are so common, you should probably avoid using only first names to name User objects.

Before creating User objects in containers, you should also familiarize yourself with and consider the following three guidelines for setting up user accounts and related login security:

- Create a template object for each container. This helps ensure that rights and default settings designed for one container do not accidentally get assigned to another container.
- Set intruder detection to **on** for each container in the Directory tree.
- Create Alias objects for users in one context who often login from workstations other than their default workstation.

You can successfully set up user accounts when you can:

- understand the function of a User object
- create User objects using the NetWare Administrator and UIMPORT utilities

Function of the User Object

Of all objects in the Directory tree, the User object is probably the most important and fundamental. User objects represent users on the network. Because the ability of users to access and use shared network resources and data is the primary purpose of having a network to begin with, the User object plays an important role in NetWare 5 networks and the Directory tree.

As part of the User object's primary function of representing users on the network, they:

- store information about the user and their working environment
- regulate a user's access to services, data, and resources on the network

Before a user can gain access to the network, they must have a User object. You create new User objects using the NetWare Administrator utility. This process creates User objects one at a time. You can also create multiple User objects in the Directory tree at the same time by using the UIMPORT utility.

Using NetWare Administrator to Create User Objects

To create one or a few user objects, use the NetWare Administrator utility. User objects are created with NetWare Administrator by following the same process you use to create other objects such as container objects like Organization or Organizational Unit objects. (Figure 3-7 shows an example of the Create User dialog.) Earlier in this chapter you

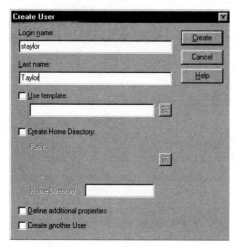

FIGURE 3-7 Example of the Create User dialog.

read instructions for creating objects such as Directory Map and Alias objects using NetWare Administrator. The basic process for creating User objects using NetWare Administrator is the same.

When creating a User object, the main differences in the process are:

- you choose **User object** instead of **Directory Map** or **Alias** from the Class of New Objects list, and
- you provide the information that is specifically required for a User object, as well as any additional information you want to provide and for which a related property is available (such as a telephone number).

Using UIMPORT to Create User Objects

While you use NetWare Administrator when you only have a few User objects to create, you may want to use the UIMPORT utility if you have:

- many User objects to create
- a database file containing user information you can export from the database software into a delimited ASCII text file, so that the exported file can be used by UIMPORT to create the User objects for you

Using UIMPORT is not a panacea for creating User objects. UIMPORT cannot put information (values) into properties associated with User objects if the information does not already exist in the database file. You will have to go back later and add that information manually. But for initially creating the User objects in the Directory tree, and filling in basic values, the UIMPORT utility is a very functional tool.

When using the UIMPORT utility, remember the following:

- you must have a database file of user information that can be exported to a delimited ASCII text file
- the default delimiter is a comma, but that can be modified
- you must create a control file to specify the format and field sequence for the data being imported with UIMPORT
- you can set certain parameters to restrict whether UIMPORT creates new User objects or simply updates existing User objects in the Directory tree
- you can specify the context into which the User objects will be placed within the Directory tree

The Novell NetWare 5 Administration course does not detail the processes associated with or the steps to follow in order to run the UIMPORT utility. If your network has a database file containing user information, and you think using the UIMPORT utility might be of benefit in creating User objects in the Directory tree, the syntax for creating the required control file is provided in Novell's NetWare 5 online documentation. You can access information about the syntax for the control file by clicking the following, beginning from [Home] in the online documentation set:

```
Reference > Utilities Reference > Utilities > UIMPORT
```

Controlling Access to Network Resources

Controlling access to network resources requires that you plan the Directory structure to optimize user access to network resources, while minimizing the work you must do as a network administrator. Keeping network administration work to a minimum wherever possible not only makes your job easier, but also reduces the opportunity for security breaches, mistakes, and so on, which could seriously jeopardize the integrity of your network and the data and resources it contains.

This chapter has already covered much of what you can do as a network administrator to control access to network resources, other than establishing and maintaining security which is discussed in detail in Chapter 4. Therefore, remember that in addition to establishing and maintaining security as discussed in Chapter 4, controlling access to network resources involves:

- using and taking full advantage of objects such as Directory Map, Group, Alias, and Application to provide access to resources when those resources are contained in different containers in the Directory tree
- providing typeful or typeless distinguished names, as appropriate, when establishing access to objects in the Directory tree
- relying on the common name to locate an object only when the object and the user's User object both reside in the same container, and the user's current context is set to the container in which the user's User object resides

Chapter Summary

This chapter discussed several important aspects of setting up a NetWare 5 network. First, it explained how to install NetWare 5 into a new Directory tree. When installing NetWare 5, be aware that:

- NetWare 5 consists of two major components: the NetWare (core) operating system (the NOS), and NLMs (NetWare Loadable Modules). While console commands are part of the operating system, NLMs are separate programs which must be loaded before they become a functional part of the NetWare file server.
- There are four different types of NLMs: Name space, LAN drivers, Disk drivers, and Utilities.
- NetWare 5's modular design reduces memory usage, allows modules to be easily loaded or unloaded when appropriate, and lets other companies provide modules to enhance the benefits of NetWare.
- To begin the installation of a new NetWare 5 file server from CD-ROM, you must first ensure the system meets the minimum hardware and software requirements, and then gather any information you may need to install the server. You start the installation by inserting the CD-ROM into the drive, changing to the CD-ROM drive, and typing Install. Most of the installation process is automatic. You generally have to provide only some information, and determine whether you want to customize the installation before you finish it.
- From the Summary screen which opens when you are almost finished with the basic installation of a NetWare 5 server from CD-ROM, you can choose to customize the NetWare 5 installation. This customization option lets you customize the NetWare 5 OS, the file system, installed protocols, and NDS.

When designing and organizing the network's resources, you should consider the following:

- how the design of the NDS tree affects the network
- how objects in the NDS tree can be accessed
- what shortcuts you can set up to simplify resource access and management
- which guidelines are available to help you effectively design and organize the network's resources

In particular, you want to be aware that you can use different resource objects, such as Printer and Directory Map objects, in the same container as the network user's User object to simplify a network user's access. Because you can set up the network to automatically specify a user's current context for them before they login, they will be able to access any resources in their current context. The current context is the location within the Directory tree to which the workstation is currently pointed. The current context is displayed as a path of containers which are listed in order from the current container to the [Root] of the Directory tree.

To successfully plan and design your network as well as to install and set it up, you also need to understand naming context. The ways in which objects can be located depends at least in part on how their naming context is specified. One way to specify an object is by using its distinguished name, of which there are two kinds: typeless distinguished name, and typeful distinguished name. A typeful distinguished name requires the use of the identifier (CN, OU, or O) and the equal sign (=) for each container in the path. For example, **.CN=STaylor.OU=EngDept.O=SSSCo** is a typeful distinguished name. A typeless distinguished name does not require the use of identifiers; an example of a typeless distinguished name for the same User object in the same Directory tree structure would be **.STaylor.EngDept.SSSCo.**

This chapter also discussed setting up user accounts and, among other things, recommended the following three guidelines for setting up user accounts and related login security:

- Create a template object for each container. This helps ensure that rights and default settings designed for one container do not accidentally get assigned to another container.
- Set intruder detection to on for each container in the Directory tree.
- Create Alias objects for users in one context who often login from workstations other than their default workstation.

This chapter introduced you to many new terms, including current context, typeful naming, and distinguished name. In order to understand all of the network design and setup tasks you must perform, and to pass the CNA and CNE certification exams, you need to ensure you understand those terms and the concepts associated with them. You should also perform at least one NetWare 5 server install in order to familiarize yourself with the process and the information you need to supply. That information is, of course, based at least in part on the network planning and designing you do for your network.

Practice Test Questions

1. The software loaded on the file server that facilitates communication between the server and workstations is/are:
   A. Config.nlm
   B. Utility modules
   C. LAN drivers
   D. Disk drivers

2. The software responsible for providing network management and other services is:
   A. Config.nlm
   B. Utility modules
   C. LAN drivers
   D. Disk drivers

3. Which three of the following are benefits of NetWare 5's modular design?
   A. Reduced memory usage
   B. Easy loading and unloading
   C. Command-line utilities that are easier to use
   D. Third parties can develop compatible modules

4. If you prefer not to take advantage of NetWare 5's GUI install, you can type what command to start the installation?
   A. Install
   B. Install -G
   C. Install /T
   D. Install +T

5. Which of the following is *not* a customization option available during installation?
   A. Properties
   B. OS
   C. File system
   D. NDS
   E. Protocol

6. To modify a volume, click **properties** after choosing the which customization option?
   A. Properties
   B. OS
   C. File system
   D. NDS
   E. Protocol

7. The DNS entry can be modified during the customization of the install by choosing which option?
   A. Properties
   B. OS
   C. File system
   D. NDS
   E. Protocol

8. In what three ways do the design of the NDS tree affect the network?
   A. Planning NDS
   B. Setting up resources
   C. Accessing resources
   D. Setting up shortcuts
   E. Planning file structure

9. The location within the Directory tree to which the workstation is presently pointed is called:
   A. Current context
   B. Preferred server
   C. Distinguished name
   D. Common name
   E. Relative distinguished name

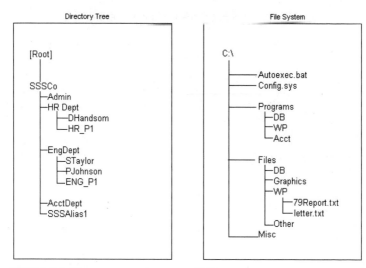

FIGURE 3-8 File system naming versus NDS name context.

10. In Figure 3-8, which type of naming convention does **.Staylor.EngDept.SSSCo** follow?
   A. Current context
   B. Preferred server
   C. Distinguished name
   D. Common name
   E. Relative distinguished name

11. Based on Figure 3-8, which of the following is an example of a typeful distinguished name?
   A. .CN=STaylor
   B. .CN=DHandsom.OU=HR_Dept.O=SSSCo
   C. .O=SSSCo.OU=EngDept.CN=STaylor
   D. .DHandsom.EngDept.SSSCo

12. In the Novell NetWare Client Properties page of a Windows 95 or Windows NT workstation, which two items of information can be provided?
   A. The user's Preferred server
   B. The name of the login script to run for the user
   C. The user's current context
   D. The name of the NDS tree

13. When using a login script to set the workstation's current context for the user, use
    A. Console nlm
    B. Config.sys file
    C. Context command
    D. The equal sign

14. Which one of the following is *not* an identifier which can be used in a typeful distinguished name?
    A. O
    B. OU
    C. C
    D. [Root]
    E. CN

15. Another name for a Common Name is:
    A. Current context
    B. Preferred server
    C. Fully distinguished name
    D. Common name
    E. Relative distinguished name

16. To locate an object in the Directory tree using its complete and unique name, specify the object's:
    A. Current context
    B. Preferred server
    C. Distinguished name
    D. Common name
    E. Relative distinguished name

17. Of the following, which one is *not* a type of object specifically designed to help simplify management of and access to resources?
    A. Alias
    B. Application
    C. Computer
    D. Directory Map
    E. Group

18. A Printer object in one container can be easily accessed by users in another container if in addition to the Printer object itself, you create which type of object in another container?
    A. Alias
    B. Application
    C. Computer
    D. Directory Map
    E. Group

19. To simplify the access by multiple users in one container to a shared subdirectory in the file system, which type of object should you create?
    A. Alias
    B. Application
    C. Computer
    D. Directory Map
    E. Group

20. Which two methods can you use to make a new object in a specific container?
    A. Click the container, then click **Create**
    B. Click the container, then click **File > Create**
    C. Right click the container, then click **Create**
    D. Right click the container, then click **File >Create**

21. If you want to simplify file system access, you should grant rights to which of the following global objects (choose four)?
    A. [Root]
    B. Group
    C. [Public]
    D. Organization
    E. Organizational Unit

22. Which two of the following are common to both NDS and file system security?
    A. Trustees
    B. Alias
    C. Directory Map
    D. Supervisor Right

23. To create User objects from an existing database of user information, run:
A. Config.nlm
B. NetWare Administrator
C. Uimport
D. Any of the above

24. Which of the following is the least important consideration when designing and organizing the network's resources?
A. How the design of the NDS tree affects the network
B. How objects in the NDS tree can be accessed
C. Availability of a user information database
D. What shortcuts can be set up

25. Of the following, which is *not* a recommended guideline for setting up user accounts and related login security?
A. Install one NetWare 5 file server before doing any planning of your Directory tree
B. Create a template object for each container
C. Set intruder detection for each container
D. Create Alias objects for users in one context who often log in from another workstation

Answers to Practice Test Questions

1. C	8. A,B,C	14. D	20. B,C
2. B	9. A	15. E	21. A,C,D,E
3. A,B,D	10. C	16. C	22. A,D
4. C	11. B	17. C	23. C
5. A	12. A,D	18. A	24. C
6. C	13. C	19. D	25. A
7. E			

CHAPTER 4

Establishing Security on a NetWare 5 Network

To successfully establish security on your NetWare 5 network, you must consider three aspects of network security. The first is that of physical security. Physical security involves such things as keeping your network file servers in locked and protected areas. For example, you may want to keep your file servers in a room to which most users do not have access. Physical security also involves such things as establishing a routine for regular backup of data on the network, and as-needed backup of the NDS tree. Physical security is not discussed in this chapter, however. For information about physical security, see the companion to this book: *Accelerated NetWare 5 CNE Study Guide*, also by this author.

This chapter does discuss the other two aspects of network security that you must consider and which you can directly manage:

- NDS security
- File system security

To ensure security on the network, NetWare implements five basic security systems. Of those five security systems, you can directly manipulate two of them (file system and NDS). You can only indirectly manipulate the other three based on how you establish and maintain security on your network through the file system and NDS. The five security systems that are implemented in NetWare 5 are:

- Login
- File system
- Server
- Network printing
- NDS

Because you can only directly manipulate file system and NDS security, this chapter concentrates on those two aspects of network security. Therefore, file system and NDS security are the main focus of the first four sections of this chapter, while login, server, and network printing security are discussed in the last section of this chapter. To ensure you have the basic knowledge you need to successfully manage network security, this chapter is designed to provide you with:

- an understanding of file system security
- an understanding of NDS security
- an understanding of rights
- instructions for implementing file system security
- instructions for managing network security

Understanding File System Security

Understanding file system security begins with a basic knowledge of the file system and its components. The file system on a NetWare file server is much the same as the file system on any Intel microprocessor-based computer. It contains a root which is the top of the structure. Below the root are files and directories. Below the directories are other files and directories.

 Do not confuse the [Root] of the NDS Directory tree with the root of the file system on a NetWare file server. They are separate entities. The root of the file system is simply the top of the file system structure. On a NetWare file server, the root of the file structure is effectively the volume, as the first place you can begin putting directories and files is just below the volume.

NOTE

Function of the File System

The purpose or function of the file system on a NetWare server is the same as that of the file system on a computer, with one exception. The function of both is to provide a place where data and programs can be stored and from which they can be accessed. On a NetWare file server, however, access to programs and data files is designed to be shared, often simultaneously, by multiple users. On a computer, the access is designed only for the single user currently working on that computer.

Components of the File System

There are five basic components of the NetWare file system:

- NetWare server
- Volume
- Directory
- Sub-directory
- Files

Because you need to be familiar with DOS and computers as a prerequisite for becoming a network administrator, those components of the NetWare file system which are the same as those of an individual computer's file system (directories, sub-directories, and files) are only mentioned here. There are still two components, however, that are specific to the NetWare file system.

The NetWare server is the first component specific to the NetWare system. You should by now also already understand what a NetWare server is. You may not fully understand what a volume is, however. A *volume* is a logical division of the NetWare server's file storage space—generally the hard disk—but it can also be something such as a CD. A volume contains a defined amount of space: it can be an entire hard disk, a

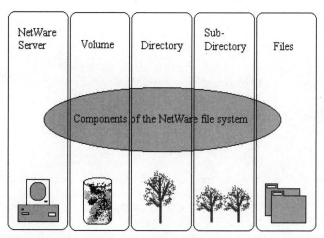

FIGURE 4-1 The five basic components of the NetWare file system.

portion of a hard disk, or multiple hard disks connected together and effectively functioning as if they were one much larger hard disk. (When a single volume exists across multiple hard disks, this is referred to as *spanning volumes*.)

All NetWare servers have one or more volumes. During the installation of a NetWare 5 file server, the **Sys:** volume is created by default. If you want other volumes created as well, you specify that fact and give each volume a name when you install NetWare 5.

All volumes have names. In the file system, you access the volumes using their volume name. In the Directory tree, each volume is represented by a Volume object. Volume objects also have names, and the Volume object in NDS that represents a volume existing on a NetWare server uses the same name as the actual volume.

In the NetWare file system, you do not store files at the volume level. Instead, you create directories below the volume level into which you can place other directories (sub-directories) and files. During the installation of NetWare 5, the install program creates directories such as **Public**, into which it places files and other directories as needed.

The install program creates only those directories and files which it needs to successfully start the NetWare 5 server, manage NDS objects, and so on. Installing application programs, saving data files, and so on are the network administrator's responsibility. For more information about managing the network file system, see Chapter 10, *Administering a NetWare 5 Network*.

Understanding NDS Security

NDS security and file system security have many things in common, including:

- **trustees** (any object with rights to access a network resource)
- **rights** (assigned ability to access or manipulate a network resource)
- **effective rights** (the combination of rights that determines what network resources an object can access or manipulate)
- **inheritance** (the ability of rights granted to one object to apply to all objects below that level in the Directory tree)
- **IRF** (Inherited Rights Filter; a process which restricts or prevents rights from one container from flowing down the Directory tree to other containers)

NDS security and file system security are separate. There are three specific ways in which NDS security differs from file system security:

- NDS security has two sets of rights: object and property, while the file system has only one set which applies to directories and files.
- In NDS, the Supervisor object and property right can be blocked by the IRF, but in file system security, the Supervisor right cannot be blocked by the IRF.
- While rights that are not blocked by the IRF in the file system flow down through the file system structure, rights in NDS (with one exception) do not flow into the file system structure. The exception is that rights granted to the Server object in NDS *do* flow down into the file system structure, but can be blocked using an IRF.

To protect the integrity of the Directory as well as the data and programs stored on NetWare file servers, and to prevent unauthorized users from accessing network resources, you must have a basic understanding of the different types of rights: NDS and file system.

Understanding Rights

Although similar in several ways, there are two separate systems of rights in NetWare 5. Each system has its own area of responsibility, and for the most part, they do not overlap with each other. There is one exception to that statement, as you will learn as you read about NDS and File system rights in NetWare 5. To successfully establish and then administer network security, you must understand both types of rights.

NDS Rights

NDS rights are those rights assigned to and for objects in the NDS tree. Concepts associated with NDS rights that you must understand if you are to successfully set up and maintain NDS security are:

- object trustees
- object rights
- property rights

OBJECT TRUSTEES

**KEY
CONCEPT**

As previously noted, a *trustee* is any object with rights to access a network resource. Trustees are commonly User objects, but other objects such as Group objects are also frequently made a trustee of one or more network resources. Trustees may be given complete and full rights to manage the properties and values of an object to which they have been assigned, or may be given more limited rights.

KEY CONCEPT The network resource (object) to which other objects have been assigned as trustees must be made aware of those trustee assignments, and of the property and object rights that were granted to those trustees. This is done through the use of the network resource object's property called the Access Control List (ACL). The *ACL* is a property of an object. It stores information about who (which objects) is allowed to access that object, and what access each object is allowed to have.

To assign a User, Group, or other object as a trustee of a network resource, such as an Organizational Unit object, you access the network resource object's (in this case the Organizational Unit object) ACL property. Then you specify which objects (User, Group, etc.) are to be trustees and which Object and Property rights they are to have. You do this using the NetWare Administrator utility (see Figure 4-2), the instructions for which are found later in this chapter in the section titled "Implementing NDS Security."

OBJECT RIGHTS

As you probably realized from the preceding section of this chapter, there are two types of rights you can grant to an object: object rights and property rights. *Object rights* control which trustee can access the object and what type of access the trustee can have. *Property rights* control what the trustee can do to the properties of the object to which the trustee has been assigned.

FIGURE 4-2 Example of an ACL.

Table 4-1 shows the types of NDS rights, identifies whether the right is an object right or a property right, and provides a brief description of what the associated right allows the trustee to do. For example, there is both a Supervisor object right and a Supervisor property right. Having the Supervisor object right gives the trustee full and unrestricted access to all properties associated with the object, while having the Supervisor

TABLE 4-1 A list of NDS object and property rights, and the effective access they provide.

NDS Right	Type of Right	Description
Supervisor	Object and Property	As an object right, it gives unrestricted access to the object as well as to all of its properties. As a property right, it gives unrestricted access to the values of all properties to which it is assigned.
Browse	Object	Allows trustees to see this object in the Directory tree.
Create	Object	Gives trustees the right to add leaf objects and other container objects to the object, if the object is a container object. Does not apply to leaf objects.
Delete	Object	Allows the trustee to remove this object from the Directory tree.
Rename	Object	Lets the trustee change the name of this object.
Compare	Property	Allows the value of one property to be compared to the value of another property, returning either a **True** or **False** to indicate whether the properties are the same.
Read	Property	Grants the trustee the right to read the values associated with the property to which it applies.
Write	Property	Lets the trustee add, change, or delete the values associated with this property.
Add or Delete Self	Property	Allows the trustee to add its User object to or remove its User object from a property when the property's value is a list of object names.

property right gives the trustee full and unrestricted access to all of the object's properties.

PROPERTY RIGHTS

Property rights control the type of access other objects have to the object for which property rights have been assigned. Unlike Object rights, which are granted to the entire object, Property rights can be granted either to all properties associated with an object or to only specific properties of that object, such as the Full Name, Department, or Telephone property of a User object.

For example, when the Write property right is granted to a user (through their User object) for a specific property of another object, that user can add, change, or delete the values of that property. In the case of the **STaylor** User object, if the User object **DHandsom** is given the Write property right to **STaylor**'s Telephone property, the user DHandsom can add, change, or delete user **STaylor**'s Telephone number.

File System Rights

As with NDS, you can assign trustees in the file system, then give those trustees various types of rights to directories and files. While some of the names of the file system rights are the same as the names of some of the NDS object and property rights, file system rights do not apply to objects in the NDS tree.

When establishing file system security, keep the following in mind:

- File system rights do not apply to objects in the NDS tree, including Server or Volume objects. They only apply to directories and files that exist on the storage devices of network file servers.
- Like NDS, the file system uses inheritance to pass rights down the file system structure to directories and files at lower levels of the directory structure. This is referred to as the *flow of rights*, and is usually discussed in relation to rights flowing down the file structure.
- You can prevent rights from flowing down the file structure by implementing one or more Inherited Rights Filters (IRF) in the file system. This is similar to how the flow of rights can be stopped in NDS, except that you use an Inherited Rights Mask (IRM) in the Directory tree, and an IRF in the file system. Although similar in function, they are two different things.
- When planning and implementing rights for a particular user, you should be primarily concerned with what the user's effective rights will be at any given directory level or file within the file system. (Effective

rights are discussed in this chapter in the section titled "Effective Rights.")

TYPES OF FILE SYSTEM RIGHTS

There are eight file system rights you can use for managing security in the file system. Some of the rights apply only to directories, while some of the rights apply only to files. The eight file system rights are:

- **Supervisor (S):** Gives full access, all rights, to the user for the directories and files to which it is granted.
- **File scan (F):** Allows the user to see the directory or file name within the file system structure.
- **Access control (A):** Lets the user change trustee assignments for the directories or files to which it applies, as it grants all of the file system rights except Supervisor.
- **Modify (M):** Lets the user change the name of the directory or file, as well as the attributes (assigned characteristics that determine what can be done with the directory or file) associated with it.
- **Erase (E):** Allows the user to delete files and directories.
- **Create (C):** Allows the user to add new files and directories.
- **Write (W):** Lets the user open a file and make changes to its content.
- **Read (R):** Lets the user open a data file and read its contents, or run a program file.

KEY CONCEPT

To help you remember these file system rights, remember that: **S**ome **FAME** **C**omes **W**ithout **R**eason. (Someday you may be a famous network administrator, but I'll bet it won't be without at least one good reason.)

KEY CONCEPT

All directories and files have certain attributes associated with them. Attributes regulate what can be done to the specific directory or file. For example, when DOS is installed on a computer, some of the system files are hidden from view. If you type the DOS command for viewing the list of files and sub-directories (DIR), you will not see any of the hidden system files because these files have been assigned the Hidden (H) attribute.

There are several attributes. Some of them apply only to files, and some of them apply only to directories. Table 4-2 lists file and directory attributes, tells you whether they apply only to files, only to directories, or to both files and directories, and provides a brief description of each attribute.

TABLE 4-2 A list of all network directory and file attributes, along with a brief description and an indication of whether the attribute can be applied to files, directories, or both.

Attribute	Application	Description
Archive needed (A)	Files	This is a DOS attribute. It indicates the file has been updated since the last time it was archived.
Can't compress (Cc)	Files	Prevents the file from being compressed, a process which reduces its size to save storage space.
Compresses (Co)	Files	Allows the file to be compressed.
Copy inhibit (Ci)	Files	Prevents this file from being copied.
Delete inhibit (Di)	Files and directories	Prevents the file or directory from being removed.
Don't compress (Do)	Files and directories	Tells the system not to compress this specific file or directory even if Compress was set on its parent directory.
Don't migrate (Dm)	Directories	Prevents this directory from being moved to another storage medium other than the server's hard disk, even though it meets the other criteria which would otherwise cause automatic migration of the directory.
Don't suballocate (Ds)	Files	Tells the system not to suballocate this file.
Execute only (X)	Files	Identifies this file as an executable, and prevents it from being modified in any way.
Hidden (H)	Files and directories	This is a DOS attribute. It prevents the file or directory from displaying when the DOS DIR command is used.
Immediate compress (Ic)	Files and directories	Allows the file or directory to be compressed immediately instead of waiting for a later time.

Migrate (M)	Files	Identifies this file as one to be moved to another storage medium other than the file server's hard disk, when certain specifications are met.
Normal (N)	Files and directories	Resets the file or directory's attributes to their original settings.
Purge (P)	Files and directories	Identifies the file or directory as one which should not be stored in the deleted.sav directory for recovery if needed at a later date.
Read only (Ro)	Files	This is a DOS attribute. It prevents anyone from modifying the file.
Read write (Rw)	Files	This is a DOS attribute. It lets the file be modified.
Rename inhibit (R) Rename inhibit (Ri)	Files Directories	Prevents the name of the file or directory from being changed.
Shareable (Sh)	Files	Allows multiple users to access the file simultaneously.
System (S)	Files and directories	This is a DOS attribute. It identifies the file or directory as being part of the operating system.
Transactional (T)	Files	Ensures the file is tracked by NetWare's Transactional Tracking System used for ensuring data integrity.

EFFECTIVE RIGHTS

Effective rights are those rights to a specific directory or file with which the user ends up when all rights or rights filters (IRFs) have been applied. Effective rights, before any IRFs are applied, are the result of three types of rights the user may receive:

- **Default rights.** Those rights a user receives simply because they were given to this user by default. For example, all rights to the entire file system are given to the administrator (user Admin) who installed the file server into the Directory tree. This occurs by default because NetWare 5 is designed to ensure that someone initially has all rights to the file system on each file server as it is installed into the Directory tree.

- **Rights assignments.** Those rights which are specifically assigned to a user at a given directory or file level within the tree.
- **Inheritance.** Those rights to directories or files that a user receives because they had the same rights to a directory at one or more levels above the current directory or file.

Once all of these rights are considered, the IRF then blocks rights from flowing any further down the file system structure. Figure 4-3 shows how the IRF modifies a user's effective rights down the file system structure from the point at which the IRF is applied.

KEY CONCEPT When the network administrator grants a user specific rights to a directory or file, those rights are not filtered out at the specific directory or file to which they were granted. They will be effected, however, by an IRF applied at a lower level in the directory structure.

KEY CONCEPT To calculate a user's effective rights at any given level in the file system structure, you may have to look at which rights a user has been specifically assigned at every directory above the level for which you are calculating the user's effective rights. When calculating the user's effective rights, consider the following at every level above the level for which you are calculating effective rights:

- whether any default rights exist
- whether any specific rights were granted to this user
- whether any IRFs were applied

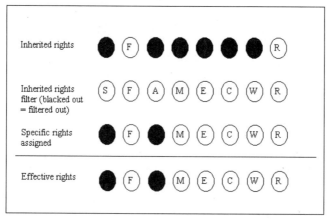

FIGURE 4-3 A diagram of how rights flow in the file system.

To determine any user's effective rights at any level in the file system:

1. Start at the highest level in the tree where the user could have received any rights, either explicitly or by default, and determine what those rights are.
2. Work your way down the file system structure to the next lowest directory level and subtract any rights which an IRF has filtered out.
3. At the same directory level of the file system structure for which you performed Step 2, add any rights the user was granted to this specific directory.

You now know what the user's effective rights are at this specific directory level in the file system structure. If you need to know the user's effective rights at a level below this directory, repeat Steps 2 and 3 of the procedure for each directory in the path leading to the lowest level in the directory for which you are calculating the users effective rights.

Effective rights = (Inherited rights) - (rights filtered by IRF) + (Specific assigned rights).

KEY
CONCEPT

Implementing NDS Security

Implementing NDS security requires that you first understand how the network is organized (the structure of the Directory tree), and which of your users need access to which of the network's resources. Once you know this, you can determine what NDS (and file system) rights you need to assign, and to which objects those rights should be granted.

To assign NDS rights to any User, Group, or other object in the Directory tree, you must first assign that object as a trustee of that User, Group, or other object. To assign an object as a trustee of another object and then give that trustee specific object and property rights, use the NetWare Administrator utility and complete the following steps:

1. Launch (start) the NetWare Administrator utility, and move through the Directory tree until you locate and select (click on to highlight) the object to which you want to assign one or more trustees. For example, to assign trustees to the User object called **STaylor**, locate then click the **STaylor** User object.
2. From the Menu bar, click **Object**, then click **Trustees of this Object**. (You can also simply locate the object, right-click on it, then click Trustees of this Object from the menu.)

3. From the Trustees of *object_name* (**STaylor** in this example) window, click **Add Trustee**.
4. Browse the Directory tree to locate the object to be made a trustee of this object, then choose it.
5. Choose which Property rights and Object rights this trustee is to have for this object.
6. Click **OK**.

If you repeat Steps 1 and 2 of this procedure, you will then see the object you just added as a trustee in the list of this object's trustees. Click **Effective Rights** to see what the newly added trustee's rights are to this object.

Figure 4-4 shows which NDS objects are trustees of the specified user (**STaylor**). In this figure, the **STaylor** user object (STaylor.EngDept.SSSCo) is a trustee of this **STaylor** User object. Users are made trustees of their own User object by default when the User object is created.

KEY
CONCEPT

When implementing NDS security, give rights only to those users or NDS objects who need to have them. To successfully implement NDS security, remember to:

1. Start with the basics all users need. For example, all users should be able to view the directory tree structure and have access to shared files and applications on the network.
2. Avoid using the **All Properties** option for assigning rights, since it gives the trustee access to all properties of the object.

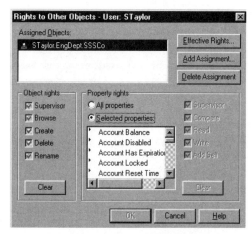

FIGURE 4-4 The Trustees of STaylor window. Displays the effective rights for the User object named **STaylor** to the **STaylor** User object.

Although you may want some users to have access to some of an object's properties, you may not want the trustee to be able to even view the information when the value associated with some of the properties is sensitive or confidential.

3. Assign specific rights using **Selected Properties** to avoid security problems. Give the user the right to modify their own User login script, but don't give them the right to change things such as their User object's name.

4. Be cautious when assigning the Write property right to the object's Trustee. If you assign this right to the Trustee, the Trustee can then make anyone on the network a Supervisor.

5. Be cautious when assigning the Supervisor object right to a Supervisor object. Doing so gives full access to all files and directories in the file system.

6. When assigning the Supervisor object right, consider its implications. Assigning the Supervisor object right grants the Supervisor right for all properties to the Trustee to whom you gave the Supervisor right.

7. Be aware that the Supervisor object right can be filtered out. If you filter out the Supervisor object right in a section of the NDS tree, you will no longer be able to manage that section of the Directory tree.

Managing Network Security

You probably recognize by now that network security regulates:

■ who accesses the network and its resources
■ how the network and its resources are accessed

Part of managing security on a network is, of course, ensuring that all users have the right access to network resources and data—no more, no less. Despite your care and diligence, there will sometimes be problems with network security. For example, you may discover that a user on the network has been adding, deleting, or modifying objects in a container without authorization. Any user with sufficient rights can do this. If this occurs, you need to find out which user it is. Maybe that user will drop you an e-mail or call to let you know it was them. Most often, however, you will have to research the security issue yourself, then modify one or more user's rights to correct the situation. To determine which user has the incorrect rights, you will need to look at the effective rights for each user.

Researching user's effective rights helps you solve another type of security problem you may have on the network as well: insufficient rights. Sometimes a user may not have access to a necessary container. Checking the user's effective rights will show you what rights they do have. However, it won't show you where those rights came from. To determine that, you must discover:

- which rights the user may have inherited
- which rights were assigned directly to a user at each of the containers in the Directory tree that reside above the container to which the user needs rights
- which rights were granted to the user because they were assigned as a member of a Group object or an occupant of the Organizational Role object
- which rights the user may have as the result of being assigned as *Security Equivalent* (a method of assigning rights to one object which are the same rights that were assigned to another object) to another object
- whether the user's rights are being screened out as the result of an IRF placed on this container or on another container at a higher level in the Directory tree

Of the five security systems provided by NetWare 5, this chapter has concentrated on NDS and file system security because they are the most complex and noticeable levels of network security, and the two systems you can directly and profoundly effect. They are also the two levels of security at which you must look when seeking to implement, modify, maintain, or troubleshoot network security. Login, server, and network printing are also important security levels, however, and thus are discussed below.

Login Security

Login security controls who can access the network, as well as when they can access it and from where. Once login security has given a user access to the network, NDS security controls access and use of the Directory, while file system security controls access and use of the data and program files stored in the file system.

When a user logs in to the network, login security performs the following process to ensure the user gets the access to the network and its resources to which they have been given rights, but does not get access to network resources or data to which the user is not authorized:

1. Verifies that the User object name with which the user is attempting to log in is a valid User object.

2. Checks to see what account restrictions apply to this user, and whether the user has met those restrictions (such as whether any time restrictions exist, and if so, whether the user is attempting to log in during the allowed times).

3. Determines if the account associated with this User object requires a password, and if so, whether the user has supplied the correct password.

4. Authenticates (automatically verifies that the log in or other requests are from the original user and have not been forged) the user to the network if all of the previous steps in this process were successful, or denies the user access if they were not.

The login process performs one additional security-related task if appropriate. If the user attempting to log in to the network provides a User object name and password which do not match, the user is considered to be an intruder. This process is known as *intruder detection*. See "Intruder Detection" later in this chapter for more details.

ACCOUNT RESTRICTIONS

In addition to requiring that a user have an authorized user account and matching password before they can log in, the network administrator can also set various related user account restrictions. To set these restrictions, the network administrator establishes or modifies settings associated with the following User object properties:

- Account balance
- Connections
- Disable/Enable
- Expiration date
- Network address
- Password
- Time

These different restrictions are set for a user by accessing the appropriate property page associated with the User object. For example, for User object **STaylor** as shown in Figure 4-5, you click the **Login Time Restrictions** page tab to open the property page where you set restrictions such as what time of the day or night or what days of the week this user can log in. Other login restriction property pages you can access when you open Details for a user are:

- Login Restrictions
- Password Restrictions

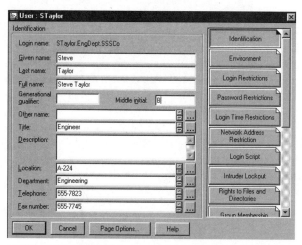

FIGURE 5-5 The Identification page which opens by default when you right-click a User object, then click **Details**. It shows other property pages you can open, including those related to login security.

- Network Address Restrictions
- Intruder Lockout

Account Balance

If accounting is installed and set up, you can use it to set restrictions on the amount of network resources the user accesses. A monetary value is set for different resources, the user is given a monetary credit associated with their account, and charges are then applied against that credit for the user's use of various resources.

Connections

Use Connections to limit the number of workstations the user can simultaneously use to log in to the network. As a license for the NetWare software is required for each user that logs in to the network, you may want to restrict users from logging in to the network from more than one workstation at a time, particularly if the number of user licenses you own is close to the number of actual users you have on your network.

Disable/Enable

With Disable/Enable, you can prevent anyone from logging in to the network using this account. You can manually disable an account. You can also automatically disable an account when needed by either requiring the user to change their password periodically, and defining how many times they can log in to the network without changing their password when required (grace logins,) or by placing an expiration date on their user account. You can also enable this account again at a later time if you choose to do so. This is particularly helpful if you have seasonal workers.

Expiration Date

Use the Expiration Date property to automatically disable a user's account. Set an expiration date; when that date has passed, the user's account is automatically disabled.

Network Address

By specifying one or more network addresses in this property, you restrict from which workstations a user can log in.

Password

Using the Password property lets you specify whether a password is required in order for a user to log in to the network using this User object name.

Time

Using the Time property lets you limit the hours during the day and the days during the week when the user can log in to the network. This restriction is one which can be set for the Group object as well as for the User object.

AUTHENTICATION

Authentication not only verifies user access, but makes it possible for a network user to log in to the network only once, and gain the full access to the network allowed by their account. Earlier versions of NetWare and some other network operating systems do not include authentication. Consequently, if a user wanted to access resources or data on multiple file servers, the user had to log in to each file server. With authentication, however, that requirement does not exist. One login is all that is necessary, and authentication takes care of the rest.

INTRUDER DETECTION

Once login security determines that the user attempting to log in may be an unauthorized user, it notifies intruder detection of the attempted unauthorized access. As a rule, when unauthorized access is identified, the account the intruder was attempting to use to gain network access is locked for a period of time.

Intruder detection settings can be defined by the network administrator when setting up the network. They are properties of each user account. The network administrator can:

- define how many attempts to log in with a mismatched login name and password are allowed during a given amount of time (such as within a 10 minute period) before this user is considered to be an intruder (number of incorrect login attempts)
- set how long a user's account is to remain locked once intruder detection occurs (the account reset time and the time until reset)

In addition, if intruder detection is set, the network address of the workstation from which the unauthorized access was attempted is recorded.

Once intruder detection occurs and an account is locked, a user with the Supervisor object right to the User object for which intruder detection has been tripped has to unlock the user's account before it can be accessed. Alternately, the user can simply wait for the amount of time the account is to remain locked as specified by the network administrator to pass; then the account will be unlocked and the user allowed to log in to the network.

Server Security

Server security is primarily concerned with the physical security of the file server. In addition to suggesting that file servers be placed in an area where they can be locked away from unauthorized access, NetWare also lets you set a password for the file server's console. If you require a password for access to the server from the console, a user must either know the console password or the administrator password in order to access the file server from the console.

Network Printing Security

Printing security controls which users can access network printers, which printers they can access, and whether they can manage network printing services. Printing security is controlled primarily by designating a printer as one of two types:

- public access printer
- controlled access printer

PUBLIC ACCESS PRINTER

A public access printer is designed to require almost no administrative intervention. Security is very low for a public access printer. All authorized network users can access a public printer as it has no corresponding NDS object.

Controlled Access Printer

A controlled access printer is the opposite of a public access printer. It does have a corresponding NDPS Printer object in the Directory tree. Security and access to this printer are implemented and controlled. It therefore requires greater management by the network administrator.

Public access printers and controlled access printers are discussed in detail in Chapter 5, *Making Print Services Available*.

Chapter Summary

To ensure security on the network, NetWare implements five basic security systems, only two (file system and NDS) of which you can directly manipulate:

- Login
- File system
- Server
- Network printing
- NDS

The purpose and function of the NetWare network file system is to provide access to and storage of data and programs. To fulfill its purpose, the NetWare file system is composed of five basic components:

- NetWare server
- Volume
- Directory
- Sub-directory
- Files

The NetWare server is the computer on which the NetWare operating system and associated software has been loaded. A volume is a logical division of the NetWare server's file storage space—generally the hard disk, but it can also be something such as a CD. Logical divisions within a volume are called directories and sub-directories, and they contain files and other sub-directories.

In the NetWare file system, you do not store files at the volume level. You store files at the directory or sub-directory level. When NetWare is installed, it creates volumes, and in those volumes it creates directories. Within those directories it stores the files needed to run the NetWare server. Other directories and files you create yourself.

File system and NDS security have a great deal in common. The following concepts and terms are common to both the file system and NDS, although their implementation may not be exactly the same:

- trustees (any object with rights to access a network resource)
- rights (assigned ability to access or manipulate a network resource)
- effective rights (the combination of rights that determines what network resources an object can access or manipulate)
- inheritance (the ability of rights granted to one object to apply to all objects below that level in the Directory tree)
- IRF (Inherited Rights Filter: a process which restricts or prevents rights from one container from flowing into the Directory tree to other containers)

Although similar in nature and implementation, NDS security and file system security are separate. There are three specific ways in which NDS security differs from file system security:

- NDS security has two sets of rights: object and property, while the file system has only one set which applies to directories and files.
- In NDS, the Supervisor object and property right can be blocked by the IRF, but in file system security, the Supervisor right cannot be blocked by the IRF.
- While rights which are not blocked by the IRF in the file system flow down through the file system structure, rights in NDS (with one exception) do not flow into the file system structure. That exception is that rights granted to the Server object in NDS do flow into the file system structure, but can be blocked using an IRF.

NDS rights are those rights which are assigned to and for objects in the NDS tree. NDS security requires that a trustee be assigned to an object before rights can be assigned. The rights are then specifically assigned to the trustee for a given object. One easy way to do this when you want to assign the same rights for a single object to several NDS objects is through the use of the Group object. Using the group object, you assign objects as members of the group, make the Group object a trustee of the object to which you want to give access, then assign rights to the Group object. All members of the Group object then have access to the object to which the Group object was assigned as a trustee.

When assigning a trustee to an object, you effectively do so by accessing the Access Control List (ACL) property of the object to which you are assigning one or more trustees. You accomplish this task using the NetWare Administrator utility.

Object trustees can be granted two types of rights: object rights and property rights. Object rights control which object the trustee can access and the type of access the trustee has. Property rights control what the trustee can do to the properties of the object.

There are eight file system rights which you can grant. To remember them, remember this phrase: Some FAME Comes Without Reason. There are five NDS property rights and five NDS object rights. Both have a Supervisor right which grants full access and allows complete control of an object or its properties. The rights are:

- **Property rights:** Compare, Read, Write, Add/Delete Self, and Supervisor
- **Object rights:** Browse, Create, Delete, Rename, and Supervisor

Directories and files also have attributes associated with them. Attributes regulate what can be done to the specific directory or file. Some attributes are DOS attributes, while others are NetWare attributes. Attributes along with rights control file and directory access and manipulation.

All the user really cares about in the end is what they can do with or to the directories, files, and objects they need to access. In the file system, the issue is effective rights. Effective rights are those rights which a user has left. To calculate effective rights, follow this formula: Effective rights = (Inherited rights) − (rights filtered by IRF) + (Specific assigned rights).

To implement security in either the NDS tree or the file system, you must make trustee assignments, assign rights to the trustees, and then judiciously use IRFs and IRMs. To assign NDS rights, use the NetWare Administrator utility. When implementing NDS security, remember to assign only the needed rights to the specific objects. Start with the basics which all users need, assign selected property rights, and remember that in NDS you can use an IRM to filter out the Supervisor object right. Be careful not to do so, however, unless you have already given a user a specific Supervisor object rights assignment to that portion of the NDS tree. Otherwise, you will not be able to manage that portion of the tree.

While NDS and file system security are what you concentrate on when managing network security, remember that there are three other types of security as well: login, file server, and network printing. Login security is controlled by the NetWare software, and involves a process of authentication and encryption which prevents unauthorized users from accessing the network. File server security is controlled by restricting physical access to the server console, and password protecting the console as appropriate. Network printing security involves, at a minimum, how you implement public access and controlled access printers.

Practice Review Questions

1. Which of the following is not a component of the NetWare file system?
   A. Volume
   B. Directory
   C. Sub-directory
   D. Object
   E. Server

2. The highest level of division of a storage device on a NetWare server is called a/an:
   A. Volume
   B. Directory
   C. Sub-directory
   D. Object
   E. Server

3. Before you can assign any user or object in the NDS tree the ability to access other objects within the NDS tree, you must first:
   A. Establish the organization of the file system
   B. Make the object a trustee of the object to which you want the object to have access
   C. Assign the Supervisor object right to the object which is to access the other object in the tree
   D. Ensure rights flow from the top of the directory structure to the location where you want the object to have rights
   E. Both steps B and D must be done first

4. The ability of rights granted to one object to apply to all objects below that level in the Directory tree is known as:
   A. Effective rights
   B. Common rights
   C. Trustee
   D. Inheritance
   E. File system flow

5. The restriction of rights which prevent them from flowing down the NDS structure is accomplished by:
   A. Applying an IRF
   B. Establishing limited effective rights
   C. Creating multiple trustees
   D. None of the above

6. One significant way in which NDS security differs from file system security is:
   A. NDS security has two sets of rights, while file system security has only one
   B. The Supervisor right cannot be blocked in NDS
   C. Rights granted to the Server object in NDS are blocked from flowing into the file system
   D. All of the above are significant ways in which NDS security differs from file system security
   E. None of the above are true statements regarding NDS versus file system security

7. When you want to give a specific set of rights to access an object in the NDS tree to multiple users at the same time, use which object?
   A. Container
   B. [Root]
   C. Group
   D. Server
   E. Organization

8. The property of an object by which you assign other objects as trustee is called:
   A. Name
   B. [Root]
   C. User
   D. Group
   E. ACL

9. Which two types of rights can be granted to a trustee of a Organizational Unit?
   A. Property
   B. File
   C. Directory
   D. Object
   E. Supervisor

10. The right which lets the trustee add, change, or delete the values associated with this property is:
    A. Read
    B. Create
    C. Write
    D. Browse
    E. Modify

11. The right which allows trustees to see this object in the Directory tree is:
    A. Read
    B. Create
    C. Write
    D. Browse
    E. Modify

12. That which regulates what can be done to a specific directory or file is called:
    A. Attribute
    B. Effective right
    C. Rights assignment
    D. IRM
    E. None of the above

13. The login process that automatically verifies that the login or other requests are from the original user and have not been forged is called:
    A. Intruder detection
    B. Verification
    C. File server security
    D. Authentication

14. The process by which a user's login name and password are matched together to ensure the user is an authorized user is known as:
    A. Intruder detection
    B. Verification
    C. File server security
    D. Authenication

15. Which three are part of account restriction security on a NetWare 5 network?
    A. Verification
    B. Account balance
    C. Connections
    D. Console password
    E. Expiration date

Answers to Practice Review Questions

1. D	6. A	11. D
2. A	7. C	12. A
3. B	8. E	13. D
4. D	9. A,D	14. A
5. A	10. C	15. B,C,E

CHAPTER 5

Making Print Services Available

In versions of NetWare before NetWare 5, printing could sometimes be a little difficult to set up, and occasionally troublesome to manage. Once you attached printers to NetWare servers or workstations, you had to create print queues (or print queue objects), printer objects, and print server objects. These aspects of printing required setup and administration. You had multiple utilities you could use to set up and administer network printing such as Pconsole, Nprinter, Nwadmin, and NetWare Administrator.

In NetWare 5, setting up and managing network printing is much easier, particularly if you have no specific need to prevent some or most network users from accessing any given network printer. NetWare 5 makes printing set up and administration easier because it implements *NDPS* (Novell Distributed Print Services).

Understanding NDPS

NDPS is the result of a joint effort by three companies—Novell, Hewlett-Packard, and Xerox—to create printing services which would be independent of network servers and which would provide better printing services by:

■ improving overall network performance as the result of reducing the overhead associated with having printers on the network

- reducing the costs, both in time and money, associated with administering printing on a network
- increasing printing performance by reducing printing problems

To successfully provide better printing services, NDPS ships with many useful features:

- enhanced support for Windows 3.1, Windows 95, and Windows NT network clients
- compatibility with non-NDPS printing services (backward compatibility)
- immediate access to network printers which have been set up then plugged in to the network (plug-and-print capability)
- ability to choose commonly-used print drivers and download them directly to workstations on the network
- delivery of current and timely information about the status of network printers and print jobs to both administrators and users (bi-directional feedback), including event notification
- elimination of SAP (Service Advertising Protocol) traffic on the network, which improves overall network performance
- multiple printer configuration creation (such as which paper tray to use and whether to print in color or in black only) which can be applied to different network users
- additional scheduling options that provide greater flexibility in scheduling print jobs
- reduced administration as printing is tightly integrated with NDS, providing NDS security and a single point for administering network printing

NDPS is successfully implemented in NetWare 5 in part because of its joint development, but also because of NetWare 5's basic design. Instead of requiring network print queues, print servers, printers, and several utilities to set up and administer printing services, NDPS can be implemented by adding a single object to the Directory tree: the NDPS Manager (although your printing implementation may require that you add other NDPS objects). In addition, NDPS uses only two types of Printers:

- public access printers, which are printers that are available to everyone on the network without any restrictions. They provide true plug-and-print capabilities, have no security associated with them, and can be managed using the Tools menu in NetWare Administrator (see Figure 5-1). In addition, public access printers are not represented as objects in the Directory tree.
- controlled access printers are printers associated with an NDS object, and which can be highly restricted and tightly administered. Because of their representation in the Directory tree, their configuration can

be manipulated, and event and status notification implemented and customized. In addition, access to them can be controlled using the NDS security options. Also, because controlled access printers are represented in the Directory tree by printer objects, those users whose User object is in the same container as the printer object automatically have rights to the controlled access printer. For users whose User object is not in the same context as the controlled access printer, you must grant them rights to the printer object.

A public access printer can easily be converted into a controlled access printer by creating a printer object for it in the Directory tree. You can then use NetWare Administrator to manage the printer object.

KEY CONCEPT

The NDPS Manager object is the object you see and work with in the Directory tree in order to set up network printing. There are actually four components of NDPS (see Figure 5-2):

- NDPS Manager
- Printer Agent
- Gateway
- NDPS Broker

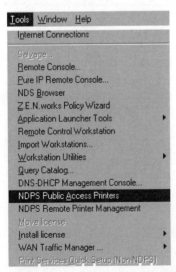

FIGURE 5-1 The tools menu in NetWare Administrator from which you can manage public access printers.

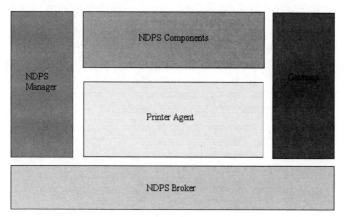

FIGURE 5-2 Components of NDPS

NDPS Manager

The NDPS Manager controls printing on the network. It is represented in the Directory tree by an NDPS Manager object. It in turn manages each of the Printer Agents on the network, and each Printer Agent then represents a single printer on the network.

Because a single NDPS Manager object can control an unlimited number of Printer Agents on the network, you will need a limited number of NDPS Manager objects in your Directory tree. As a rule, you should create an NDPS Manager object for each server on your network, if you want those servers to have NDPS printers assigned to them.

Creating one or more NDPS Manager objects in the Directory tree is the first step to setting up network printing using NDPS.

KEY CONCEPT

Once created, the NDPS Manager objects take responsibility for:

■ storing the information that **NDPS.nlm** needs in order to interface with Printer Agents
■ providing access to the NDPS Manager console, from which you can perform some limited management and configuration tasks

With the NDPS Manager, you can control multiple printers, but you only have to load the NDPS Manager on one server. However, if the

NDPS Manager is controlling a local printer (a printer attached to a file server,) the one server you choose to load the NDPS Manager on should be the server to which the printer is attached.

Printer Agents

The network administrator can control multiple printers using the NDPS Manager because the NDPS Manager can control multiple Printer Agents. A *Printer Agent* is a physical printer's logical representative in the network. A Printer Agent represents only one printer, so each printer must have a Printer Agent to represent it. A Printer Agent helps reduce set up and management of printers because it takes the place of and performs the functions which once were handled by the printer it represents, as well as the functions once handled by a print queue, print server, and spooler.

The Printer Agent (see Figure 5-3) can be implemented as:

- software running on a server
- part of the printer which is directly attached to the network.

If the Printer Agent is software running on a file server, it can represent:

- a printer attached to a file server
- a printer attached to a workstation

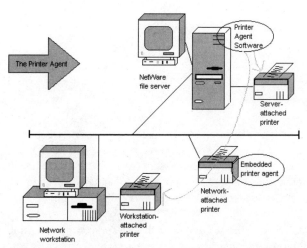

FIGURE 5-3 Examples of how the Printer Agent can be implemented.

Otherwise, the Printer Agent for a printer attached directly to the network is embedded in the printer itself.

KEY CONCEPT

One printer agent exists for each printer on the network. Therefore, if you have a printer attached to a file server, and a printer attached to a workstation, each printer must have a corresponding Printer Agent.

The Printer Agent is responsible for:

- managing the many and varied tasks the printer performs, including the processing of print jobs
- providing network clients with information about a particular print job, document, or attributes of the printer itself
- ensuring successful printing to a wide range of print devices in various document production environments
- notifying the appropriate network clients of printing issues such as problems, completion, change of status, and errors

Gateways

A *gateway* is software loaded on the NDPS server (server on which the NDPS broker is loaded) that ensures that printers—as well as some systems such as UNIX and Macintosh, which are not NDPS-aware, or systems which must have queues from which to take print jobs—can process print jobs in an NDPS environment. A gateway must be specifically configured for the print system or printer it is supporting. At present, NDPS currently supports the following gateways:

- HP (Hewlett-Packard)
- Xerox
- Novell

NOTE

The Novell gateway consists of two components: a Print Device Subsystem, and a Port Handler. The Novell gateway makes it possible to use NDPS printing services in Novell's older non-NDPS aware printing environments which use Nprinter, or which place print jobs into a print queue before sending them to printers. Also, you use the Novell gateway for most non-HP or non-Xerox printers.

When you create a new Printer Agent, you choose and configure a printer gateway for the printer supported by this gateway. A gateway's configuration includes the make and model of the printer it supports. This is necessary because the gateway takes the NDPS commands and print queries, translates them into a language the printer can understand, and then forwards them to the actual printer.

PRINT DEVICE SUBSYSTEM

The Print Device Subsystem (PDS) is an NLM which provides a user interface where you can create a Printer Agent. When you create a Printer Agent, this NLM is automatically loaded on the file server. It stores information such as the make and model of the printer in a database.

You must use the PDS utility whenever you create a Printer Agent for a printer that is not connected directly to the network (when it is connected through a workstation or a file server). You also use the PDS utility when the printer does not have a specific NDPS gateway. In addition, if the printer is providing printing services using Pserver, you use the PDS utility to create the Printer Agent.

PORT HANDLER

The Port Handler's primary responsibility is to ensure that the PDS can communicate with the printer, regardless of how the printer is actually connected to the network. The port handler allows the printer's network interface to use any number of methods, including:

- parallel ports
- serial ports
- QMS protocol
- remote/network printer protocol

NDPS Broker

The NDPS Broker is a module that is loaded on the network and added as an object to the NDS tree when NDPS is installed. (See Figure 5-4 to view the identification page for a NDPS broker.) Its primary duty is to provide network printing services which were not available in earlier versions of NetWare. Those services are:

- **Service Registry Service (SRS):** Makes it possible for one of the two types of NDPS printers (public access) to advertise themselves on the network so that users can take advantage of the printer's services.
- **Event Notification Services (ENS):** Makes it possible for printers to send specific notices about the printer's status or the status of jobs it is servicing to the appropriate network users.

FIGURE 5-4 Identification page for an NDPS broker.

- **Resource Management Services (RMS):** Makes it possible to install and update resources in one centralized network location, and then download those installed or updated resources to network clients, including printers, as needed

The NDPS Broker is created when NDPS is installed. One NDPS Broker is sufficient to service any file server that is no more than three hops along the communications media away from an existing NDPS Broker. If the file server containing the NDPS Broker is more than three hops away from the server on which you are currently installing NDPS, then another NDPS Broker is automatically created.

Setting Up Print Services

Setting up print services using NDPS requires that you complete several basic steps, including:

1. Verifying that each of the servers on which you plan to load NDPS meet the minimum hardware requirements for an NDPS server, and that you have the proper object rights.
2. Installing the NDPS software.
3. Creating and running the NDPS Manager.
4. Ensuring the NDPS Broker and NDPS Manager are running on the server.
5. Creating Printer Agents.

Meeting Minimum Requirements

Each file server which is to provide NDPS printing services must meet these minimum hardware requirements:

- 80 MB of disk space on the SYS volume
- 4 additional MB of RAM
- a CD-ROM drive

As the individual installing NDPS, you must meet these minimum rights requirements:

- Supervisor Object right to the Server object (if this is the first NDPS server you are installing)
- Browse, Create, Delete, and Rename rights to the container in which the server on which you are installing NDPS is located (if this is other than the first NDPS server you are installing)
- Read, Write, Modify, Create, and File Scan rights to the file system at the root of the volume (to create Printer Agents for public access printers)
- Browse and Create object rights to the container in which the NDPS Printer object exists (to create controlled access printers)

Installing the NDPS Software

There are two ways you can install the NDPS software:

- by choosing to install it during the NetWare 5 server installation
- by installing it using the Other Products option of the **Nwconfig.nlm** run on the server after the NetWare 5 server software has been installed

If you choose to install it during the NetWare 5 server install, you do so when you are prompted to choose other products to install. At the Other Products window which opens during the NetWare 5 server install, a list of check boxes with associated products is presented. The box titled **Install Novell Distributed Print Services** (NDPS) is already checked so that NDPS will be installed to this server by default. Click the box to uncheck it if you do not want to install NDPS. When you accept the default and install NDPS, the command for loading the **NDPS.nlm** is placed into the **Autoexec.ncf** startup file to ensure the **NDPS.nlm** is loaded on the server each time the file server is booted.

You use the **Nwconfig.nlm** to load the NDPS software when you did not choose the **Install Novell Distributed Print Services** (NDPS) check box during the Other Products installation portion of the NetWare 5 server install. To install NDPS software using the **Nwconfig.nlm**, load the **Nwconfig.nlm** at the file server console, then choose the **Install an item or product listed above** option. Specify that you want to install NDPS software, and follow the prompts to complete the installation.

Creating and Running the NDPS Manager

The NDPS Manager is an NDS object; you create it using NetWare Administrator in the same way you create other NDS objects. First, you locate the container into which you want to place the NDPS Manager. You should choose the same container in which the Server object representing the NDPS server (the server with NDPS loaded on it) is loaded. To create the NDPS Manager object, complete the following steps:

1. Right-click the container object into which the NDPS Manager object is to be placed.
2. Click **Create**. The New Object dialog opens displaying the Class of new object list (see Figure 5-5).
3. Scroll through the list until you see NDPS Manager, then click **NDPS Manager** to select it, and click **OK** to begin the create process. The Create NDPS Manager dialog opens (see Figure 5-6).
4. In the Create NDPS Manager Object dialog, provide a name for the NDPS Manager object, then browse the tree to locate the file server on which NDPS has been loaded, and the volume on which you want NDPS to store the NDPS database.

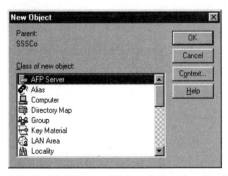

FIGURE 5-5 The New Object dialog showing the list of objects you can create. You will notice that the NDPS Manager object does not display. To see it, you must scroll down the list.

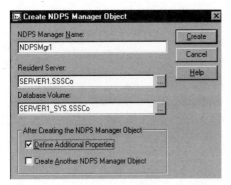

FIGURE 5-6 The Create NDPS Manager Object dialog showing the list of objects you can create.

5. Make sure the box next to Define Additional Properties is checked.
6. Click **Create** to create the NDPS Manager Object.
7. Specify additional information associated with the NDPS Manager object you created. In particular, you must assign the Admin object for each container in the Directory tree to be Managers of this NDPS Manager object.
8. Click **OK** to create the NDPS Manager object.

Once you create the NDPS Manager, you must load it at the file server. You can either add the **Load** command to the **Autoexec.ncf** file, or enter the command manually at the server console prompt. If you do not add the command to the **Autoexec.ncf** file, you will have to manually load the NDPS Manager each time you bring the server down and reboot it.

Whether entering the command at the server console prompt, or placing it into the Autoexec.ncf file, follow this format:

```
Load Ndpsm.nlm name_and_context
```

Replace name_and_context with the name and context of the NDPS Manager. For example, if you named the NDPS Manager **NDPSMgrS1**, and placed it into the SSSCO container where the Server1 server object exists, the command would read as follows:

```
Load Ndpsm.nlm NDPSMgrS1.SSSCO
```

Creating Printer Agent and Printer Objects

After you create the NDPS Manager and load **Ndpsm.nlm** at the file server, you create one or more Printer Agents.

NOTE

You must have the **Ndpsm.nlm** loaded before you create Printer Agents. If you do not load it first, you are prompted to do so when creating the first Printer agent.

Part of creating the Printer Agents involves creating printers, either public access or controlled access. Therefore, the procedures in this section explain how to create a Printer Agent, as well as how to create public and controlled access printers.

CREATE A PRINTER AGENT

As with the NDPS Manager, you create Printer Agents using NetWare Administrator. To create a Printer Agent, complete the following steps:

1. Browse the Directory tree until you locate the NDPS Manager object, then right-click it and choose **Details** to open the Identification page associated with the NDPS Manager object (see Figure 5-7).
2. Click Printer Agent List, then click New. The Create Printer Agent dialog opens (see Figure 5-8).
3. Provide a name for this Printer Agent, then browse the tree to provide the name and context for the NDPS Manager to associate it with.

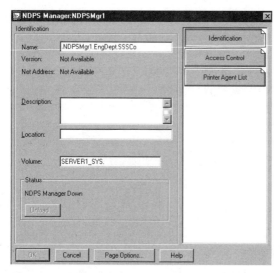

FIGURE 5-7 Example of the Identification page associated with an NDPS Manager object.

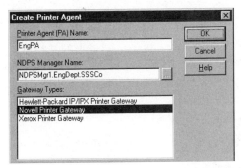

FIGURE 5-8 Example of a Create Printer Agent dialog.

4. Choose the type of gateway to be associated with this Printer Agent.
5. Configure the gateway you chose. (See "Create a Public Access Printer" below for more information on configuring the gateway.)
6. Once you have provided all of the information required to create the chosen gateway, click **Finish** or **OK**, depending on the type of gateway you chose to configure.

CREATE A PUBLIC ACCESS PRINTER

When you create a Printer Agent list to associate with the NDPS Manager, you configure the gateway as well. When you configure the gateway, you are effectively creating a public access printer for the printer you choose. Therefore, to configure the gateway and create a public access printer, complete one of the following:

■ If you chose to create a Hewlett-Packard Gateway, first choose the protocol (IP or IPX). Next, choose either the printer from the Printer/JetDirect list if it is a Jet Direct printer, or the IP address for the printer. Then, click **OK**.

■ If you chose to configure the Xerox Gateway, follow the on-screen instructions form the Xerox Setup Wizard. If the Xerox printer you are using is connected directly to the network, click **Next**, then follow the prompts. If the Xerox printer you are using is connected to a server using a parallel port, click **Cancel** and choose the **Novell Printer Gateway** instead.

NOTE

If you do not have a Hewlett-Packard or Xerox printer for which you need a gateway, choose the **Novell Printer Gateway**. It is designed to provide generic functionality so that you can use all types of printers.

- If you chose to create a Novell Printer Gateway, choose the Printer Type, then choose the Port Handler Type, and click **OK**. When specifying the Novell Port Handler, the Configure Port Handler for Printer Agent dialog opens. Within this dialog you choose the Connection Type and Port Type, then click **Next**. Depending on the Connection Type you chose, you may be prompted to provide additional information.

CREATE A CONTROLLED ACCESS PRINTER

If you want to create a controlled access printer, you need Browse and Create object rights to the container where you want to create the controlled access printer. You also must be designated as a manager of the NDPS Manager object that controls the associated Printer Agent.

NOTE

If you are logged into the network as Admin, and you completed Step 6 of the procedure for creating an NDPS Manager, you already are designated as a manager of the NDPS Manager object. If you did not complete Step 6 of that procedure, or you are logged in to the network as a user other than Admin or as a user without Admin equivalent rights, you must either go back and perform Step 6, or assign rights to your current User object.

To create a controlled access printer, complete these steps:

1. Using NetWare Administrator, locate the container where you want to create the controlled access printer, then right-click the container's name.
2. Click **Create**. The New Object dialog opens.
3. Click **NDPS Printer** in the Class of New Object list, then click **OK**. The Create NDPS Printer dialog opens (see Figure 5-9).
4. In the NDPS Printer Name field, type a name for this controlled access printer.
5. Make sure the **Create a New Printer Agent** radio button in the Printer Agent Source area is active.
6. Click either **Define Additional Properties** or **Create Another NDPS Printer**.

NOTE

Unless you are simultaneously creating multiple NDPS Printer objects, after which you will be going back into the Details of each object to provide additional information, click the **Define Additional Properties** checkbox.

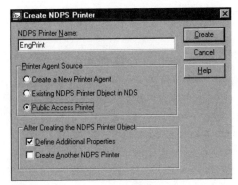

FIGURE 5-9 Example of a Create NDPS Printer dialog.

7. Provide the required additional information, creating the controlled access printer following the same process now as if you were creating a public access printer.

Managing Network Printing

After you have created public and controlled access printers, there are three types of printer management tasks you may want or need to complete. First, you may determine that one or more of the public access printers you have created should actually be controlled access printers. If so, you can convert a public access printer to a controlled access printer. Second, you will need to set up access to printers from client workstations. Third, you may want to manage printer access and print jobs.

Convert a Public Access Printer to a Controlled Access Printer

To convert a public access printer to a controlled access printer requires only that you create an NDPS Printer object for that printer in the appropriate container. When creating the NDPS Printer object, you specify the Public Access Printer as the Printer Agent source. In addition, because you are converting a public access printer to a controlled access printer, the system presents you with a warning designed to prevent you from accidentally converting a public access printer to a controlled access printer. When you see the warning, simply click **OK**.

Set Up Printer Access for Client Workstations

To set up printer access for client workstations, use NetWare Administrator. From within NetWare Administrator, you can create and configure printers as well as designate printers to be automatically installed to all workstations. To automatically install printers on workstations, however, the workstation must be running either Windows 3.1, Windows 95, or Windows NT. You cannot automatically install printers on workstations that are running only DOS.

You can also update printer drivers or add new ones to the database provided by NDPS. In addition, you can change the default values associated with printer properties.

Manage Printer Access and Print Jobs

Both you as a network administrator and users can manage print jobs, although users can manage only the print jobs they submitted. Users run the Novell Printer Manager from their workstation to manager NDPS printing tasks. With it, users can perform such tasks as seeing existing print jobs, and pausing, resuming, or deleting their print jobs.

MANAGE PRINTER ACCESS

You manage a user's printer access by installing a printer on a workstation, and by configuring a printer for a workstation. Installing a printer on a workstation is simply a matter of running the related Windows printer setup. For example, on a workstation running Windows 95, you launch NetWare Tools, then click **Printer Manager**. This runs the **Nwpmw32.exe** program (located in **sys/public/win32**), and opens the Novell Printer Manager.

Within the Novell Printers dialog you:

1. In the printer menu, click **New**. A list of available printers displays.
2. Click the printer you want to install, and then click **Add**.
3. (Optional) Specify settings for this printer by clicking **Filter**, selecting the features you want to add (such as a description, whether the printer is a color printer, or the mechanism by which the printer prints—ink jet, dot matrix, and so on,) then clicking **OK**.
4. Click **Install**.
5. (Optional) If desired, change the printer's name.
6. Click **OK** and then click **Close**.

The print driver is downloaded to the workstation. The user will then be able to print to the specified printer.

MANAGE PRINT JOBS

After you install the client software, a list of available printers is displayed in the main window of the Novell Printer Manager. You can use the Novell Printer Manager to manage various aspects of print jobs including:

- adding or deleting printers
- viewing a list of existing print jobs and getting real-time status for each
- adding print jobs with a hold status
- modifying the status of print jobs (pause, resume, or delete print jobs, or change their print order)
- configuring print job spooling

Using NetWare Administrator, you can also specify who has access to the printer. Open the NDPS Printer object in NetWare Administrator, then click **Access Control**. Identify users to have access to the printer by assigning users as:

- **Managers** (can configure—add/delete users, configure notification profiles, and manage printer configurations, and troubleshoot the printer)
- **Operators** (can set configuration defaults, maintain the printer's status, and manipulate print jobs)
- **Users** (can specify which users can send print jobs to this printer, and manipulate or delete their own print jobs)

In order to manipulate print jobs other than their own, users must be assigned as Operators or Managers to the printer containing the jobs to be manipulated.

NOTE

You also can control functions related to controlled access printers using NetWare Administrator. To do so, open the Details page for the NDPS Printer object. Then click the appropriate button on the page to:

- display services and attributes of the printer (Features)
- modify the job list and spooling configuration, or reset the printer (Jobs and Control)
- learn more about the printer and its current status (Identification and Status)
- change the status of a print job (Pause Output and Pause Input)

You can also perform other management tasks associated specifically with a given print job:

- to view information about an existing print job
- modify a print job once it has been sent to the printer but before it prints
- change the order of print jobs
- copy or move a print job
- delete a print job

View Information About an Existing Print Job

To view information about an existing print job:

1. Start NetWare Administrator. Right-click the printer object to which the print job was sent, then choose **Details**.
2. Click **Jobs**.
3. Click **Job List**.
4. Click the print job you want to view information about.
5. Click **Information**.

Modify a Print Job

To modify a print job once it has been sent to the printer but before it prints:

1. Start NetWare Administrator and choose the printer object to which the print job was sent.
2. Click **Jobs**.
3. Click **Job List**.
4. Click the print job.
5. Click **Job Options**.
6. Click **Configuration**.
7. Click the appropriate properties tab.
8. Change the options or properties, then click **OK**.

Change the Order of Print Jobs

To change the order in which print jobs are scheduled to be printed:

1. Start NetWare Administrator and choose the printer object to which the print job was sent.
2. Click **Jobs**.
3. Click **Job List**.
4. Click the print job.
5. Click **Job Options**.
6. Click **Reorder**.
7. Choose its new position.
8. Click **OK**. (If the list does not update, click **F5** to update the order.)

Copy or Move Print Jobs

To copy or move a print job:

1. Start NetWare Administrator and choose the printer object to which the print job was sent.
2. Click **Jobs**.
3. Click **Job List**.
4. Click the print job you want to move or copy.
5. Click **Job Options**.
6. Click either **Move** or **Copy**, depending on which you want to do.
7. Move or copy the print job to its new location, then click **OK**. (If the job list does not update, click **F5** to update the list.)

Delete a Print Job

To delete a print job:

1. Start NetWare Administrator and choose the printer object to which the print job was sent.
2. Click **Jobs**.
3. Click **Job List**.
4. Click the print job you want to delete.
5. Click **Job Options**.
6. Click **Delete**.
7. Click **OK** to confirm that you want to delete the job.

Chapter Summary

Printing is an important network service, but its setup and maintenance can be time-consuming and sometimes frustrating for the network administrator. Before NDPS, setting up and maintaining print services on a NetWare network required knowledge of and the ability to set up and maintain:

- print queues
- print servers
- spoolers
- printers

It also required that you become familiar with several utilities by which you managed these different aspects of printing. For example, you would use the **Capture** command-line utility to direct print requests, **Pconsole** to manage print jobs, or any of the other printing utilities such as **Rprinter**, **Nprinter**, and **Pserver**.

With NDPS, however, you use the NetWare Administrator tool and manage printing primarily from it. The major task you have to fulfill with NDPS is that of creating the NDPS Manager object, from which you can then manage various aspects of network printing.

There are four major components of NDPS:

- **NDPS Manager:** Responsible for creating and controlling printer agents. It is represented as an object in the Directory tree.
- **Printer Agent:** Responsible for representing a single printer in the network, and for performing the tasks related to this printer that used to be done with print queue, printer, and print server objects, and spoolers.
- **Gateway:** Responsible for ensuring that printing to non-NDPS printers and to printers which require a print queue is possible.
- **NDPS Broker:** Responsible for allowing public-access printers to make their presence on the network known, as well as for letting printers send customized notices related to printing to the appropriate user, and for allowing resources to be centrally located and then downloaded to various network entities as they are needed.

There are two types of printers in NDPS:

- public access printers
- controlled access printers

Public access printers take full advantage of their plug-and-print capabilities. There is little to no security surrounding a public access printer. No object in the Directory tree exists for it, thus no object has to be managed. It does not allow much configuration, however, nor does it do much in the way of event notification. If the default setups for a public-access printer are not sufficient, you may prefer to use a controlled access printer.

Controlled access printers let you configure and manage the network's printing services. You can set up strict security around a controlled access printer. With a controlled access printer, you can ensure anyone and everyone gets notified when there is a problem, error, or just whenever a job is finished, if you choose to do so. There is an equivalent Printer object in the Directory tree for each controlled access printer; thus, you can manage that object and apply security to it as you would other objects in the Directory tree.

To set up NDPS printing, you must set it up on a file server which meets the minimum system requirements for NDPS:

- 80 MB minimum of available disk space

- 4 MB minimum of RAM in addition to the minimum needed for NetWare 5
- CD-ROM drive

Once you meet the minimum system requires for NDPS, the basic process for setting up an NDPS server includes:

- installing the NDPS software
- creating and loading the NDPS manager
- ensuring the NDPS Broker is installed
- creating a Printer Agent for each network printer

To install NDPS, you can do so by either:

- clicking the **Install Novell Distributed Print Services (NDPS)** box in the Other Products window during the installation of the file server
- loading the **Nwconfig.nlm** at the file server, and then choosing **Install an Item or Product Listed Above**.

Then you load NDPS manager. You can either load it automatically when the server boots by placing the **Load NDPSM.NLM <name>** command in the server's **Autoexec.ncf** file (replacing <name> with the name of the NDPS Manager), or manually by typing the same command at the server console prompt. By default, the command to load the NDPS manager is placed into the **Autoexec.ncf** file when you install NDPS manager. If you choose to load it manually, be sure to include the context when providing the name of the NDPS Manager object.

To create Printer Agents, open the details page for the NDPS Manager, click **Printer Agent List**, click **New**, then provided the required information. You will need to provide a name, gateway type, and printer driver for each Printer Agent you create. You create a Printer Agent for each printer on the network.

If you choose, you can later convert a public access printer to a controlled access printer. Whenever possible, however, use public access printers to simplify printing set up and management on your network.

Even when most of your printers are public access printers, there are still some tasks you may need to perform such as:

- modifying a printer's configuration or a print job's properties
- reordering the print order of two or more print jobs
- copying or moving print jobs from one printer to another
- viewing various information about a specific print job
- deleting a print job completely before it prints

Remember, you must have the appropriate rights to perform any of these various tasks. The rights you must have depend on the task you want to perform. Basic rights requirements are:

- Supervisor Object right to the Server object (if this is the first NDPS server you are installing)
- Browse, Create, Delete, and Rename rights to the container in which the server on which you are installing NDPS is located (if this is other than the first NDPS server you are installing)
- Read, Write, Modify, Create, and File Scan rights to the file system at the root of the volume (to create Printer Agents for public access printers)
- Browse and Create object rights to the container in which the NDPS Printer object exists (to create controlled access printers)

Managing network printing involves many different tasks, including:

- Creating at least one NDPS Manager, loading the Ndpsm.nlm at the associated file server, and creating one or more Printer Agents, which you do using NetWare Administrator. (Note that use of the word "load" when loading an NCM is optional in NetWare 5.)
- Creating public access printers. When you create a Printer Agent list to associate with the NDPS Manager, you configure the gateway as well. When you configure the gateway, you are effectively creating a public access printer for the printer you choose.
- Creating controlled access printers. Use NetWare Administrator to create controlled access printers. Doing so is primarily the result of creating a NDPS Printer object in the Directory tree. To do so you must have Browse and Create object rights to the container where you want to create the controlled access printer. You also must be designated as a manager of the NDPS Manager object which controls the associated Printer Agent.
- As needed, convert one or more public access printers to controlled access printer. To do so only requires that you create an NDPS Printer object for that printer in the appropriate container.
- Setting up client workstations so they can access network printers. To do so, you use NetWare Administrator. From within NetWare Administrator, you can create and configure printers as well as designate printers to be automatically installed to all workstations. To automatically install printers on workstations, however, the workstation must be running either Windows 3.1, Windows 95, or Windows NT. You cannot automatically install printers on workstations that are running only DOS.
- Managing all aspects of printing including printer configurations, and print jobs. To do so, use the Novell Print Manager and NetWare Administrator. You assign Managers, Operators, and Users to printers as needed. You set up and modify print job configurations. And you manip-

ulate print jobs as needed by changing their print order, deleting them, changing their configuration, and making other associated changes.

Practice Test Questions

1. The NDPS component which controls Printer Agents is:
   A. Printer Gateway
   B. NDPS Broker
   C. Port Handler
   D. Print Device Subsystem
   E. NDPS Manager

2. The NDPS component which provides a bridge between NDPS clients and non-NDPS compliant (legacy) printing systems is:
   A. Printer Gateway
   B. NDPS Broker
   C. Port Handler
   D. Print Device Subsystem
   E. NDPS Manager

3. The software process which manages a single physical print device is:
   A. Printer Agent
   B. NDPS Broker
   C. Port Handler
   D. Print Device Subsystem
   E. NDPS Manager

4. The NDPS component which ensures that the print device subsystem can communicate with the printer regardless of its physical connection type is:
   A. Printer Agent
   B. NDPS Broker
   C. Port Handler
   D. Printer Gateway
   E. NDPS Manager

5. This NDPS component knows the make and model of the printer, ensuring that it can control and query the printer in the printer's language:
   A. Printer Agent
   B. NDPS Broker
   C. Port Handler
   D. Print Device Subsystem
   E. NDPS Manager

6. Among other tasks it performs, which NDPS component provides resource management and event notification?
   A. Printer Agent
   B. NDPS Broker
   C. Printer Gateway
   D. Print Device Subsystem
   E. NDPS Manager

7. If this is not the first NDPS server you are installing, which of the following object rights for the container in which the server resides do you *not* need to have?
   A. Supervisor
   B. Browse
   C. Create
   D. Delete
   E. Rename

8. If this is the first NDPS server you are installing, you must have at least which object right to the Server object?
   A. Supervisor
   B. Browse
   C. Create
   D. Delete
   E. Rename

9. Of the following, which is *not* a print-job related task a user can perform without being a Manager or Operator?
   A. Delete their print job
   B. Copy their print job
   C. View information about their print job
   D. Change the order of their print job

10. When you configure a Gateway, you are effectively creating a/an:
    A. Controlled access printer for the printer you chose
    B. Public access printer for the printer you choose
    C. Print job configuration to be associated with jobs using the Gateway
    D. None of the above

11. Creating a controlled access printer primarily involves:
    A. Creating an NDPS Manager object
    B. Choosing a name for the printer
    C. Configuring a Gateway
    D. Creating an NDPS Printer object in the Directory tree

12. You create Printer Agents by
    A. Loading **Ndps.nlm** on the server
    B. Creating a Printer Agent object in the Directory tree, providing information as prompted
    C. Clicking Printer Agent on the details page for the NDPS Manager, and providing the needed information
    D. None of the above

13. Of the following, which three are requirements for setting up NDPS printing?
    A. 80 MB minimum of available disk space
    B. 8 MB minimum of RAM in addition to the minimum needed for NetWare 5
    C. A CD-ROM drive
    D. A file server

14. Which of the following will correctly load the NDPS Manager?
    A. Load NDPS.NLM
    B. Load Ndpsm.nlm name_and_context
    C. Load Ndpsm.nlm
    D. None of the above

15. Which of the following is *not* a responsibility of the Printer Agent?
    A. Managing the various tasks the printer performs
    B. Providing network clients with information about a particular print job, document, or attributes of the printer itself
    C. Ensuring successful printing to a wide range of print devices in various document production environments
    D. Notifying the appropriate network clients of printing issues such as problems, completion, and change of status.
    E. None of these tasks are responsibilities of the Printer Agent.

Answers to Practice Test Questions

1. E	6. B	11. D
2. A	7. A	12. C
3. A	8. A	13. A,C,D
4. C	9. C	14. B
5. D	10. B	15. E

CHAPTER 6

Setting Up and Customizing Network Access for Users

There are five major tasks you must perform if you are to successfully set up and customize your network user's access to the network. In addition, to be an effective network administrator, you need to understand how to explore the network using Windows and browsers. The five major tasks you must perform, as well as how to explore the network using Windows and browsers, are discussed in this chapter.

The five major tasks are:

- installing the Novell client
- managing NetWare user licenses
- understanding the login process
- understanding login scripts
- creating and modifying login scripts

Installing the Novell Client

NetWare 5 ships with support for three Novell clients:

- DOS/Windows 3.1
- Windows 95
- Windows NT

Because workstations running DOS only or Windows 3.1 are becoming less common, and Windows 95 as well as Windows NT workstations are becoming more common, the Novell NetWare 5 Administration course concentrates only on installing the Windows 95 and Windows NT clients. Therefore, only the install process for those two Novell clients are covered in this chapter.

There are several ways you can install the Novell client. The easiest way when installing the client on one workstation at a time is by using the client install on the Novell Clients CD-ROM. That is the install method concentrated on in this chapter. However, you can also install these Novell clients by following any of several other install processes, including:

- Z.E.N.works Application Launcher
- Automatic Client Upgrade (ACU)
- Msbatch

If you are installing a Windows 95 Client or a Windows NT client from CD-ROM, complete the following steps:

1. Insert the Novell Client CD-ROM into the CD-ROM drive at the client workstation. The Client install automatically launches and opens to the Novell Client main window.

If the Novell Client installation does not start automatically, open **My Computer** and double-click the CD-ROM drive letter to open the Novell Client main window.

NOTE

2. Click the language you want to install. For example, click **English**.
3. Click either **Windows 95 Client** or **Windows NT Client**. The associated Windows Components window opens (see Figure 6-1).
4. Click **Install Novell Client**. The Novell Client Installation screen opens (see Figure 6-2).
5. Click **Install** to install the client using the Typical Installation. If you want to, you can choose Custom Installation, but Typical Installation is much simpler to do and is generally the best option.

You should view the read me file before continuing the installation, since it contains information which is pertinent to the Novell Client.

NOTE

6. Follow the prompts to complete the installation of the Novell Client.

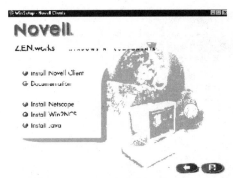

FIGURE 6-1 Example of the Windows NT Components window from which you choose Install Novell Client.

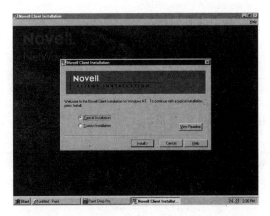

FIGURE 6-2 Example of the Novell Client Installation window from which you choose Typical Installation.

Managing NetWare User Licenses

NetWare 5 is a licensed application. Each user that wants to log in to the network must have an associated license. You do not have to give a specific license to each user, however. What you must do is manage a group of NetWare user licenses on the network.

When NetWare 5 is installed, two types of license objects are added to the Directory tree (see Figure 6-3):

- License container objects
- License certificate objects

FIGURE 6-3 View of NetWare Administrator showing the two installed License objects. The container License object is highlighted. The server License object is found immediately below the container License object.

There are two types of License container objects:

- User license (connection license)
- Server license

License object names are defined by stringing together the following three items of information, based on the license being installed:

- publisher's name
- product name
- version (which can identify the number of users)

For example, the user License container name for a 250 user version of NetWare 5 would appear as: **Novell+NetWare 5 Conn SCL +250**, while the server License container would appear as: **Novell+NetWare 5 Server +250**.

Within each type of License container object, related License Certificate objects are stored. You need a License Certificate object in the user License container object for each user on your network.

To manage licensing on your network, you must assign User, Group, Organization, or Organizational Unit objects to the License Certificate objects. In addition, managing licensing on your network means you also install additional licenses as needed.

Assign Objects to License Certificates

To assign an object to a License Certificate object, use NetWare Administrator to complete the following steps:

1. Because you are assigning license certificates to objects and not objects to license certificates, open the Licensing container, then double-click the License Certificate object you want to assign. The License Certificate's General page opens (see Figure 6-4).
2. Click **Assignments** to open the Assignments page.
3. Click **Add** to open the Select Object dialog, then choose an Object (see Figure 6-5).
4. Click **OK** on the Select Object page to add the chosen object with its context to the User Assignment field.
5. Click **OK** to complete the assignment of the chosen object to this License Certificate.

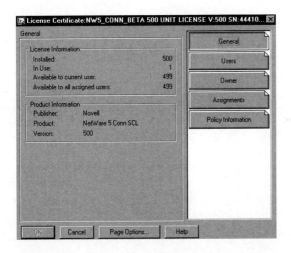

FIGURE 6-4 The General page for a Licensing certificate.

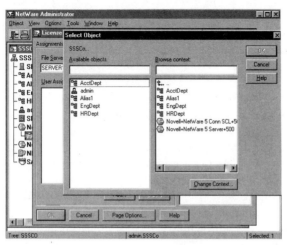

FIGURE 6-5 Example of the Select Object dialog, from which you choose the object to which this Licensing certificate will be assigned.

Install Additional Licenses

Installing additional licenses is a relatively easy task. To install additional licenses, complete the following steps:

1. Click **Tools** on the NetWare Administrator menu bar. The Tools menu opens.
2. Click **Install License**. The related list of licenses install options opens.
3. Click **Install License Certificate**. The Install a License Certificate dialog opens (see Figure 6-6).
4. Browse for and then choose the file of the License Certificate. The path and file name for the License Certificate displays in the related field.
5. Browse for and then choose the context into which this License Certificate is to be installed. The current context is displayed in the related field by default. In Figure 6-6, the current context was the SSSCo container for the SunShoeShine Company.
6. Click **OK**.

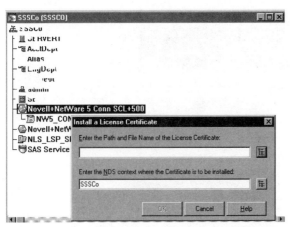

FIGURE 6-6 The Install a License Certificate dialog which opens when you open NetWare Administrator and choose **Tools > Install License > Install License Certificate.**

Understanding the Login Process

When a user opens the Novell Login dialog and provides their user name and password, the result is that the login process logs the user into the network, not into a specific server on the network. As part of logging in to the network using the Novell Login dialog, the server from which **Login.exe** is run in order to accomplish the network login can be specified, but the login is to the network, not to that specific server.

Because the login is to the network and not to a specific file server, a process known as authentication occurs when the user logs in. During authentication, the User object (or any other object seeking access to network resources) is checked against the NDS database to ensure that the object is a valid NDS object. The object's rights are verified, and any login restrictions which might apply are checked and applied. Various measures of security are applied to the entire login process.

You cannot access network resources unless you first log in to the network. However, once your current context is set, you can view that part of the Directory tree. Logging in to the network requires that you use the Novell Client (see Figure 6-7) to log in. On the Novell Client login window, you provide the network with:

- your User object name
- the password associated with your User object

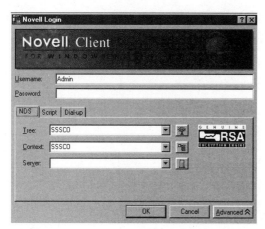

FIGURE 6-7 Example of the Novell Client for Windows 95 login dialog as set up for the Admin user, with the Advanced NDS tab open.

- the name of the Directory tree in which your User object is located
- the context within the Directory tree in which your User object is located
- the name of the server from which you want the Login.exe file to run
- settings and variables associated with both the login script and profile script to be run, if applicable
- information associated with using Dial-up Networking to log in, if appropriate

This sounds like a lot of information just to log in. However, most of it is supplied by default for the user, and once the user logs in, this information does not have to be specified during future logins (except for the user's name and password).

Setting up the defaults, particularly those related to login scripts, is the network administrator's responsibility. Before you can set up login scripts, however, you need to understand what they are.

Understanding Login Scripts

Login scripts are files which contain various commands that run when a user logs in. There are four types of login scripts:

- Container
- Profile
- User
- Default

The container login script exists to provide basic configuration for any user with a User object in the same container as the container login script. When a user logs in to the network, the container login script is the first login script to be run. It runs for every user in the same container for which the container login script was created. When setting variables common to multiple users, such as a drive mapping to the Public directory on a file server, you should set the majority of those variables in the container login script.

The profile login script exists to customize configuration for several users when those users all have the same configuration needs. However, to create a profile login script, you must first create a Profile object. If it exists, the profile login script runs after the container login script, and it only runs for those users to which it has been assigned. In addition, because the profile login script runs after the container login script, the result of some of the commands in the profile login script can overwrite the result of similar commands in the container login script. For example, if the container login script assigns a specific letter to identify the path to a certain network directory (using the MAP command) and the profile login script reassigns that letter to another path, the reassigned path is the one the users will end up with once the profile login script is run.

The user login script exists to customize configuration for a single user. If it exists, the user login script is run after the profile login script. Because it runs after both the container login script and the profile login script, it too can modify settings established by either of the first two login scripts, for the same reason that settings in the profile login script can overwrite settings in the container login script.

The default login script exists to provide minimum configuration for a user who logs in to the network when none of the other three types of login scripts exist. It is possible to prevent even the default login script from running, however, by using a command called **NO DEFAULT**. (Login script commands are discussed in more detail in the section "Creating and Modifying Login Scripts" later in this chapter.)

Before any login script can be applied or run, the login script must be created. The only exception to that is the default login script which runs for the user if no other login script exists, and if it has not been prevented from running by using the **NO DEFAULT** login script command.

Creating and Modifying Login Scripts

How you create a login script depends on the type of login script you want to create. For example, to create a container login script:

1. Right-click the container to which you want the container login script to apply, then click **Details**.
2. Click **Login Script**. The Login Script page opens (see Figure 6-8).
3. Type the appropriate commands into the Login script field, following the syntax required for creating login scripts, and using the appropriate commands.
4. When you have finished typing in the login script commands, click **OK**.

NOTE
Modifying a login script simply requires that you follow the same procedure you used to create the login script, however, when the login script is displayed, you modify the appropriate commands, then save the modified login script by clicking **OK**.

As you may have noticed, Figure 6-8 shows login script commands which have already been entered into the Login Script field. However, no commands are included in this field when you first open this page. You must add them yourself.

NOTE
Creating login scripts can be time consuming and troublesome, particularly if you don't follow all of the conventions exactly. To ease this effort, Novell has provided sample login scripts that you can copy from the help file into a container, profile, or user login script you create for your system.

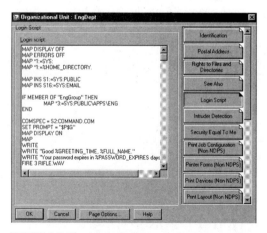

FIGURE 6-8 The Login Script page that opens when selecting a container in the Directory tree displayed in NetWare Administrator, then clicking **Details > Login Script**.

To take advantage of the help Novell has provided, open the Login Script page for the login script you want to create, then click **Help**. The NetWare Administrator help opens. Next, click **Login Script Help** under Related Topics, then click **Types of Login Scripts**. On the Types of Login Scripts help page, click the link which jumps to a sample of the type of login script you want to create. For example, click the **sample container login script** link under the Container Login Script heading. A sample of the chosen type of login script opens. Select the text of the entire login script. Then, click **Edit** on the menu bar, and click **Copy**. The sample login script is copied to the Windows clipboard.

You can now copy the sample login script from the Windows clipboard to the Login Script field for the login script you are creating. First, however, you may want to close the help file, then return to the login script page. Copy the sample login script to the Login Script field by placing the cursor in the Login script field, then pressing **Ctrl-V** on the keyboard. The sample login script you copied from the help file is pasted into the Login Script field. Now you can edit and modify the login script as needed, but the overall amount of work to create a login script is greatly reduced.

You can follow this process of copying a sample login script and pasting it into the login script you are creating for any of the three types of login scripts: container, profile, and user.

Remember, to create a Profile login script, you must first create a Profile object. The profile login script is a property of the Profile object, just as the container login script is a property of a container and the user login script is a property of a user. Once you create a Profile object, the procedure for creating a profile login script is the same as that for creating a container login script, with two differences:

- you choose a Profile object instead of a Container object
- you must add User or other objects as trustees to the Profile object and grant them at least the Browse object right and either the Compare and Read All Properties right, or the Compare and Read rights to the Login Script selected property (see Figure 6-9)

To create a User login script, you perform the same steps as in creating a Container login script, but you click the **User** object instead of the Container object.

In the sample login script in Figure 6-8, several commands such as MAP, IF...THEN, and others are used in login scripts. The MAP command assigns a drive letter to a specific directory path on a specific volume. .

FIGURE 6-9 The Rights to Other Objects dialog in which you add an object as a Trustee of the Profile object so you can then grant them rights to the Profile object's login script.

The MAP command can be used to create either a search drive or a network drive. A network drive is a direct pointer to a specific location in the file system, and is used to store or retrieve data files. The search drive is also a pointer to a specific location in the file system, but it tells the network that this path is one in which to search when looking for an executable program file such as a .dll, .exe, and so on.

KEY CONCEPT

The important thing to remember about search drives is that they establish the order in which the network is searched when looking for an executable file. The first search drive is checked first, then subsequent search drives are checked until all mapped search drives have been searched. When NetWare assigns a drive letter to a search drive, it begins by assigning the drive letter Z, and works its way backwards through the alphabet. You can map up to 16 search drives.

Network drives can be assigned any letter after those letters which are reserved for the equipment on the computer. For example, letters A, B, and C are reserved for floppy and hard disk drives respectively. If a CD-ROM drive exists in a computer, it is usually assigned the D drive letter.

That leaves the letters beginning with E and working down through the alphabet available for network drive mapping.

There are several commands you can use in a login script. For more information about other login script commands, you can refer to the Help associated with the login script property of an object, or read about the available commands and how to use them in the online documentation that ships with NetWare 5. Some of the common login script commands which are referenced in the NetWare 5 Administration course, and thus which you should make an effort to become familiar with are:

- `BREAK`
- `FDISPLAY`
- `FIRE PHASERS`
- `GREETING_TIME`
- `HOUR24`
- `IF...THEN`
- `INCLUDE`
- `LOGIN_NAME`
- `MAP`
- `MAP DISPLAY`
- `NDAY_OF_WEEK`
- `NO_DEFAULT`
- `PAUSE`
- `REM` (or `REMARK`, semi-colon, or asterisk)
- `STATION`
- `WRITE`

Exploring the Network

You can explore the network by browsing the Directory tree using the Network Neighborhood on your Windows desktop. In addition, you can use browsers such as Netscape Navigator and Microsoft's Internet Explorer to access Web servers. Through the interface and utilities provided by the Novell Client and many current browsers, you can:

- log in to the network
- view resources on the network
- access resources on the network including printing, file storage, and applications (although you cannot access NDS and NDS objects other than trees and containers)

Taking Advantage of Windows to Explore the Network

To explore the network using Network Neighborhood, follow these steps:

1. Double-click the **Network Neighborhood** icon on your Windows desktop.
2. Double-click **Entire Network**.
3. Double-click one of the following, depending on what you want to see in the Directory tree:
   - **NDPS Public Access Printers**
   - **NetWare Servers**
   - **Novell Directory Services**
4. Move through the Directory tree by expanding containers as needed until you locate a specific object for which you are looking, or just to get an overview of the Directory tree.

KEY CONCEPT

In addition to making it possible to browse the directory tree and view network resources using Network Neighborhood, the Novell Client provides two other browsing features. Those two features are support for long filenames, and integration with Windows.

By supporting long filenames, you can see all objects in the directory tree, regardless of how many characters were used to name the object. Some object names are quite long. Licensing container names are a good example. A typical Licensing container name can resemble the following: **Novell+NetWare 5 Server +250**.

Using Browsers to Explore the Network

Because the Novell Client is integrated with Windows, you can use the Windows Explorer utility from the start/programs menu to access Web servers. The Novell Client also provides support for other common browsers, such as Netscape Navigator.

NOTE

The NetWare 5 online documentation is presented in HTML format. While you can use Internet Explorer or other browsers to view it, the online documentation ships with search and print engines optimized for use with Netscape Navigator. The best way to find information that you need in the online documentation, then, is to use the version of Netscape Navigator included with it.

Most browsers generally support only the TCP/IP protocol. TCP/IP is the main Internet protocol. The Novell Client supports TCP/IP, but it also supports IPX. In addition, browsers rely on the workstation's operating system to function. Some newer versions of browsers, particularly Microsoft's Internet Explorer, actually become part of the operating system on the workstation.

KEY CONCEPT

The browser is the main environment in which Java programs run. Many Internet Web sites today are based on Java. As Java-based programs can run on virtually any computer platform including Windows, Macintosh, mainframes, and others, Java-based programs are likely to increase in the future. Thus it is important that any browser you use support Java.

When you install the Netscape Navigator browser included with the Novell Client, it enables your workstation to run Java programs. The Winsetup.exe program that installs the Novell Client also installs the Netscape Navigator browser. After installation, an icon added to the desktop lets you launch the Netscape Navigator browser. When you boot your workstation, the Novell Client is installed. Therefore, you can still launch the Netscape Navigator browser even before you open the Novell Login dialog box and log in and authenticate yourself to the network. However, until you do authenticate yourself to the network, your access to the Internet or intranet may be limited.

Chapter Summary

To successfully set up and customize your user's access to the network, you must:

- install the Novell Client
- manage NetWare user licenses
- understand the login process and login scripts
- be able to create and modify login scripts

You can install the Novell Client using any of the following:

- Z.E.N.works
- Automatic Client Upgrade (ACU)
- Msbatch

The installation method described in this chapter relies on the CD-ROM which includes the Novell Client (and Z.E.N.works) software. To install the Novell Client, you put the CD-ROM into the CD-ROM drive, use **My Computer** to locate the CD-ROM drive, then double-click the drive letter to launch the Install program. After choosing the language you want to install, you click the client you want to install, then follow the on-screen prompts to complete the Novell Client installation.

NetWare 5 is a licensed application. Each user that wants to log in to the network must have an associated license. You do not have to give a specific license to each user, however. What you must do is manage NetWare user licenses on the network. To do that, you work with the two types of license objects which are added to the Directory tree during the installation of NetWare 5: License container objects (of which there are two types—Connection License and Server License), and License certificate objects.

As with other NDS objects, License objects have names assigned to them. The names are created by stringing together the following three items of information based on the license being installed:

- publisher's name
- product name
- version (which can identify the number of users)

Within each type of License container object, related License Certificate objects are stored. You need a License Certificate object in the user License container object for each user on your network. You assign User, Group, Organization or Organizational Unit objects to the License Certificate objects. When needed, you install additional licenses by first choosing **Tools** from the NetWare Administrator menu bar; after which you choose **Install Licenses**, then **Install License Certificates**.

When a user opens the Novell Login dialog and provides their user name and password, the result is that the login process logs the user into and then authenticates them to the network, not into a specific server on the network. During authentication, the User object (or other object seeking access to network resources) is checked against the NDS database to ensure that the object is a valid NDS object. In addition, the object's rights are verified and any login restrictions that might apply are checked and applied. Various measures of security are applied to the entire login process.

A login script is a file containing commands designed to set up the network environment for network users. Login scripts run when a user logs in to the network. There are four types of login scripts (including the Default login script), but you can create only three of them: Container, Profile, and User. NetWare 5 provides the Default login script.

The container login script exists to provide basic configuration for any user with a User object in the same container as the container login script. It runs for every user in the same container for which the container login script was created. It is the first login script to run when a user logs in.

The profile login script exists to customize configuration for several users when those users all have the same configuration needs. If it exists, the profile login script runs after the container login script, and it only runs for those users to which it has been assigned.

The user login script exists to customize configuration for a single user. It is run after the profile login script, if a user login script exists.

The default login script exists to provide minimum configuration for a user who logs in to the network when none of the other three types of login scripts exist. It is possible to prevent even the default login script from running, however, by using a command called **NO DEFAULT**.

If you choose to create login scripts, you create them as properties of their associated objects. For example, the user login script is a property of the User object. To create them, therefore, you use NetWare Administrator, open the associated details pages for the object (User, Organization, Organizational Object, or Profile), then open the Login Script page. You create (or modify) a login script on the Login Script property page.

For login scripts to be useful, they must contain specific commands. For example, you can include the MAP command to assign drive letters to specific paths in the directory structure of a file server. Several commands are available. Some of them have been listed in this chapter, including such commands as IF...THEN, NO_DEFAULT, MAP, and WRITE. As the commands included in this chapter are specifically listed as common commands in the NetWare 5 Administration course manual, you should look at the online help or the Help associated with the Login Script page and familiarize yourself with the function of these various commands.

Login scripts set up a user's environment, and features of the Windows desktop help to make the network more accessible for the user. You can explore the network by browsing the Directory tree using the Network Neighborhood on your Windows desktop. In addition, you can use browsers such as Netscape Navigator and Microsoft's Internet Explorer to access Web servers. Through the interface and utilities provided by the Novell Client and many current browsers, you can:

- log in to the network
- view resources on the network
- access resources on the network including printing, file storage, and applications

Novell's NetWare 5 online documentation is in HTML format and uses the Netscape Navigator browser bundled with NetWare 5. While you can use most browser software to view the online documentation, the online documentation ships with special search and print engines that only function with the version of Netscape Navigator provided.

Practice Test Questions

1. Of the following, which is *not* a client installation method?
   A. Z.E.N.works
   B. ACU
   C. Mssetup.exe
   D. Msbatch

2. Which two types of license objects are added to the Directory tree when you install NetWare 5?
   A. License container
   B. Publisher license
   C. User license
   D. License certificate
   E. Server license

3. Which of the following cannot be assigned to License Certificate objects?
   A. User objects
   B. Group objects
   C. Organization objects
   D. Workstation objects
   E. Organizational Unit objects

4. If you need to install additional licenses on your server,
   A. Run NetWare Administrator and click **Tools > Install Licenses > Install License Certificate**
   B. Run NetWare Administrator and click **Tools > Install License Certificate > Install Licenses**
   C. Right click the server object and click **License page > Add License Certificate**
   D. None of the above will install additional licenses on your server

5. During authentication:
   A. A user's rights to network resources are verified
   B. The User object and password are checked against the NDS database to ensure the User object is a valid object, and the password matches the user object
   C. Login restrictions for the specific user are applied
   D. A, B, and C are all true
   E. Only A and B are true

6. The login script which runs last and runs only when no other login script exists is:
   A. Default
   B. Container
   C. Profile
   D. User

7. The login script to use if you want to customize configuration for several users, even when their User objects reside in multiple containers is:
   A. Default
   B. Container
   C. Profile
   D. User

8. The first login script to run when a user logs in to the network is:
   A. Default
   B. Container
   C. Profile
   D. User

9. Which statement about login scripts is *not* true?
   A. A login script is a property of an object
   B. Login scripts contain commands which set up and configure a user's environment
   C. You create login scripts by running the Login Script Create utility
   D. A profile login script can only be associated with a Profile object

10. Search drives:
    A. Establish the order in which the network is searched when looking for a data file
    B. Receive D as the first drive letter assigned by default unless the computer has a CD-ROM drive, then it is E
    C. Are generally mapped starting with the letter Z and working backwards up the alphabet
    D. Up to 16 in quantity can be mapped for any given user

11. If you want to display text on a user's workstation when they log in, which command can you add to the login script to accomplish this task?
    A. INCLUDE
    B. BREAK
    C. MAP DISPLAY
    D. WRITE
    E. REM

12. Which of the following is not displayed in Network Neighborhood when you double-click **Entire Network**?
    A. NDPS Public Access Printers
    B. NetWare Servers
    C. Novell Directory Services
    D. Novell Client

13. Two browsing features provided by the Novell client are:
    A. Support for long filenames
    B. Integration with Windows
    C. Licensing certificate display
    D. Network Neighborhood icon
    E. NetWare Servers

14. Which three of the following is the Novell Client fully integrated with?
    A. Windows Explorer
    B. Network Neighborhood utilities
    C. Windows desktop
    D. Macintosh desktop

15. Which two does the Novell Client support?
    A. TCP/IP
    B. MSWinset.exe
    C. IPX
    D. CLU

Answers to Practice Test Questions

1. C	6. A	11. D
2. A,D	7. C	12. D
3. D	8. B	13. A,B
4. A	9. C	14. A,B,C
5. D	10. C	15. A,C

CHAPTER 7

Using Application Launcher

Z.E.N.works (Zero Effort Networking) is a snap-in to NetWare Administrator. When installed on file servers in your network, Z.E.N.works reduces the time it takes to administer your network and the workstations on it. When you install Z.E.N.works, you add to NDS' capabilities by allowing a new object to be included in NDS: Workstation objects. By adding a new object to NDS, the NDS schema is extended. The NDS schema defines what objects can be included in NDS, and defines their requirements, limitations, and relationships with other objects in NDS.

Z.E.N.works provides several advantages to both you (the network administrator) and your network users:

- installation is integrated and thus much easier to do
- applications can be distributed and managed from a central location
- workstations can be managed and maintained remotely using workstation objects
- administrators and users on Windows 95 or Windows NT workstations can schedule programs to run on those workstations at a predetermined time and without other administrator or user intervention, including installing, running, and correcting problems with applications
- users can send and administrators can respond to requests for help with problems on their workstation

Network administrators can use Z.E.N.works to:

■ distribute and manage applications
■ configure and manage workstations
■ remotely repair workstation problems

Application Launcher is the component of Z.E.N.works that allows you to distribute and manage applications. Application Launcher itself consists of four product components:

■ the Application Launcher snap-in to NetWare Administrator
■ snAppShot (**Snapshot.exe**, **Snappe16.exe** and **Snappe32.exe**)
■ the user's Application Launcher window (Nal.exe)
■ the Application Launcher Explorer (Nalexpld.exe)

Of these four components, the first two (Application Launcher snap-in for NetWare Administrator and snAppShot) are used by the network administrator. Application Launcher window and Application Launcher Explorer are used by network users, although they are initially set up by the network administrator for distribution to the user's workstation.

Although there are other components of Z.E.N.works, Application Launcher is the only one discussed in this chapter. Chapter 8, *Using Other Z.E.N.works Features*, discusses how Z.E.N.works lets users make the network administrator aware of workstation problems, and lets the network administrator configure, manage, and make software repairs to workstations without actually having to be physically at the workstation.

This chapter discusses:

■ what application launcher is, and what you must do to take advantage of its features and benefits on your network
■ how to create and work with Application objects
■ how to distribute and manage network applications

Learning About Application Launcher

Application Launcher is the part of Z.E.N.works that makes it possible for network administrators to install and update applications which run either on individual workstations, or which are stored on a network file server for access by multiple users. Because networks are designed to allow users to share resources, networked applications are the preferred choice. There may be times, however, when you do not want an application to be shared. For example, you may have only one user who does all of the payroll using a single payroll application. You could store this application on the network and require that the user log in and access the application from a file server. On the other hand, it may be that management prefers the payroll software and its accompanying sensitive information not be on the network. In that case, you can install the application to the user's individual workstation, updating it as needed. Using Application Launcher, however, you can still install and maintain this application from the network administrator's workstation, and never have to physically be at the user's workstation.

Application Launcher is flexible about how you install and update applications for users. Implementing a feature referred to as *push-and-pull software distribution*, Application Launcher lets you decide whether the network administrator or the user has control over installing and updating applications.

If you choose to administer one or more applications using the pull distribution method, users actually initiate the installation or update process. As the network administrator, you provide an icon on the user's desktop. When the user clicks the icon, Application Launcher:

- starts the application
- makes workstation configuration changes, if needed
- runs the related installation program to install the software directly to the hard disk on the workstation
- creates associated application objects

If you choose to use the push distribution method instead, the same tasks are accomplished. The difference is that the user does not have a choice over when the tasks are performed. The tasks are done as a Forced Run (which is also a property of the Application object). Push distribution is the better choice when:

- certain important software, such as client software, must be updated on the user's workstation
- certain programs should be started automatically whenever a user logs in

As the network administrator, you are responsible for implementing Application Launcher. Choosing to implement Application Launcher benefits both you and your network's users in many ways. Benefits to the network administrator are:

- Ability to administer applications from a central location, usually the administrator's workstation
- Ability to maintain and control applications from a central location
- Ability to distribute software using either the push or the pull distribution methods

Benefits to the user are:

- Applications can be accessed by the user without the user having to be concerned about which file server the application is stored on, or without having to first map a drive to access that application (location-independent access)
- Applications are fault tolerant because if one file server running a specific application becomes unavailable for any reason, Application Launcher automatically locates that application on another file server, and presents it to the user without the user knowing where it came from
- Applications' work loads are automatically balanced by Application Launcher, as Application Launcher can detect an overworked application and route users to another licensed copy of the application
- Users receive automatic support when they are working from a workstation other than their default workstation, as Application Launcher automatically detects the use of a roaming profile and provides the necessary components to run applications

How to Set Up Application Launcher on Your Network

There is a defined process you must follow in order to take advantage of Application Launcher's features and benefits. The process is described in general terms in the procedure which follows. Once you understand the process, you can then move on and perform the detailed steps. To set up Application Launcher on your network, you must:

1. Decide which application you want to distribute.

   For example, you may choose to distribute the NetWare Administrator utility to users on the network from whom you want assistance with network administration.
2. Determine which workstation has the hardware and configuration that is typical of the workstations to which you will be distributing the application.

   For example, if you will be distributing the NetWare Administrator utility, determine which workstation your potential network administrators have which is typical in its hardware and configuration.
3. If you have not already done so, install Z.E.N.works on the network file server.
4. Go to the workstation you chose as the baseline workstation, and run **Snappshot.exe** (from the file server) on that workstation. (The section of this chapter titled "How to Use SnAppShot to Capture a

Workstation's Pre-Installation Configuration" explains how to perform this task.)

Snappshot.exe is what is called a wrapper file. Its function is to determine which operating system the workstation is running, and then launch the appropriate Snappshot executable: Snappe16.exe or Snappe32.exe, for 16-bit and 32-bit workstations respectively. Running Snappshot.exe creates an .AOT and other needed files. You can then use the .AOT file to define associated properties when creating the Application object in the Directory tree.

5. From your administrator's workstation (or another workstation from which you have logged in to the network as user Admin), start NetWare Administrator, create an Application object, then associate other objects with the Application objects. (The procedure in the "Creating and Working With Application Objects" section later in this chapter describes the detailed steps you must follow to create the Application object.)

6. Identify where the Application object's icon is to be placed when the user logs in to the network and the installation of this application is automatically launched.

7. Place the appropriate executable program (**Nal.exe** for the Windows Launcher or **Nalexpld.exe** for the Windows Explorer) into either the Startup folder on the workstation, or into a login script.

How to Use SnAppShot to Capture a Workstation's Pre-Installation Configuration

You use the snAppShot utility to create application object templates. You can then use this template to identify the Application object. You create the typical workstation configuration. Then, when the application is installed and configured on each user's workstation, its configuration will be set to work best for the typical network workstation from which the user will run the application.

In snAppShot, you identify what the utility is to search for when it looks for the current workstation's settings (settings the workstation has before the user launches the application for the first time). Then you install the application and complete the search process.

To use snAppShot to capture a workstation's initial configuration, you must first have installed Z.E.N.works to the server. Installing Z.E.N.works to a server ensures that, among other things, you have access to **Snapshot.exe** and associated files.

To capture a workstation's pre-installation configuration using snAppshot, complete the following steps:

1. From the user's workstation, log in to the network.
2. Locate and double-click **Snappshot.exe**. The Z.E.N.works install puts the file into the **SYS:Public\snapshot** directory.
3. Click the type of snapshot you want to take, such as Standard (see Figure 7-1). The Novell Application Launcher snAppShot dialog opens for the type of operating system the workstation is running (Windows 95, Windows NT or Windows 3.1).

> You can see a description of each available type of snapshot you can take by running the mouse over the list. A description for the option to which the mouse is currently pointing is displayed below
>
> NOTE   the list.

4. Enter an NDS Application object name and application icon title.
   Once you have entered an Application object name, press the Tab key and the same name appears in the Application Icon Title field.
5. Click **Next**. The dialog showing the location into which the application files will be stored opens. It defaults to **C:\Snapshot\ NDS_Application_Object_name** (the **NDS_Application_Object_ name** is actually the name you typed into the NDS Application object name field in Step 4). If you want the files stored in a different location, click the **Browse** button and choose where you want the files stored.
6. Click **Next** again to continue running snAppShot.

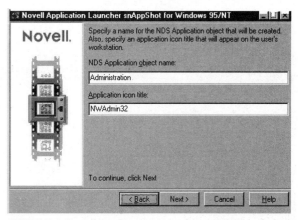

FIGURE 7-1 Novell Application Launcher snAppShot for Windows 95/NT dialog, into which you type a name for the NDS Application object and a name for the Application icon's title.

If the directory does not exist, you are prompted to create it. Click **Yes** to create the directory.

NOTE

7. Click **Next** to accept the default Application object template (AOT name and location), or change the default, then click **Next** again. The default is the same default path displayed after you completed Step 4. If the default is not acceptable, you can Browse for a different location, then choose a different filename.
8. Choose the drives you want snAppShot to scan, then click **Next**. Available drives are displayed. You can accept the default or you can add or remove drives as needed using the **Add** or **Remove** buttons. A summary of snAppShot settings is displayed.
9. Click **Next** to continue (see Figure 7-2).

You can first click Save Preferences and follow the prompts if you want to use these same settings to generate other snAppShot settings.

NOTE

10. Wait while the scanning process runs (see Figure 7-3).

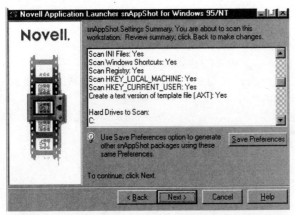

FIGURE 7-2 Dialog displaying the preferences used to create the snAppShot package.

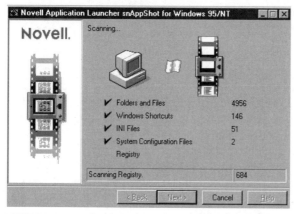

FIGURE 7-3 Sample of the dialog as it is displaying the progress of the scanning process.

11. Click **Run Application** to install and run the set up for the application you are preparing to install. The Select Setup Program dialog opens to display your choice of setup programs.
12. Browse the file system until you find the executable program for the application you want to run, then click it to add its name to the File name field. For example, browse to **SYS:Public\win32** to locate and choose **Nwadmn32.exe** to run the NetWare Administrator utility set up.
13. Click **Open**. The window identifying that the system is waiting for the application installation to finish is displayed.
14. Click **Next**. The dialog requesting the Application's install directory opens.
15. Browse for and choose or type in the path into which you want this application's files installed, then click **Next**. The file scanning process starts, and the template (.AOT file) is generated.

This path is then represented in the .AOT file by the %TARGET_PATH% variable.

NOTE

16. When the snAppShot Completion Summary dialog opens, click **Print** to print the .AOT file and store it with your other network documentation. (A sample of what you can expect to see in the summary area of the dialog is shown in Figure 7-4.)

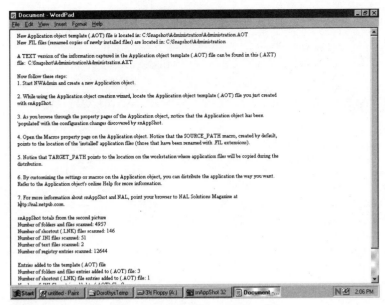

FIGURE 7-4 Sample of the contents of the summary dialog.

17. Click **Finish** to exit snAppShot.

As helpful text in the summary dialog indicated, the next step to configuring Application Launcher for your network is to create a new Application object.

Creating and Working with Application Objects

The major benefit of using Application Launcher to network administrators is that applications can be administered for the entire network from a single point. That single point is usually the administrator's workstation.

Single-point network administration requires that you create an Application object for each application you want to install and administer. You use NetWare Administrator to create Application objects in the directory tree. Each Application object you create and the properties associated with it then become part of the NDS database, and are subject to all of the security associated with NDS.

In addition to creating the Application object, you must identify where on the user's workstation (system tray, desktop, start menu, or in Application Launcher) the Application Launcher software is to put the application's icon or startup program when the user logs in to the network and the application's installation automatically begins. How to create an Application object in the NDS tree, and how to specify the location of the application for the user are both discussed below.

How to Create an Application Object in the NDS Tree

When you create an Application object in the NDS tree, it has a defined set of properties, the values of which you supply. Some of the properties associated with Application objects are:

- the location on the network of the actual application, provided as a drive mapping or UNC path to the executable file
- the printer port to which printing from this application is to be directed
- the registry and INI entries needed so that Windows can recognize and run the actual application
- the program files required to run the application
- the network and search drives needed to run the application and store and retrieve associated data files

To create an Application object, start NetWare Administrator from your administrator's workstation, and complete the following steps. When completing this process, note that the steps may differ slightly the very first time you complete this process.

1. Right click the container object (Organization or Organizational Unit) into which you want to place the Application object.
2. Click **Create**. The New Object dialog opens, displaying the Class of New Object list.
3. Click **Application**, then click **OK**. The Create Application Object dialog opens (see Figure 7-5).
4. Click on the associated radio button to choose the specific option you want to use when the Application object is created. To use the .AOT file you created from running Snapshot.exe on the user's workstation, click: **Create an Application object with an .aot/.axt file**.

NOTE

The AOT file is created in a format which cannot be read in a text editor, while the AXT file is created in a format which can be read in a text editor. Either way, the purpose of this file is to record what happened to the workstation when the application was installed on the workstation. (The online Help provides more detailed information about these two files, and why and when you might want to use them.)

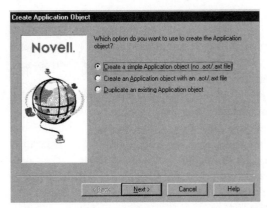

FIGURE 7-5 Create Application Object dialog showing the default option:
Create a simple Application object (no .aot/.axt file).

5. Click **Next**, The Create Application Object dialog opens (see Figure
7-6). Browse for and choose or type in the path to the location of the
executable file for the application.

If you choose the defaults while creating the AOT file, the file is
located in **c:\snapshot\NDS_Application_Object_name.**

NOTE

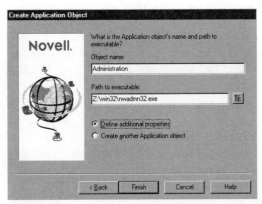

FIGURE 7-6 The Create Application Object dialog into which you type an
object name, and specify the path to the executable file.

6. Provide the needed information in the Object name and Path to executable fields, then if displayed, click either **Define additional properties** or **Create another Application object**. Generally, you want to create one Application object at a time, so click the radio button next to **Define Additional Properties**.

7. Click **Finish**. The Application object's details opens with the Identification page displayed.

8. Click any of the other page tabs and provide any additional information. For example, click **Fault Tolerance** to open the Fault Tolerance property page, then click the **Fault Tolerance** check box, the **Load Balancing** check box, or both check boxes to enable one or both of these features.

NOTE You must associate other objects with the Application object if users are to be able to run the application. You do this on the Associations property page (see Figure 7-7). Instructions for associating objects with this Application object are provided below in "Associating the Application Object with Other Objects."

9. Click **OK** when you have finished supplying the needed information on the various property pages to complete the creation of this Application object.

Associating the Application Object with Other Objects

Once you create an Application object and provide information in different property pages, you must associate it with objects on the network for it to be of any use. Associating the Application object also requires a change to the Application object's properties, which you do through the Association property page.

You can associate Application objects with the following object classes:

- Organization
- Organizational Unit
- Group
- User
- Country

Associating an Application object with Organization, Organizational Unit, Group, User, or Country objects provides users with access to that Application object. Being associated with the Application object gives the associated User, Group, or container object the right to run the application for which the Application object was created. Once you associate the Application object with a User, Group, or container object, NDS security controls access to the Application object and the application it represents, just as it controls access to other objects in the Directory.

By associating User objects or Group objects with an Application object, only those specific users identified by the User objects or those who are members of the specific Group objects will have access to the Application object. By associating a container object with the Application object, all users whose User object or who are a member of any Group within that container are granted access to the Application object.

To associate another object in the Directory tree with an Application object, start NetWare Administrator, then follow these steps:

1. Right click the application object, then choose **Details** to open the Application object's details which contains page tabs to each of the Application object's property pages. (Alternatively, you can just double-click the Application object.) By default, the Application object's Identification page opens (see Figure 7-7).
2. Click the **Associations** page tab to open the Associations property page (see Figure 7-8).
3. Click **Add**. The Select Object dialog opens.
4. Browse the context until you find the object you want to associate with this Application object.
5. In the Available Objects list (on the left side of the window), click the object to be associated with this Application object. For example, to associate the Admin user, click the **Admin User** object (see Figure 7-9).

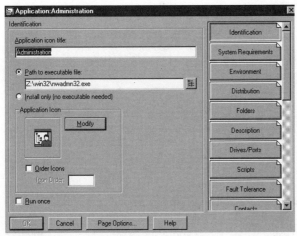

FIGURE 7-7 The Application object's Identification page.

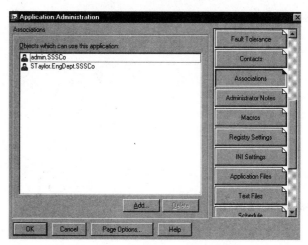

FIGURE 7-8 The Application object's Associations page to which you add User, Organization, Organizational Unit, Group, or Country objects.

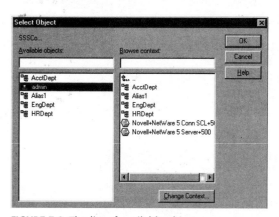

FIGURE 7-9 The list of available objects.

6. Click **OK**. The Select Object dialog closes and the object is added to the list of objects on the Associations page.

7. Click **OK**.

After you have completed this process, you can see what rights the associated object has to the Application object by right-clicking the Application object in the NDS tree, clicking **Details** in the menu that opens, then clicking **Trustees of this Object**. Once the Trustees of Object_name window opens, click the trustee whose rights you want to see, then click **Effective**

rights. For example, click **STaylor.EngDept.SSSCo** to see the STaylor User object's effective rights (see Figure 7-10).

Distributing and Managing Network Applications

When you created the Application object, you had the option to use the template (.AOT file) that was created when you ran the Snapshot program. The purpose of creating and using the template was to allow Application Launcher to automatically install, configure, and if necessary restore the settings, drive mappings, and icons associated with the application on the user's workstation.

The installation and configuration take place when the user logs in to the network and launches the application. In addition, if a user makes changes to the application's settings at any time in the future, the AOT restores the original, correct settings the next time the user launches the application. Enabling this installation and configuration process and providing the user with a means to see and run the application entail the basic processes associated with distributing and managing applications.

Distributing and managing applications is relatively easy. Two prerequisites must be met first, however:

FIGURE 7-10 View of User object STaylor's effective rights to the Administration Application object.

- Users who will be accessing the applications must have file system rights to the directory where the application is located.
- Z.E.N.works must be installed on the file server so that Application Launcher is installed and available.

Distributing and managing an application requires that you:

1. Create the Application object as described in the previous procedure. (See "How to Create an Application Object in the NDS Tree.")
2. Associate the Application object you created with User, Group, Organization, Organizational Unit, or Country objects. (See "Associating the Application Object with Other Objects.")
3. Specify where the icon for the user will display: in the System tray, on the desktop, in the Start menu, or in Application Launcher.
4. Place the appropriate executable program (**Nal.exe** or **Nalexpld.exe**) into either the Startup folder on the workstation or into a login script which will run for the user when the user logs in to the network.

By following the procedures previously described in this chapter; you have already accomplished Steps 1 and 2. Now you must specify where the icon for the user is to display, and place the appropriate executable program where the user can access it.

Specifying Where the Icon Displays

Specify where the icon for the user will display (Step 3 above): in the System tray, on the desktop, in the Start menu, or in Application Launcher by completing these steps:

1. In NetWare Administrator, right click the object you associated with the Application object. For example, right click the Admin User object.
2. Click **Details**.
3. Click the **Applications** page tab to open the Applications page (see Figure 7-11).
4. Locate the executable program file you want the user to be able to access and run.
5. Click the appropriate check boxes next to the executable program file you located.

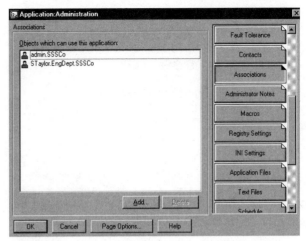

FIGURE 7-11 The Application object's Applications page.

 There are four check boxes from which to choose. The Application Launcher check box is already marked. You can also choose to mark any or all of the following:

- Start Menu
- Desktop
- System Tray

6. Click **OK**.

Distributing the Application Launcher

You can place the appropriate executable program (**Nal.exe** or **Nalexpld.exe**) into either the Startup folder on the workstation or into a login script (Step 4). If you place it into the login script, the executable program will run for the user when the user logs in to the network.

During these two procedures, you can specify either the Application Launcher or the Application Explorer to run for the user at their workstation. To have the Application Launcher run, you need to set it up to run the **Nal.exe** program file. To have the Application Explorer run, you need to set it up to run the **Nalexpld.exe** program file.

AT THE USER'S WORKSTATION

To have either Application Launcher or Application Explorer run at the user's workstation, complete the following steps:

1. At the user's workstation, right-click the **Start** button.
2. Right click **Explore**. This opens the Explore window.
3. Expand the folder view on the left of the Explore window until you locate the drive mapping to **Sys:Public** on the file server, then expand that folder.
4. Scroll through the Contents of the Public directory (on the right side of the Explore window), until you find either the Nal.exe or Nalexpld.exe file.
5. Click and drag the file (**Nal.exe** or **Nalexpld.exe**) from the Contents of the Public directory list on the right of the Explore window to the C:/Windows/Start Menu folder on the left side of the Explore window. This copies the file (usually as a shortcut) into the Program folder.
6. Double-click the file you just dropped to launch the associated program (Application Launcher or Application Explorer). The Application Launcher or Application Explorer program runs, its icon is displayed on the user's workstation desktop, and the application you set up to load and configure is also installed and made available to the user.

NOTE

This procedure is time consuming to do for more than one or two workstations. If your network has more workstations than this, you will find it less time consuming to follow the "From a Login Script" procedure (see below).

FROM A LOGIN SCRIPT

To have either Application Launcher or Application Explorer run at the user's workstation from instructions you include in a login script, complete the following steps:

1. In NetWare Administrator, right-click the object to which you associated the Application object. The associated Identification property page for this object opens. For example, if you associated the Application object with a user's User object, right-click the user's User object.
2. Click the **Login Script** tab to open the user's Login Script property page.
3. Place the appropriate command into the user's login script at the bottom. (Do not place it before any existing login script commands. Put it in last so that it will be the last command to execute.)
   For example, put one or the other of the following commands into the login script replacing Server1 with the name of the file server:

```
@\\Server1\SYS\PUBLIC\Nalexpld.exe or @\\Server1\
SYS\PUBLIC\Nal.exe
```
4. Click **OK**.

When the user logs in to the network, the command you placed into the user's login script will run. The Application Launcher or Application Explorer program will run (depending on which one you specified to run), and the applications you identified to be installed and set up will also run.

By following all of the procedures detailed in this chapter, you will have successfully set up and configured Application Launcher for your network. Now, the next time the users affected by the configuration and setup you just completed log in to the network, the configuration and set up of their workstations to access the specified applications will automatically occur.

Chapter Summary

Z.E.N.works (Zero Effort Networking) is a snap-in to NetWare Administrator. When installed on file servers in your network, Z.E.N.works reduces the time it takes to administer your network and the workstations on it. One way in which it accomplishes that is through the Application Launcher component of Z.E.N.works. Application Launcher simplifies the distribution and maintenance of applications on the network.

Application Launcher is the component of Z.E.N.works which allows you to distribute and manage applications. Application Launcher itself consists of four product components:

- the Application Launcher snap-in to NetWare Administrator
- snAppShot
- the user's Application Launcher window
- the Application Launcher Explorer

As the network administrator, you are responsible for implementing Application Launcher. Choosing to implement Application Launcher benefits both you and your network's users in the following ways. Benefits to the network administrator are:

- Centralized application administration
- Centralized application maintenance and control
- Push or pull distribution of software

Benefits to the user are:

- Automatic, location-independent access to applications
- Fault tolerance of network applications
- Automatic balancing of an application's workload
- Automatic support of roaming profiles

Before you can administer applications on your network using Application launcher, you must create an Application object for each type of application on your network, and provide the needed property values for that Application object. You must then associate the application object with other objects on the network for it to be of any use. You can associate Application objects with:

- Organization objects
- Organizational Unit objects
- Group objects
- User objects
- Country object

Associating an Application object with Organization, Organizational Unit, Group, or User objects provides users with access to that Application object, and thus to the application it represents.

When you create an Application object in the NDS tree, like other NDS objects, it has a defined set of properties; you supply the values. The properties associated with Application objects are:

- the location on the network of the actual application, provided as a drive mapping or UNC path to the executable file
- the printer port to which printing from this application is to be directed
- the registry and INI entries needed so that Windows can recognize and run the actual application
- the program files required to run the application
- the network and search drives needed to run the application and store and retrieve associated data files

When you created the Application object, you had the option to use the template (.AOT file) that was created when you ran the Snapshot program. The purpose of creating and using the template was to allow Application Launcher to automatically install, configure, and if necessary restore the settings, drive mappings, and icons associated with the application on the user's workstation.

The installation and configuration take place when the user logs in to the network and launches the application. In addition, if a user makes changes to the application's settings at any time in the future, the AOT restores the original, correct settings the next time the user launches the application. Enabling this installation and configuration process, and providing the user with a means to see and run the application entail the basic processes associated with distributing and managing applications.

Distributing and managing applications is relatively easy. However, two prerequisites must be met first:

- Users who will be accessing the applications must have file system rights to the directory where the application is located.
- Z.E.N.works must be installed on the file server so that Application Launcher is installed and available.

To distribute and manage an application requires that you:

1. Create the Application object.
2. Associate the Application object you created with User, Group, Organization, Organizational Unit, or Country objects.
3. Specify where the icon for the user will display: in the System tray, on the desktop, in the Start menu, or in Application Launcher.
4. Place the appropriate executable program (**Nal.exe** or **Nalexpld.exe**) into either the Startup folder on the workstation, or into a login script which will run for the user when the user logs in to the network.

When you have finished these tasks (which takes longer to explain on paper than they actually take to do), you will have successfully set up Application Launcher on your network.

Practice Test Questions

1. Of the following, which one is not an advantage of running Z.E.N.works on your network?
   A. Integrated install
   B. Program scheduling
   C. Central application management
   D. Automated error messaging

2. The feature of Z.E.N.works which allows you to distribute and manage applications is:
   A. Application Explorer
   B. Application Launcher
   C. Windows Launcher
   D. Windows Explorer

3. To ensure application software is updated at the user's workstation, set which value in one of the Application object's property pages?
   A. Launch always
   B. Forced run
   C. Push distribution
   D. Pull distribution

4. The feature of Application Launcher which ensures that if one file server running an application becomes unavailable, another server can take its place is:
   A. Fault tolerance
   B. Load balancing
   C. Roaming profile
   D. Location-independence

5. A user receives automatic support when working from other than their default workstation because of which Z.E.N.works feature?
   A. Fault tolerance
   B. Load balancing
   C. Roaming profile
   D. Location-independence

6. You can create an .AOT file using either (choose two):
   A. **Snappe16.exe**
   B. **Snappe32.exe**
   C. **Nwadmin32.exe**
   D. **Nal.exe**

7. The AOT file represents the path to where an application's files are to be stored as:
   A. `%SOURCE_PATH%`
   B. `SOURCE_PATH`
   C. `%TARGET_PATH%`
   D. `TARGET_PATH`

8. The two properties for which you must provide values when creating an Application object are:
   A. Forced run
   B. Path to executable
   C. Fault tolerance
   D. Load balancing

9. You set load balancing for an Application object on which property page?
A. Identification
B. Associations
C. Fault tolerance
D. Load balancing

10. You can associate any of the following objects with an Application object except:
A. Organizational Unit
B. User
C. Alias
D. Country

11. Users accessing applications must:
A. Have file system rights to the directory where the application is stored
B. Have NDS rights to the directory where the application is stored
C. Have NDS rights to the Windows Explorer
D. Have file system rights to where Snapshot.exe is stored

12. The application icon can be displayed for user access anywhere except:
A. Start menu
B. System tray
C. Windows desktop
D. Property page

13. The last step you must perform when distributing and managing an application is:
A. Place **Nal.exe** or **Nalexpld.exe** into Startup
B. Create the Application's NDS object on the user's desktop
C. Run **Snapshot.exe**
D. Associate the application object with the user

14. To get Windows Explorer to run on the user's workstation, you can make it launch using (choose two):
A. Explore
B. Desktop
C. Login script
D. System tray

15. Which of the following is the correct format to use when placing the command to run Application Explorer into a login script?

A. `@\\server_name\sys\public\Nal.exe`

B. `@\\server_name\sys\public\Nalexpld.exe`

C. `@\\sys\public\Nalexpld.exe`

D. `@\\sys\public\Nal.exe`

Answers to Practice Test Questions

1. D	6. A,B	11. A
2. B	7. C	12. D
3. B	8. B,D	13. A
4. A	9. C	14. A,C
5. D	10. C	15. B

CHAPTER 8

Using Other
Z.E.N.works Features

Z.E.N.works (Zero Effort Networking) is a directory-enabled networking service designed to provide network administrators the
ability to manage their network with less effort and at a lower overall cost. The Z.E.N.works product name is not intended to give the
impression that administrators won't have to do any work to manage the
network. It is instead intended to reflect the fact that Z.E.N.works was
designed to make it effortless for users to access the network resources
that they need. Since network administrators must set up the network as
conveniently and quickly as possible and then keep it fully functioning
for the user's access to be effortless, Z.E.N.works concentrates on making that job easier and quicker.

Z.E.N.works combines the best features of three Novell products in
order to make a network administrator's set up and maintenance as easy
and inexpensive as possible. Two of these three features were previously
available for separate purchase. The third feature, however, was still under
development before the release of Z.E.N.works. These three features are:

- Novell Application Launcher (NAL) v2.50, which was updated and
  renamed Application Launcher. Its purpose is to let network administrators distribute and maintain applications across the network.
  Application Launcher was discussed in detail in Chapter 7, *Using
  Application Launcher.*

- Novell Workstation Manager v1.10, which was updated to include some additional functionality. Its purpose is to let network administrators configure parameters such as printer or workstation settings for Windows 95 and Windows NT workstations, and then implement those settings for all associated workstations without having to physically be at each workstation to do so.
- Remote Control, which was a previously unreleased product. Its purpose is to let users electronically notify a help desk when they have problems with their workstation, so help desk personnel can remotely look at the workstation and resolve errors as quickly and easily as possible.

Z.E.N.works is tightly integrated with NDS. You install Z.E.N.works to your network server, install the Novell Client software on the workstation, and then you access and use Z.E.N.works through NetWare Administrator. Z.E.N.works is referred to as a *snap-in* to NetWare Administrator. You install it separately from the NetWare 5 server installation, and it hooks up with and is accessed by running the NetWare Administrator utility.

Z.E.N.works provides its network management capabilities by using NDS objects. When you install Z.E.N.works, the Policy Package object class is added to the Directory tree, and the NDS schema is extended to accept Policy Package, Policy, and Workstation objects.

You use NetWare Administrator to tell the network to create Policy Package objects, which Z.E.N.works then populates with a variety of Policies, depending on the type of Policy Package object you chose to create. You can then change the settings and configurations associated with one or more of those Policies, and distribute the Policy Packages and the configuration settings they contain to specific users on the network. Z.E.N.works also includes a scheduler you can run to specify when an action such as the distribution of a Policy Package to a user's workstation is to take place. In addition, Z.E.N.works includes a desktop version of the scheduler which your network users can run as a separate utility. With it, they can schedule actions to take place at their own workstations. For example, a user can schedule an automatic regular backup of some or all of the contents of their workstation's hard drive to the network.

KEY CONCEPT

When you register and import workstations into your NDS tree, Z.E.N.works creates workstation objects. Each Workstation object represents an actual workstation on the network. A Workstation object has two primary functions: collecting and storing inventory-related information about the workstation, such as the type of CPU it has and how much memory it has; and enabling the network administrator or other authorized user to remotely control that workstation.

There are two Z.E.N.works packages available. The first is called the Z.E.N.works Starter Pack. It is included when you purchase NetWare 5. The second is called Z.E.N.works Full. It is a separate product you purchase which enhances the capabilities of Z.E.N.works. While the Z.E.N.works Starter pack provides the Application Launcher and Policy Package and Policy desktop management software, the Z.E.N.works full package provides additional features. If you purchase Z.E.N.works Full and install it to your network, you also get the following Z.E.N.works functionality:

- Workstation inventory
- Help requester
- Remote Control

Chapter 7, *Using Application Launcher*, explained how to take advantage of the Application Launcher features of Z.E.N.works. This chapter concentrates on explaining Policy Packages and Policies, and on showing you how to take advantage of the basic desktop management features included in the Z.E.N.works Starter Pack. You'll learn how to create Policy Package objects in the Directory, and how to enable and configure desktop management Policies within Policy Packages. Chapter 9 explains the three additional Z.E.N.works features you get when you buy and install the Z.E.N.works Full product for NetWare 5.

This chapter discusses two basic functions:

- managing network workstations using policy packages and policies
- customizing the user's desktop and printing environments

There are five major steps you must perform if you are to take full advantage of Z.E.N.works:

1. Create Policy Package objects and enable and modify the configuration of various policies within those packages.
2. Register each workstation in the Directory tree.
3. Import registered workstations into the Directory tree.
4. Set up remote control.
5. Set up the help requester.

Issues and procedures associated with the first step are discussed in the sections of this chapter titled "Managing Network Workstations Using Policy

Packages and Policies," and "Customizing the User's Desktop and Printing Environments." Issues and procedures associated with the four remaining steps are discussed in Chapter 9, *Taking Full Advantage of Z.E.N.works.*

Before you complete the procedures associated with each of these steps, however, you will find it useful to have a good understanding of Z.E.N.works. The first section in this chapter, "Understanding Z.E.N.works" is designed to give you an overview of Z.E.N.works. It includes a discussion of the features included in the Z.E.N.works Starter Pack, as well as those features included in the Z.E.N.works Full product.

Understanding Z.E.N.works

Z.E.N.works reduces the costs and complexities of administering networks because it provides you as the network administrator with services that let you manage your network from your own workstation. Z.E.N.works creates what is called a *digital persona*. The digital personal is a combination of the resources a specific user can access, and the rights that user has to those resources. By establishing and maintaining a digital persona for each network user, you have greater administrative control of your network. Because Z.E.N.works lets you manage digital personas from your own administrator's workstation, the cost in dollars and time of administering and managing the network is reduced.

KEY CONCEPT

To take full advantage of Z.E.N.works to manage your network means that you:

- develop and follow a consistent cycle of maintenance to make sure that the NDS accurately reflects the workstations in use
- update NDS when workstations are added, removed, or moved; when you find that not all workstations are represented in NDS; you replace network boards, or IPX numbers are changed
- create and update Z.E.N.works policies, and associate policies with containers, groups and users

Minimum Requirements for Using Z.E.N.works

To take full advantage of Z.E.N.works, your network must be configured as follows:

- Running NetWare 5
- Running the latest Novell Client on your workstations
- Policy Packages must be created and managed

- Running **Nwadmin32.exe** to use NetWare Administrator instead of other older versions of Nwadmin

Setting Up Policy Packages in Z.E.N.works

Policy Packages are objects that let you set rules for managing workstations and allow you to troubleshoot your network without leaving your office. They can be associated with containers, groups, users, and workstation groups. (A Workstation group is a new NetWare 5 NDS object. It allows you to apply policies to multiple workstations, just as a user Group allows you to apply rights and login scripts to multiple users.)

There are seven policy package objects, each of which fall into one of three types: container, user, or workstation:

- **Container:** This policy package object contains only a policy: a Search policy. The search policy allows you to determine which policy packages are associated with a container. Because policy package associations flow down the tree like rights, you can search up the tree to see who has what rights. You may find this necessary if security is breached by someone having too many rights, or if unnecessary LAN traffic is generated in search levels.
- **Workstation:** There are three types of workstation policy package objects, one for each Windows platform: Win3x, Win95, and WinNT. You use these policy packages to set up the environment for workstations. Within these policy packages there are 10 different policies which you can enable and configure. For example, you can enable a policy to set controls (restrictions) for workstations, then associate the workstation policy package with containers, workstation group objects, or workstation objects. The controls you set are then applied regardless of who uses the workstation.
- **User:** There are three types of user policy package objects, one for each Windows platform: Win 3x, Win95 and WinNT. User policy packages set up the working environment for a specific user when they log in to the network. There are nine user policies you can configure. When you configure these policies, you set up the working environment for those users associated with the policies in the user policy package. The user policy package can be associated with containers, user (not workstation) group objects, and user objects.

NDS Issues and Z.E.N.works

Using Z.E.N.works on your network will reduce the time you spend implementing and maintaining your network, but it does have other impacts as well. In particular, there are two issues you might want to consider:

- the number of objects in the directory tree
- the importance of pre-planning

NUMBER OF OBJECTS IN THE DIRECTORY TREE

When you implement Z.E.N.works on your network—particularly when you begin utilizing the workstation inventory feature of Z.E.N.works—both you and NetWare can create many NDS objects in the directory tree. For example, if your network includes 1500 workstations and you implement workstation inventory, 1500 workstation objects are added to NDS. Therefore, using Z.E.N.works can greatly increase the number of objects in NDS. You must consider the potential for a large increase in object count when considering implementing policies.

For example, if you do have 1500 workstations on your network, make sure you still have the ability to allow 1500 more objects to be created in the partition in which these workstation objects will be added. You also need to have the workstation objects added to the same partition where the related users' User objects are located. In addition, you need to consider the network size, Windows platforms you have, and whether you need to make multiple policy packages for the same containers. (Using multiple policy packages facilitates giving differing rights to users, such as administrators and regular users.)

IMPORTANCE OF PRE-PLANNING

When implementing Z.E.N.works, you may want to do some pre-planning. Deciding which policy packages you need in NDS and which NDS objects should be associated with these policy packages is a good first step. You may also want to take into consideration how you can customize the policies you create. In addition, consider:

- creating policy packages at the highest level you can to minimize administration
- creating user packages in the containers where user's User objects are, and workstation policies where Workstation objects are

Avoid creating single-use containers, because they slow down the network and reduce scalability.

NOTE

- determining how these policy packages will be associated with users, groups, workstations, and workstation groups before you create them

Registering and Importing Workstations

Registering and importing workstations is another task you perform, and another feature of Z.E.N.works. You must register workstations with NDS before they can be added (imported) as objects. You register workstations with NDS through the Workstation Registration agent included with Z.E.N.works. When a workstation running the latest Novell Client logs into the network, its network address is sent to NDS and placed on a list of registered workstations. NDS then creates a Workstation object for each imported workstation.

Before importing workstations, you must configure the Workstation Import policy in the Workstation Policy package for each platform. Doing so specifies how the workstation is to be displayed in the Directory tree once it is imported. The Workstation Import policy will then be able to create the workstation object in the correct container following the correct naming conventions.

Once you have created the needed Workstation Import policies and each workstation registers with NDS, those workstations can then be imported into the NDS tree. The associated workstation registration agents, **WSREG32.EXE**, **WSREG16. EXE**, and **WSREG32.DLL**, are run to import workstations into the NDS tree. You can use the Workstation Registration Agents through Application Launcher, Scheduler, or Login Scripts. However, scheduler works only for Windows 95 and NT workstations.

When a workstation is registered, a log file is created at the root of the workstation's local drive and a list of workstations that have been registered appears in the NDS container object's Registered Workstations page. You can check either place to verify that the workstation has successfully been registered.

Once a workstation is registered, you must import it to NDS to create an NDS object for that workstation. Periodically, you can re-import workstation objects to update information when changes occur in the workstation hardware (network board), location, or address.

Understanding What You Can Do with Policies

There are two primary tasks you can perform using policies:

- configure the workstation environment
- configure printing environments

CONFIGURE THE WORKSTATION ENVIRONMENT

The appearance and functionality of a user's Windows desktop can be customized through User System and Computer System policies. Using these policies, you can define what applications are visible and available to users. Any changes you make to a user's desktop occur immediately, and affect only those workstations associated with these policies. You can set other desktop preferences in the Desktop Preferences policy of the user policy package. For example, you can set which wallpaper displays on the desktop, which screen saver runs, and what sounds the system makes when different events (such as a user logging out of the network, or a system processing error) occur.

CONFIGURE PRINTING ENVIRONMENT

You can use policies to help you install the correct priner drivers to the workstations, and to configure the printing environment through NDS. You can associate users or workstations with a specific printer and printer drivers. When users log in, the associations are created and the printer driver is installed.

Using Z.E.N.works through NetWare Administrator, you can also set up and use remote control and the help requester. Information about remote control and the Help Requester are covered below.

Understanding Remote Control

Remote Control allows the administrator to remotely control a target workstation for troubleshooting and repair (if the problem is software and not hardware) through NetWare Administrator. Remote control access is granted through the NetWare Administration Tools menu. When you use the Tools menu to set up and use remote control, you see a representation of the target workstation's desktop which you can then control.

Remote control of a workstation is accomplished by distributing the User agent application (**WUSER.EXE** or **WUSER32.EXE**) using Application Launcher or Login Scripts. User agent application objects appear in NDS during Z.E.N.works installation. Make sure that:

- you have the correct rights
- the workstation object has been created in NDS
- the User Agent application object has been associated with the user groups or user objects in NDS

The Remote Control policy also allows you to set security measures to ensure network security. Controlling a workstation is done through a set of buttons that appear in the upper right corner of the desktop window, or through a set of shortcuts. For information on how to control security on a workstation using the buttons, see the section of this chapter titled "Establish a Remote Control Connection to the Workstation."

Understanding the Help Requester

The help requester simplifies how users get help for workstations, applications, etc. Help Desk policies allow you to determine how users will contact technical support—either through email or call contact. If you use email, you must have GroupWise, or a MAPI service.

Help Requester can be added to all desktops using Application Launcher (**HLPREQ16.EXE** and **HLPREQ32.EXE**). You must also configure the Help Desk policy in the User Policy Package to provide the Help Requester with the correct NDS information. This includes choosing whether contact will be made via email or telephone, complete contact information, and subject line topics for messages.

Help Desk policies can be added to existing User Policy Packages. If a User Policy Package does not exist, it must be created; the Help Desk Policy must then be configured.

When the Help Requester is distributed and the Help Desk Policy is created and associated, users can launch the Help Requester and report problems. You can review user's help requests, and then remotely control the workstations to fix the problem, providing you first have implemented remote control.

 The Info button in the Help Requester supplies users with information about their workstations that is useful when tech support is needed.

NOTE

As identified previously, there are five steps associated with managing network workstations using Policy Packages and Policies:

1. Create Policy Package objects and enable appropriate policies (the Workstation Import policy, for example, if you want to use the workstation information gathering and storing capabilities of Z.E.N.works).

2. Register each workstation in the Directory tree.

3. Import registered workstations into the Directory tree.

4. Set up remote control.

5. Set up the help requester.

The overview and conceptual information associated with these steps were covered earlier in this chapter. Now, the processes associated with the first of the five steps are covered below. The processes associated with the last four steps are covered in Chapter 9, *Taking Full Advantage of Z.E.N.works.*

Managing Network Workstations Using Policy Packages and Policies

To manage network workstations using policy packages and policies requires that you first create policy packages, and then enable and configure the policies they contain which you want to apply to users on your network. To complete the procedures outlined in both this and the next chapter, you need to have NetWare Administrator running on your workstation, and you need to be logged into the network as the Admin user, or a user with equivalent rights.

Create Policy Package Objects and Enable Policies

Creating a policy package consists of a series of simple steps. Once you create a policy package, you can then decide which policies to enable within it and make configuration changes to those policies. In addition, you can then schedule policy packages to be run.

CREATE POLICY PACKAGE OBJECTS

You create Policy Package objects the same way you create other objects in the Directory tree. This section shows you how to create any of the different types of Policy Package objects, but concentrates on creating User and Workstation Policy Packages.

To create a policy package, complete the following steps:

1. Right-click the container object into which you want the Policy Package object to be placed. A menu opens.
2. Click **Create**. The New Object dialog opens (see Figure 8-1).
3. Click **Policy Package**. A list of available Policy Packages is presented.
4. Click to choose one of the seven available types of Policy Packages, then click **Create**. The dialog for the chosen policy package opens. The seven Policy Packages you can create are:
   - Container Package
   - WIN31 User Package
   - WIN31 Workstation Package
   - WIN95 User Package
   - WIN95 Workstation Package

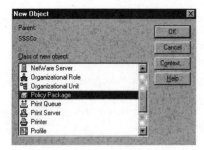

FIGURE 8-1 The New Object dialog from which you choose to create a Policy Package object.

- WINNT User Package
- WINNT Workstation Package

User policy packages are the ones you will use most often. Figure 8-2 shows the Create Policy Package dialog for a WIN95 User Package.

5. Type a name for the Policy Package, click the box next to the **Define Additional Properties** field, then click **Create**. The Policies page opens. It displays a check box and name for each of the types of policies you can enable within this policy package.

Now you have successfully created a policy package, but for that policy package to be of any use, you must enable the policies within it that you want to have applied, configure the policies you enabled, and then associate the policy package with users. The following procedures explain how to accomplish these tasks.

ENABLE AND CONFIGURE POLICIES ASSOCIATED WITH A POLICY PACKAGE

When you create a policy package, the associated Policies property page opens (see Figure 8-3). The Policies property page displays all policies

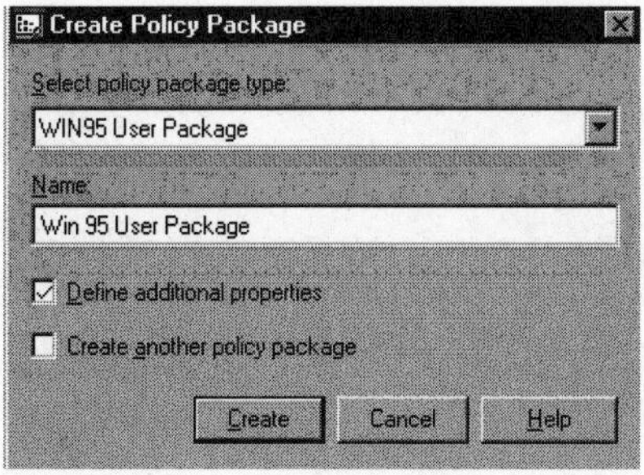

FIGURE 8-2 Create Policy Package dialog for creating a WIN95 User Package.

associated with this policy package. Each listed policy has a check box next to it. To enable a policy, click the check box. A check mark is placed into the check box indicating that the policy has been enabled. You can disable it by clicking in the check box again to remove the checkmark.

Once you enable a policy, you must configure that policy. For example, if you enable the Workstation Inventory policy, you need to specify how workstation's object names are to be determined and specified in the Directory tree when workstations are imported.

KEY CONCEPT

Each policy has a default configuration set for it. Sometimes, the default is no configuration information. Once you have enabled the policies you want enabled in the package, you can modify the associated default configurations. You modify the default configuration to suit your requirements by clicking the policy whose defaults you want to modify, then clicking **Details**.

What you choose to set or modify depends on what policy you selected before clicking **Details**. For example, if you clicked **95 User System Policies**, then clicked **Details**, you would see a configuration page similar to the one shown in Figure 8-4.

From that configuration page, you click the plus (+) button to expand any of the items listed under Default User. A list of those features for which you can modify configuration information is then displayed. Modify those features which you want to modify, then click **OK** to save your changes.

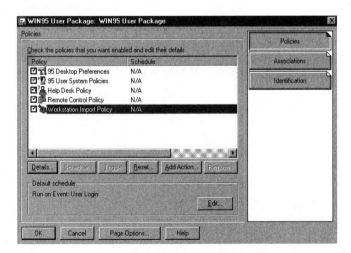

FIGURE 8-3 Policies page for a WIN95 User Package.

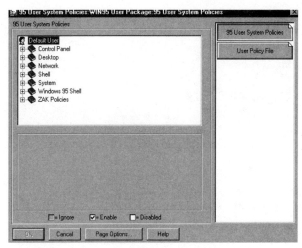

FIGURE 8-4 The Windows 95 User System Policies page.

For example, if you expand System, then expand Restrictions (see Figure 8-5), you have four restrictions you can set:

- **Disable Registry editing tools:** Clicking the associated box enables the disabling of Registry editing tools. In other words, it prevents the user from being able to run any of the Registry tools which would allow them to modify their Windows Registry settings.

- **Run only allowed Windows applications:** Clicking the associated box prevents the user from running any Windows applications you have not specifically added to the list of those applications they can run. When you enable this restriction, the Show button opens on the lower part of this window. You must click the **Show** button, then click **Add** and type in the name of the Windows application you want them to run. If allowing them to run more than one Windows application, you will have to click **Add** and type the application's name for each one you want them to run. Figure 8-5 displays the windows associated with this process.

- **Disable MS-DOS prompt:** Prevents the user from accessing the MS-DOS prompt.

- **Disable single-mode MS-DOS applications:** Prevents the user from running single-mode (non-network), DOS-based applications.

Now that you have created a policy package, enabled the policies you want it to use, and made configuration changes as needed, you must associate appropriate objects with this policy package.

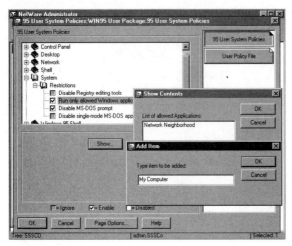

FIGURE 8-5 Dialogs associated with restricting the Windows applications for users with this policy.

Associating Objects with Policy Packages

A policy package is not complete until it has one or more other objects associated with it. As a rule, you associate specific User objects, but you can associate other objects as well.

To make these associations, complete the following steps:

1. With the Policy Package details open (right-click the Policy Package object in NetWare Administrator, then click **Details**), click the **Associations** page tab. The Associations page opens.

2. Click **Add**. The Select Object dialog opens.

3. Browse the Directory tree until you find the object you want to associate with this policy package displayed under the Available Objects area of this dialog.

4. Click the object, then click **OK**. The object displays in the Associations list (see Figure 8-6).

5. Click **OK** to accept the associations you made and close the policy package.

To manage network workstations using Policy Package objects and policies, you must create the appropriate Policy Package object, enable the policies you deem appropriate, make configuration changes, and make associations if appropriate. Configuring the user's desktop and printing environments is a typical use for policy packages and policies.

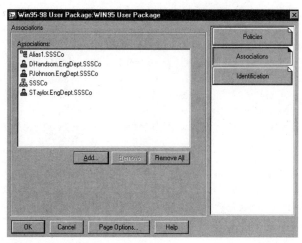

FIGURE 8-6 The Associations page for a WIN95 User Package.

Customizing the User's Desktop and Printing Environments

The sample used in the previous section showed you one way to customize a user's desktop environment. The procedure is the same regardless of which desktop configuration you want to set up. However, you can also configure the user's desktop environment by configuring Control Panel options associated with the desktop preferences policy of a User Package.

Configure the User's Desktop Environment by Configuring Control Panel Options

To configure Control Panel options in the Desktop Preferences Policy, complete the following steps:

1. Open the details page of the User or Workstation Package.
2. Click **95 Desktop Preferences** or **NT Desktop Preferences**, depending on whether this is a WIN95 or a WINNT User or Workstation Package, then click **Details**. The Control Panel page opens.
3. Double-click **Display**. The Display Properties page opens.
4. Click one of the available Display Properties page tabs to open its associated display page. For example, click **Appearance** to open the Appearance page.

5. Click the associated check box to enable configuration of this property. For example, if you opened the Appearance page, click the check box next to Color Scheme (see Figure 8-7).
6. Provide the required information. For example, if you opened the Appearance page, click the arrow to open the list of available color schemes from which you then click to choose the color scheme you want to set as the configuration for associated objects.
7. Click any of the other page tabs and change any of the configurations for the open page if you want to do so, then click **OK**. The Display Properties page closes.
8. If you want the workstation's configuration that you just set to be updated when the user on this workstation is authenticated to NDS, check the **Always update Workstation During NDS Authentication** check box at the bottom of the Desktop Preferences page.
9. Click **OK**.

NOTE

Microsoft provides a method for setting desktop preferences. Microsoft refers to it as policy solutions. The Z.E.N.works Control Panel page options such as Display interface with Microsoft Windows to make the desktop settings function. Z.E.N.works lets you establish mandatory profiles using these Control Panel settings.

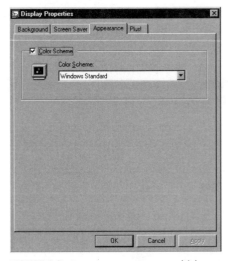

FIGURE 8-7 Appearance page on which you set the configuration for the Windows desktop color scheme.

Establish Printing Policies for Users

To establish printing policies for users on the network, follow these steps:

1. Open (or create and then open) a Workstation Package.
2. Click the associated check box to enable the 95 or NT Computer Printer policy.
3. Click **Details**.
4. Provide the needed information to configure the Computer Printer policy.
5. Click **OK** to save the configuration for this policy.

Chapter Summary

Z.E.N.works (Zero Effort Networking) is a directory-enabled networking service designed to provide network administrators the ability to manage their network with less effort and at a lower overall cost. The Z.E.N.works product name reflects the fact that it was designed to make it effortless for users to access the network resources that they need. Network administrators must set up the network as conveniently and quickly as possible and then keep it fully functioning for the user's access to be effortless, Z.E.N.works concentrates on making that job easier and quicker.

Z.E.N.works combines the best features of three Novell products in order to make a network administrator's set up and maintenance as easy and inexpensive as possible: Novell Application Launcher (NAL) v2.50, which was updated and renamed Application Launcher, Novell Workstation Manager v1.10, and Remote Control, which was a previously unreleased product.

To take full advantage of Z.E.N.works, your network must meet several minimum requirements:

- You must have first installed NetWare 5 on your server.
- You must be running the latest Novell Client on your workstations.
- You must run the **Nwadmin32.exe** version of NetWare Administrator instead of one of the other older versions of **Nwadmin.exe**.

Once you meet the minimum requirements and install Z.E.N.works, you create policy packages, enable those policies they contain that you need to use on your network, configure those policies you enabled, then distribute whatever software needs to be distributed to user's workstations. Policy packages are objects that let you set rules for managing workstations and allow you to troubleshoot your network without leaving your office. They can be associated with containers, groups, users, and workstation groups. To be used, however, you must associate them with one or more objects.

You create policy packages to accomplish a variety of tasks. For example, you create policy packages and enable policies which allow you to configure a user's workstation. You can set what their display will look like, as well as other environment configurations which you would otherwise only be able to do by sitting at the user's workstation and accessing Windows' Control Panel.

Practice Test Questions

1. The three features of Z.E.N.works are:
   A. Application Launcher
   B. Workstation Manager
   C. Policy Packages
   D. Remote Control
   E. Policies

2. When you install Z.E.N.works, which class is added to the Directory?
   A. Policy
   B. Policy Package
   C. Help Requester
   D. Remote Control
   E. All of the above

3. Which two objects are not added to the schema as the result of installing Z.E.N.works?
   A. Policy
   B. Policy Package
   C. Help Requester
   D. Remote Control
   E. Workstation objects

4. The combination of resources a specific user can access, and the rights that user has to those resources, is referred to as:
   A. Z.E.N.works
   B. Workstation inventory
   C. Digital persona
   D. User view

5. Of the following, which two are *not* specific tasks you must perform if you are to take full advantage of Z.E.N.works to manage your network?
  A. Troubleshoot your network using Help Requester
  B. Develop and follow a consistent cycle of maintenance
  C. Update NDS when changes to workstations occur
  D. Create and update policies
  E. Run **Nwadmin.exe**

6. The three types of policy package objects you can create are:
  A. Container
  B. Workstation
  C. User
  D. Group
  E. Organization

7. The two main NDS issues you need to consider when implementing Z.E.N.works on your network are:
  A. The number of objects in the Directory
  B. The method of registering and importing workstations
  C. The types of Z.E.N.works objects you create
  D. The workstation registration agents you use
  E. The importance of pre-planning

8. Which of the following statements about policies is *not* true?
  A. You can use policies to help you install the correct printer drivers to the workstations.
  B. The appearance and functionality of a user's Windows desktop can be customized using User System and Computer System policies.
  C. The Remote Control policy lets you access a user's workstation without having to be physically sitting at it.
  D. Any changes you make to a user's desktop affect only those workstations associated with the User System or Computer System policy.
  E. None of the above are not true.

9. Of the following, which is *not* a true statement regarding the Remote Control policy?
  A. You must have the correct rights to run it.
  B. The user's Workstation object must exist in NDS.
  C. The User Agent application object must be associated with the appropriate user groups or user objects in NDS.
  D. All of the above are true statements.
  E. None of the above are true statements.

10. To enable a policy in a policy package you must:
   A. Name the policy
   B. Click the check box next to the policy
   C. Click **Details**
   D. Click **Edit** and specify when the policy will be run
   E. Create the policy package

11. To modify the defaults associated with a specific policy, you first enable that policy then:
   A. Name the policy
   B. Click the check box next to the policy
   C. Click **Details**
   D. Click **Edit** and specify when the policy will be run
   E. Create the policy package

12. Of the following, which is not a configuration you can modify in a Windows 95 user System Policy?
   A. Disable registry editing tools
   B. Run only allowed DOS applications
   C. Disable MS-DOS prompt
   D. Disable single-mode DOS-based applications

13. Configuring which of the following is a typical use for policy packages and policies?
   A. A user's desktop and printing environments
   B. The Help Requester application
   C. A workstation registration policy
   D. None of the above
   E. All of the above

14. Two important NDS issues to consider when implemening and maintaining your network with Z.E.N.works are:
   A. The number of objects in the directory tree
   B. If your network has any Windows 3.1x workstations
   C. The importance of pre-planning your network
   D. Only A and B

15. The Help Requester can be added to all desktops using Application Launcher by specifying which two of the following executable files?
   A. **NalRqstr.exe**
   B. **Hlpreq16.exe**
   C. **Hlpreq32.exe**
   D. **Nal16.exe**
   E. **Nal32.exe**

Answers to Practice Test Questions

1. A, B, D	6. A, B, C	11. C
2. B	7. A, E	12. B
3. C, D	8. C	13. E
4. C	9. E	14. A, C
5. A, E	10. B	15. B, C

CHAPTER 9

Taking Full Advantage of Z.E.N.works

A s Chapter 8 stated, there are five major steps you must perform if you are to take full advantage of Z.E.N.works. The first step (creating Policy Package objects and enabling and modifying the configuration of various policies within those packages) was discussed in detail in Chapter 8. To take advantage of the workstation inventory, help requester, and remote control features provided in the Z.E.N.works Full package, you must complete these additional steps:

1. Register each workstation in the Directory tree.
2. Import registered workstations into the Directory tree.
3. Set up remote control.
4. Set up the help requester.

This chapter explains how to take advantage of these three added features found in the Z.E.N.works Full product. You'll learn how to:

- Make NDS aware of network workstations
- Set up and use remote control
- Set up and use the help requester

Making NDS Aware of Network Workstations

NDS becomes aware of network workstations when those workstations are registered with NDS (imported into the NDS tree). Registering a workstation with NDS results in the creation of a Workstation object. Each workstation on the network that is registered with NDS has an associated Workstation object in the NDS tree.

Importing workstations into NDS requires that the workstation meets minimum qualifications. First, the workstation must be capable of being imported into NDS. That is, the workstation must be running a current Novell Client for Z.E.N.works. Second, a user must currently be logged in to the network from the workstation for importing to function.

KEY CONCEPT

Importing workstations into NDS also requires that you follow a specific process. First, you must create a User Policy Package. Then, you must enable the Workstation Import policy within that User Policy Package, make modifications as needed to the Workstation Import policy, and associate the User Policy Package with users. (Because the Workstation objects are automatically created in NDS, and because NDS requires that every object have its own name, there must be a means whereby unique names can be determined and assigned to each Workstation object when it is imported. That is the function of the Workstation Import policy.) Next, you must register the workstations in your Directory tree, and finally you must import the registered workstations.

Once you have accomplished all of these tasks—workstations have been imported and now display as Workstation objects in the Directory tree— you may also want to view the workstation information these Workstation objects have collected and stored.

Create a User Policy Package

As with other policy packages, the User Policy Package is created by following the same process used to create any object in the Directory tree. First, you right-click the container into which the object is to be placed, then you click **Create**. Next, you click the class of object to be created (Policy Package in this case), then click **OK**. You then choose to create the User Policy Package.

Enable, Modify, and Associate a Workstation Import Policy

To enable the Workstation Import Policy, simply create or open an existing User Policy Package, then click on the check box next to Workstation Import Policy. This enables the Workstation Import Policy with default configurations. You will probably want to customize the policy rather than just accepting the defaults. For example, you may want to customize how names are assigned to workstation objects. To do so, modify the Workstation Import policy.

To modify the Workstation Import policy:

1. Run NetWare Administrator and open the User Policy Package which has the Workstation Import policy enabled.
2. Click **Workstation Import Policy** to select it, then click **Details**.
3. Click **Allow importing of Workstations** (see Figure 9-1).
4. Specify where the Workstation objects are to be created. The path you specify is relative to the path in which this Policy Package resides. If you want the Workstation objects to be imported into a container above the current container, for example, click the **Browse** button (the button with three dots on it, next to the Path field) and type a single period (.) into the path.
5. Click the **Workstation Naming** page tab. The Workstation Naming page opens (see Figure 9-2).

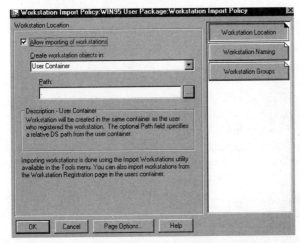

FIGURE 9-1 The Workstation Location dialog. This is where you identify the location in the Directory tree where the Workstation objects are to be created when they are imported into the Directory tree.

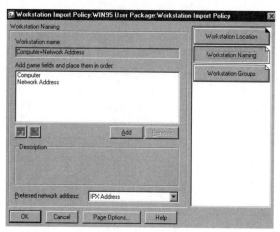

FIGURE 9-2 Workstation Naming properties page.

6. Using the **Add** button to include name fields in the order in which you want them to appear, define how you want the workstation to be named. For example, if **Computer** and **Network Address** appear in that order in the **Add name fields and place them in order** list, the name of each imported workstation will consist of its computer name followed by its network address in one long stream.

7. Choose the preferred network address such as IPX Address.

8. Click **OK** when you have finished providing the needed information.

To associate a User Policy Package with network users, complete the following steps:

1. With the User Policy Package Policies page open, click **Associations**.

2. Click **Add**.

3. Choose the objects you want to associate with this User Policy Package. For example, if you choose a container object, all users whose User object resides within that container will be associated with this User Policy Package.

4. Click **OK**. The User Policy Package closes, and the associations are made.

Register and Import Workstations

Once the registration process is configured, the workstation a user logs in on will automatically be imported into NDS the next time the user logs in if the WSReg32 program is executed from the user's login script. Before that occurs, however, you must prepare workstation registration.

PREPARE WORKSTATION REGISTRATION

Part of ensuring that the import is successful is granting users the necessary rights to the container where their Workstation object is created when the registration process occurs. To set up rights, you prepare workstation registration by completing the following steps:

1. From the menu on NetWare Administrator, click **Tools**.
2. Click **Workstation Utilities**.
3. Click **Prepare Workstation Registration**. The Workstation Registration dialog opens (See Figure 9-3).
4. Browse to find the container where the Workstation object is to be created in NDS (see Figure 9-4), then click **OK**.

IMPORT ONE OR MORE WORKSTATIONS

You can import a single workstation or multiple workstations. Import a single workstation as follows:

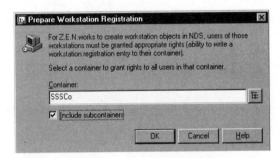

FIGURE 9-3 Workstation Registration dialog.

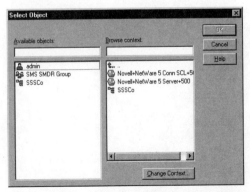

FIGURE 9-4 Browse to locate the container where the Workstation object is to be created.

1. Within the Directory tree view of NetWare Administrator, right-click the container where you chose to import the workstation. A menu opens.
2. Click **Details**. The Identification property page for this container opens by default.
3. Click **Workstation Registration** to open the Workstation Registration property page.
4. Select the workstation you want to import.
5. Click **Import**.
6. Click **OK**.

To import multiple workstations, use the Import Workstations option on the NetWare Administrator Tools menu. (See Figure 9-5.)

After completing either of these processes, the workstations are imported into the chosen container. Now you must enable workstation inventory, and if you want to, change its schedule.

By default, the scheduling process is automatic. It occurs based on the default schedule, which is set up to have each workstation register when a user logs in from that workstation. You can change the schedule, however, using the **Edit** button on the Workstation Package.

To change the default schedule, select the **Workstation Inventory policy** in the Workstation Package, then click **Edit**. The Default Schedule page opens. Modify the settings from their default to reflect when you prefer to have the Workstation Inventory policy run. For example, you can change it from running when the user logs in, to running monthly on the last day of the month between 08:00 am and 05:00 pm (see Figure 9-6). When finished modifying the default schedule, click **OK**.

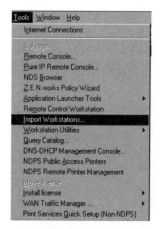

FIGURE 9-5 The Import Workstations option on the NetWare Administrator Tools menu.

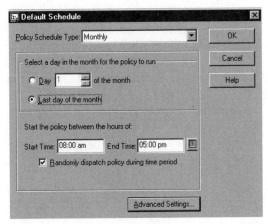

FIGURE 9-6 The Default Schedule dialog, where you modify when the Workstation import is to occur.

You can use the Z.E.N.works scheduler to register workstations in NDS if all of the Z.E.N.works components were installed when you installed Z.E.N.works. (If you chose **Typical Install** when you installed Z.E.N.works, all components were installed.) You can also use the Application Launcher feature of Z.E.N.works to register workstations, or if you chose not to install all Z.E.N.works components when you installed Z.E.N.works, you can use a login script to register workstations.

View Information Associated with Each Workstation Object

Once workstations have been imported, you may want to view the information stored for each workstation. For example, you may want to see what disk drives each workstations have, how much RAM is present, or what the interrupts, I/O ports, DMA channels, or memory address settings are for one or more workstations. To view this information, follow these steps:

1. From the list of Workstation objects displayed in the Directory tree view of NetWare Administrator, double-click the Workstation object whose information you want to view.
2. Click the **Workstation Inventory** page button to open the Workstation object's associated Workstation Inventory property

page. Basic workstation inventory information such as the operating system this workstation is running, how much memory it has, and which CPU it has is displayed on the opening Workstation Inventory property page.

3. To view additional information about this workstation, click the **Advanced Information** button. A dialog with five tabs opens.

4. Click one of the tabs (Drives, Buses, Services, Resources, or Display Adapter) to view related information. The associated page opens.

You can view the information on each of the associated tab pages by simply clicking the tab to change to that page. On some pages, you can change how the related information is displayed. For example, on the Drives page, you can choose to display the workstation's list of drives by either the type of drive (removable, logical, or CD-ROM), or by the drive letter (in alphabetical order).

5. Click either **OK** or **Cancel** to close the workstation's dialog boxes.

Setting Up and Using Remote Control

Remote control is that feature of Z.E.N.works that lets you sit at your own workstation and work as if you were sitting at a user's workstation. Its primary benefit is that of making it easier and quicker for you to repair software problems on the workstation. The assumption is made that you will receive a request from a user to assist with a software problem on their workstation, and you will respond by taking control of their workstation, making the necessary corrections, and then notifying the user that you have fixed the problem.

 To use remote control, the user's workstation must first be registered with NDS as a workstation. Therefore, you must have followed the procedure for setting up and importing workstations into the network before you can take advantage of the remote control feature of Z.E.N.works.

To make the process of problem reporting to problem resolution a relatively easy one, both the Help Requester feature as well as the Remote Control feature of Z.E.N.works have been provided. This section explains remote control and how to use it. "Setting Up and Using the Help Requester" later in this chapter explains how to make the Help Requester available to users so that they can notify the appropriate person when they have a software problem on their workstation.

Setting Up Remote Control

There are three steps to setting up remote control: meeting minimum requirements, distributing the appropriate User agent application, and (optionally) modifying remote control security.

MEETING MINIMUM REQUIREMENTS

To take advantage of remote control, you must meet requirements for rights as well as for software. The following are the rights and software requirements for using remote control:

- **Software:** The server must be running NetWare 5, the network administrator's workstation must be running the **Nwadmin32.exe** version of NetWare Administrator, and each workstation must be running the Novell Client supplied with Z.E.N.works. In addition, each workstation must be connected to the network (an NDS connection is required; a bindery connection will not work), registered in NDS, and have an associated Workstation object in the Directory tree.

- **NDS rights:** The network administrator must have at least the Write right to the DM Remote Verification attribute of the Workstation object, and the Read right to all attributes in the Workstation object. (The Read right comes from the [Public] object.)

- **File system rights:** Users must have the Read and File Scan rights to the directory in which Application Launcher is installed, as well as to the directory containing the User agent application. By default, this directory is Public. Also by default, users already have Read and File Scan rights to the Public directory.

DISTRIBUTING USER AGENT APPLICATIONS

A User Agent application is the application which allows the network administrator to connect to and manage a user's workstation with the remote control utility in NetWare Administrator. The User Agent application must be running on the workstation for you to access that workstation. For the User Agent application to be running on the workstation, the associated User Agent Application object must exist in the Directory tree. It is created automatically when you install Z.E.N.works. In addition, for the User Agent application to actually be running on the user's workstations, you must install it to the workstation. Which version of the User Agent application you install, however, depends on what operating system the workstation is running. On a Windows 3.x or Windows 95 workstation, install the **Wuser.exe** application object. On a Windows 95 workstation, install **Ntstacfg.exe**.

Installing the User Agent Application

You can install the User Agent application (Wuser.exe or Ntstacfg.exe) using Application Launcher. Do so as follows:

1. Associate the User Agent application object with an NDS object.
2. Right-click the object you associated with the User Agent application object.
3. Click **Applications**. The Applications property page opens.
4. Mark the check box associated with **Force Run**.
5. Click **OK**.

Set Up Application Launcher to Run the Application Launcher Explorer

KEY
CONCEPT

You must set up Application Launcher to run the Application Launcher Explorer so that the User Agent application will be put on the user's workstation the next time the user logs in. To accomplish this task, place the following command (replacing `server_name` with the actual name of the file server) in the container login script for those containers where the User Agent application object is located:

```
@\\server_name\sys\public\nalexpld.exe
```

The **Wuser.exe** (for Windows 3.x and Windows 95 workstations) and **Ntstacfg.exe** applications are stored in **sys\public** on the file server. Depending on what operating system the workstation is running when the user logs in, one of these files will run.

The **Ntstacfg.exe** application needs to be launched through Application Launcher on a Windows NT workstation the first time only. After that, Windows NT starts it automatically at startup.

Make the Appropriate Application Executable Available to Users

You must make the **Wuser.exe** or **Ntstacfg.exe** files available to users. You can do this by placing commands into the container's login scripts. The first command you need to put in the login script maps a search drive to the **sys\public** directory. Subsequent commands identify which program is to run depending on the workstation's operating system.

Put the following commands into the container's login script:

```
MAP ROOT INS S1:=server_name\SYS:PUBLIC
    IF "%PLATFORM"="W95" THEN begin
        @Wuser.exe
    End
```

```
IF "%PLATFORM"="WNT" THEN begin
  @Ntstacfg.exe
End
IF "%PLATFORM"="WIN" THEN begin
  @Wuser.exe
End
```

MODIFYING REMOTE CONTROL SECURITY

You don't want just anyone to be able to access and control a user's workstation. To ensure that only authorized personnel remotely access user's workstations, you need to set up remote control security. Although you can do this for individual workstations by assigning trustees and granting specific rights to the Workstation objects in the Directory tree, you can do it for larger numbers of workstations using the Remote Control policy in either a User or Workstation Policy Package. You only need to do this, however, if you want to change the default which automatically enables remote control access when the Workstation object is created.

KEY CONCEPT

The process is simple. Create either a User or Workstation Policy Package, or open an existing one. Enable the Remote Control policy in the Policy Package, then configure security parameters (see Figure 9-7). Next, associate the Policy Package with the NDS objects to which the policy is to be applied.

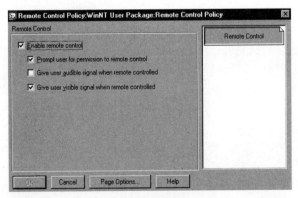

FIGURE 9-7 The Remote Control Policy page, from which you enable remote control and define security.

You can set up the following parameters for remote control security:

- Disable remote control so the workstation cannot be controlled from a remote location.
- Prompt the user when remote control is being attempted. This requires that the user confirm remote control before the remote control process can actually take control of the workstation.
- Enable an alert to sound while the workstation is being accessed from a remote location.
- Display a remote control icon while the workstation is being accessed.

You set up remote control security in either a User or a Workstation object by completing the following steps:

1. Within the Directory display in NetWare Administrator, right-click the User or Workstation object, then click **Details**.
2. Click the **Remote Control** page tab. The Remote Control properties page opens.
3. Click the **Use These Settings and Ignore Remote Control Policy** check box to enable these settings to override any Remote Control policy which exists.
4. Click one or more of the check boxes to set security settings to your specifications. For example, click the **Disable Remote Control** box to prevent anyone from remotely accessing this workstation.
5. Click **OK**.

Establish a Remote Control Connection to the Workstation

Once remote control access has been set up, you can access a user's workstation when necessary. For example, if a user contacts you with a problem that you determine to be a software problem, you can run NetWare Administrator and establish a remote connection to their workstation.

NOTE

Before starting the remote control connection, notify the user that they may be prompted to allow remote control. Tell them to quickly click the **Yes** button if they are prompted. You must also tell them not to touch the keyboard while you are remotely accessing their workstation, as their keyboard will still be active.

To establish a remote connection to a user's workstation, complete the following steps:

1. Click once to select the Workstation object representing the user's workstation (the target workstation).
2. Click **Tools**. The Tools menu opens.
3. Click **Remote Control Workstation**. A connection to the target workstation is started, and a window displaying the status of that connection attempt is displayed. When the connection is successful, the Viewing window showing the target workstation's desktop opens.

NOTE

If you set security to prompt the user for permission for you to have remote access to their workstation, the user is prompted. They have five seconds to respond. If they do not respond with permission within that time, the connection is not made, and the status window displays a message telling you that the user did not respond.

4. You can now make any changes you would have done had you been sitting at the user's workstation.

The viewer screen that opens when you remotely access a workstation provides several buttons and key combinations which you can use to work with the user's workstation. The buttons you can use, and their function are:

- **Start button:** Sends a **Ctrl-Esc** key sequence to the workstation. It opens the target workstation's Start menu or task list, depending on the version of the Windows operating system running on the workstation. With the Start menu or task list open you can perform various tasks using the cursor and mouse. For example, you can use the **Run** command to run a program.
- **Application Switcher button:** Lets you choose an application that is currently open on the user's workstation. To use this button, click it, then press **Tab** to choose the open application.
- **System Key Pass-Through button:** Turns on or off your workstation's ability to use **Ctrl** and **Alt** keys on your keyboard as if you were using them directly at the target workstation's keyboard. Unless you click this button first, your **Ctrl** and **Alt** keys do not function on the target workstation. Click it a second time and you return the function to inactive.
- **Navigation button:** Minimizes the desktop of the target workstation so that you can frame an area of the target desktop and change the view to be that of the area you framed. This makes it easier for you to navigate the target desktop when you reduce the Viewing window's size, which you may want to do if you are working with more than one target workstation at a time.

The key combinations you can use and their associated function are:

- **Ctrl+Alt+A:** Increase the refresh rate of the Viewing window without changing the target workstation's refresh rate.
- **Ctrl+Alt+H:** Enable the Control Options hot key on the target workstation.
- **Ctrl+Alt+M:** Size the Viewing window to your monitor's screen size and do not display window borders.
- **Ctrl+Alt+R:** Refresh the target workstation's window.
- **Ctrl+Alt+S:** Pass Windows reserved keystrokes, such as Alt+Tab, to the target workstation so all keystrokes affect only the target workstation and not your own.
- **Ctrl+Alt+T:** Reconnect your workstation to the target workstation and refresh the Viewing window.

Ending a Remote Control Session

To disconnect from a remote controlled workstation:

1. Click the dash (–) button in the upper left corner of the viewing window. This opens a pull-down menu.
2. Click **Close**.

You can also disconnect by clicking **Alt+F4** if you have toggled the use of Alt and Ctrl keys to be active, or you can use the key sequence assigned for stopping the view, which is **Left-Shift+Esc** by default.

Setting Up and Using the Help Requester

The Help Requester is an application users can run to request help when experiencing problems with their workstation, network, or software. As the network administrator, you decide how you want to receive help requests, then you create Help Desk policies. The policies establish what options the users have when using the Help Requester.

Users can access the Help Requester for two purposes. One is to locate contact information so they know who to notify when they are having problems. The other is to send an email to the appropriate help person. Of course, only a network with an email application can take advantage of this second purpose.

Load Help Requester on the User's Workstation

As with remote control, for the user to run the Help Requester application, it must to be loaded to their workstations. You can use Application

Launcher to load the Help Requester application on user's workstations. Depending on the operating system the user's workstation is running, you load either **Hlpreq16.exe** (for Windows 3.x workstations) or **Hlpreq32.exe** for Windows 95 and Windows NT workstation.

Make Sure Users Have Sufficient Rights to Run Help Requester

Because the Help Requester is part of Z.E.N.works, the application objects mapped to these two versions of the Help Requester are created in the Directory tree when you install Z.E.N.works. As with the Remote Control programs, these Help Requester programs reside in the **sys\public** directory on the file server. By default, users automatically have Read and File Scan file system rights to this directory, so they have the necessary rights to run these programs. In addition to file system rights, users also need the Read and Compare All Property Rights to the application objects. Because those rights are also automatically assigned to any container, group, or user object associated with the application object, you only need to associate one or more of these objects to the application object for the users to have all the rights they need to access this application object.

Meet Minimum Software Requirements for Running Help Requester

The Help Requester also has the same software requirements as Remote Control:

- The server must be running NetWare 5.
- The network administrator's workstation must be running the **Nwadmin32.exe** version of NetWare Administrator.
- Each workstation must be running the Novell Client supplied with Z.E.N.works.
- Each workstation must be connected to the network (an NDS connection is required; a bindery connection will not work), registered in NDS, and have an associated Workstation object in the Directory tree.
- If the email feature of Help Requester is to be used, the network must provide a messaging service, such as GroupWise.

Enable and Configure a Help Desk Policy

The Help Desk policy is a policy in User Policy Packages. To Enable and Configure a Help Desk policy, complete the following steps:

1. Create or open an existing User Policy Package.
2. Click the check box next to the Help Desk policy to enable it, then click **Details**. Now you can configure the Help Desk policy to suit your network needs and environment.
3. Click the **Information** page tab. The Information property page opens.
4. In the **Contact Name** field, provide the name of the individual users are to contact when they have a software problem.
5. In the **Email Address** field, provide the full email address for the person you named in the Contact Name field.
6. In the **Telephone Number** field, provide the contact's complete telephone number. An area code may not be needed if this contact will never be called from any number other than a number in the same area code.
7. Click the **Configuration** button. The Configuration property page opens (see Figure 9-8).
8. If you want users to be able to launch the Help Requester, click **Allow users to launch the Help Requester**.
9. Click **Allow users to send trouble tickets from the Help Requester**.
10. Select the trouble ticket delivery mode from the pull-down menu. For example, select GroupWise 5.0.
11. In the **Trouble Ticket Subject Lines** field, identify subject lines to be used for help requests.
12. Click **OK** to finish configuring the Help Requester and accept the configuration information you entered.

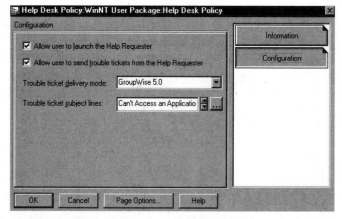

FIGURE 9-8 Configuration page for a Help Desk Policy.

Now that the Help Desk policy is configured, you must associate it with one or more objects for it to be effective. However, if the User Policy Package which contains this Help Desk policy has already been associated with other objects in the Directory, you do not need to modify that association unless you specifically want it changed. If this User Policy Package has not been associated with other objects in the Directory, click the Associations button to open the property page from which you associate this User Policy Package (and thus this Help Desk policy) with other objects in the Directory.

Now that the Help Desk policy has been enabled and its User Policy Package associated with other objects in the Directory tree, you must distribute the Help Desk policy to workstations.

Distribute the Help Desk Application to Workstations

Once you have enabled and configured a Help Desk policy, you can distribute the Help Desk application to workstations using Application Launcher. The process is the same as for distributing Remote Control because you need the Application Launcher or the Application Explorer running on the user's workstation. That requires that you distribute the **Nal.exe** or **Nalexpld.exe** software to the user's workstation. You can simply put the appropriate command (@\\server_name\sys\public\nalexpld.exe or @\\server_name\sys\public\nal.exe) into the container login script to accomplish this.

Use the Help Requester

You create a Help Desk policy and then distribute its associated application to the user's workstations so that they can make the appropriate contact or notification when a problem occurs. The user needs to know how to use the Help Requester in order to make that contact or notification.

When the Help Requester is running, a window is presented to the user. That window contains four buttons: Mail, Call, Info, and Help. The user clicks on these buttons to perform the following associated tasks:

- **Mail:** Identify the subject topic (choose which subject reasonably describes the problem), provide a message (generally a brief description of the problem), click **User** and if necessary provide your user name and context, then click **Send** to mail the help request. The User tab generally already contains your user information. You can reference it if needed to tell the contact person your user context and workstation ID.

- **Call:** Use to find the name, email address, and phone number for the person who is available to help with problems. You use this page primarily when you cannot email the help request because email does not exist on your network, or when you want to follow up on a help request you previously sent.

- **Info:** Use to see both the information contained in the Help Desk tab in the Call for Help window, and in the User tab of the Help Desk policy.

- **Help:** View information on how to use the Help Requester utility.

The workstation inventory, help requester, and remote control features of Z.E.N.works all function together to help you manage your network with the least amount of work and time. This helps keep your company's network management costs as low as possible, frees up some of the network administrator's time for such tasks as optimizing the network, and simplifies problem reporting and repair.

Chapter Summary

The Z.E.N.works full product provides three features not available in the Z.E.N.works Starter Pack version which ships with NetWare 5: Workstation Inventory, Remote Control, and Help Requester. This chapter explained how to take advantage of workstation inventory, which you can do once you register workstations with NDS. Once registered, workstations then can be added (imported) into NDS as Workstation objects. You register workstations with NDS through the Workstation Registration agent included with Z.E.N.works. When a workstation running the latest Novell Client logs into the network, its network address is sent to NDS and placed on a list of registered workstations. NDS then creates a Workstation object for each imported workstation.

Before importing workstations, you must configure the Workstation Import policy in the Workstation Policy package for each platform. Doing so specifies how the workstation is to be displayed in the Directory tree once it is imported. The Workstation Import policy is then able to create the workstation object in the correct container following the correct naming conventions.

Once you have created the needed Workstation Import policies and each workstation registers itself with NDS, those workstations can be imported into the NDS tree. The associated workstation registration agents: **Wsreg32.exe**, **Wsreg16. exe**, and **Wsreg32.dll**, are run to import workstations into the NDS tree.

This chapter also discussed the remote control feature of Z.E.N.works. You use remote control to remotely control a target workstation for troubleshooting and repair (if the problem is software and not hardware) through NetWare Administrator. Remote control access is granted through the NetWare Administration Tools menu. When you use the Tools menu to set up and use remote control, you see a representation of the target workstation's desktop, which you can then control.

Remote control of a workstation is accomplished by distributing the User agent application (Wuser.exe or Wuser32.exe) using Application Launcher or Login Scripts. User agent application objects appear in NDS during Z.E.N.works installation.

This chapter also discussed the help requester feature of Z.E.N.works. You use help requester to simplify how users get help for workstations, applications, etc. Help Desk policies allow you to determine how users will contact technical support either through email or phone contact. If you use email, you must have GroupWise or a MAPI service.

Help Requester can be added to all desktops using Application Launcher (Hlpreq16.exe and Hlpreq32.exe). You must also configure the Help Desk policy in the User Policy Package to provide the Help Requester with the correct NDS information. This includes choosing whether contact will be made via email or telephone, complete contact information, and subject line topics for messages.

Help Desk policies can be added to existing User Policy Packages. If a User Policy Package does not exist, it must be created and then the Help Desk Policy must be configured.

When the Help Requester is distributed and the Help Desk Policy is created and associated, users can launch the Help Requester and report problems. You can review user's help requests, and then remotely control the workstations to fix the reported problem, providing you first have implemented remote control.

Practice Test Questions

1. Which two are primary functions of the Workstation object?
   A. Collecting information about the workstation
   B. Displaying CPU information
   C. Establishing the Help Requester
   D. Enabling remote control of workstations

2. If a user has requested help for a workstation, server, or other software problem, the help desk personnel may ask the user to click which button to provide information about the workstation which the help desk personnel can use to resolve the problem?
   A. Mail
   B. Call
   C. Info
   D. Help
   E. Add

3. NDS becomes aware of network workstations when those workstations are:
   A. Imported into NDS
   B. Created as objects in NDS
   C. Associated with a Workstation object in NDS
   D. Assigned a unique name in NDS

4. The Import Workstations option is found:
   A. On the Workstation Policy
   B. On the Workstation Policy Details page
   C. On the Tools menu in NetWare Administrator
   D. On all of the above.

5. Of the following, which is *not* one of the tabs you can choose to view workstation inventory information?
   A. Drives
   B. Buses
   C. Services
   D. Resources
   E. See Also

6. Which of the following is *not* one of the steps associated with setting up remote control?
   A. Meeting minimum requirements
   B. Distributing the appropriate User Agent application
   C. Running the Help Desk application
   D. Modifying remote control security

7. Which of the following is *not* one of the parameters you can set for remote control security?
   A. Prompting the user to approve remote control access when it is being attempted.
   B. Disabling remote control so the workstation cannot be accessed and controlled from a remote location.
   C. Displaying a remote control icon at the administrator's workstation when the administrator is accessing a workstation.
   D. Enabling an alert to sound when the workstation is being accessed from a remote location.

8. To establish a remote connection to a user's workstation, you must run NetWare Administrator and:
   A. Click to select the **Workstation** object, click **Tools** in the menu bar, then click **Remote Control**.
   B. Double-click the **Workstation** object, then open the **Remote Control** property page.
   C. Open the **Options** menu in NetWare Administrator, then click **Remote Control**.
   D. None of the above.

9. To open the Start menu or task list on a user's workstation during a remote control session, click which button in the remote control viewer screen?
   A. Start
   B. Application Switcher
   C. System Key Pass-Through
   D. Navigation

10. When running remote control, to refresh the target workstation's window, click:
    A. **Ctrl+Alt+A**
    B. **Ctrl+Alt+H**
    C. **Ctrl+Alt+M**
    D. **Ctrl+Alt+R**

Answers to Practice Test Questions

1. A, D   6. C
2. C   7. C
3. A   8. A
4. C   9. A
5. E   10. D

CHAPTER 10

Administering a NetWare 5 Network

A s you have progressed through the chapters of this book, you have opened and worked with NetWare Administrator several times. You should recognize that it has the same capabilities of any Windows-based utility when it comes to changing the size of the window, opening and closing it, scrolling through its contents, and so on.

While you have performed several tasks using NetWare Administrator, there are other basic tasks you can do with it. This chapter provides more information about NetWare Administrator, and how to use it to perform basic network administration tasks.

In addition, this chapter discusses:

- Tasks associated with maintaining the network's file system
- How to use role-based administration to help distribute some of the administrator's workload

Configuring NetWare Administrator

You can modify the presentation of NetWare Administrator by changing the appearance of the tool bar and the status bar. You can also change the order in which objects are displayed in the Directory tree, and how each object's property pages are displayed.

Change the Appearance of the Toolbar and Status Bar

KEY CONCEPT

You can change the appearance of the toolbar and status bar by showing, hiding, or selecting items to be included. To show or hide either the toolbar or status bar, open the View menu from the menu bar, then click one of the following:

- Show Toolbar
- Show Status Bar

If the Toolbar or Status Bar is showing at the time you click one of these options, a checkmark is shown next to the option. When you click the option, the opposite action occurs and the Toolbar or Status bar is closed. The checkmark is also removed.

KEY CONCEPT

Using the View menu, you can also specify whether Hints or Quick Tips are displayed. Click on either option to change its status (active if a checkmark appears next to it, inactive if there is no checkmark.) Figure 10-1 shows the View menu as it appears when you open it in NetWare Administrator.

KEY CONCEPT

You can also configure the buttons on the toolbar. With the toolbar you want to configure open and active, right-click the toolbar, then click **Configure Toolbar and Status Bar**. The Configure Toolbar and Status Bar dialog opens (see Figure 10-2).

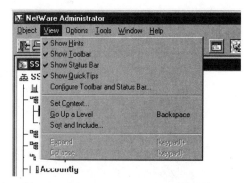

FIGURE 10-1 Example of the View pull-down menu opened from the menu bar in NetWare Administrator.

FIGURE 10-2 Sample Configure Toolbar and Status Bar dialog.

You can then:

- Use the Toolbar-Main Features tab or the Toolbar-View Features tab to select and arrange the main toolbar buttons, or the view-specific toolbar buttons.
- Add, remove, or reorder information on the status bar.

When you have finished making changes, click **OK**.

Filter How Objects Are Displayed

You can also modify the presentation of NetWare Administrator by filtering the way objects are displayed in the Directory tree. When you filter the tree view you specify how objects are to be ordered for display in the Directory tree.

KEY
CONCEPT

To change the order in which objects are displayed in the Directory tree, activate the window whose object view you want to change, click **View** on the menu bar, then click **Sort and Include**. The Sort and Include by Object Class page opens (see Figure 10-3). Using drag-and-drop, simply move the order of the object classes until you are satisfied with the new order, then choose **OK**. Alternately, you can click on a class that you want to move, then click either the **up** or **down arrow** button to move the class inside the list.

If you choose, you can prevent some class types from displaying in the list at all. To do so, click the class of object you want to prevent from displaying, then click the **right arrow** button to remove it from the

Included classes list and place it into the Available classes list. You can also reverse the process and add a class back into the view of the Directory tree. Click the class in the Available classes list, then click the **left arrow** button.

To see your changes take affect, collapse the Directory tree view, then expand it again. The objects now display in the order you specified.

Being able to change how various items such as the toolbar and Directory objects appear in NetWare Administrator should help you customize NetWare Administrator to your personal preferences. Whether you modify NetWare Administrator's appearance or not, you should know how to view the detailed information associated with each object in the Directory tree.

View and Change Object Information

KEY
CONCEPT

The process is simple. To view or change information about an object, you must open the object's details. To do that, simply right-click on the object, and then click **Details**. The Identification page for the object whose details you chose to view opens by default. You can then click on one of the property page tabs to view information about the object's properties.

Manipulating the view you see with NetWare Administrator and knowing how to get more information (view the property pages of) any object

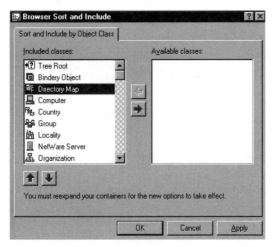

FIGURE 10-3 Sort and Include by Object Class browser view.

in the Directory tree are basic to using NetWare Administrator. Figure 10-4 shows the Users property page for the Server object called Server1. Notice that the User's button on the right of the graphic is depressed. If you click any of the property page buttons associated with the details for an object, the associated property page opens.

Using NetWare Administrator to Perform Basic Tasks

When using NetWare Administrator, there are some basic tasks you will want to be able to perform. For example, when you first launch NetWare Administrator, the Directory tree structure you see generally does not begin at the [Root] of the tree. Instead, it usually begins at the highest container level within which your User object is set. It opens to your current context.

Changing the view of the Directory tree structure is an easy task providing you have sufficient rights to view higher levels of the Directory tree. As a network administrator, you have all rights to the Directory tree.

To change the view of the Directory tree to include any container at a level lower than your current context, all you do is expand the container object. To expand any container object in the Directory tree simply double-click the object.

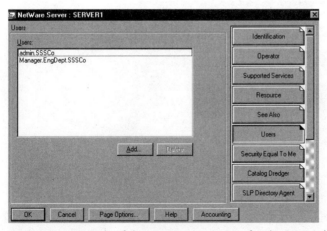

FIGURE 10-4 Example of the Users property page for the Server object named Server1.

Viewing a level of the Directory tree higher than the highest level currently shown requires a little more effort. To see all levels of the Directory tree, you must change your current context to [Root].

To change your current context to [Root] using NetWare Administrator when you are only one level below [Root], open the View menu, then click Go Up a Level. To change your current context to [Root] using NetWare Administrator when your current context is deeper than one level below [Root], complete the following steps, the windows for which are shown in Figure 10-5):

1. Click **View** on the NetWare Administrator menu bar.
2. Click **Set Context**. The Set Context dialog opens.
3. Click the **Browse** button next to the Context field. The Select Object dialog opens.
4. Click the **up arrow** icon on the Browse context side of the Select Object dialog, or click on one of the container objects, depending on which direction in the directory tree you want to go (up the tree structure or down).
5. Continue to click the appropriate icon until the container object of the context to which you want to change shows on the Available objects side of the Select Object dialog.
6. Double-click the container object you want to set as your current context.
7. Click **OK**.

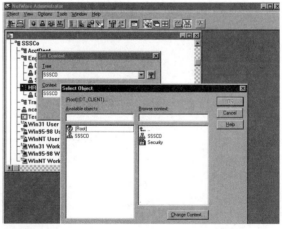

FIGURE 10-5 The dialog boxes which open when you choose to change your current context using the Set Context option in the View menu.

You can also change your current context without browsing the directory tree if you know what the context is to which you want to change. For example, if you know you want to change to [Root], complete the following steps:

1. Click **View** on the NetWare Administrator menu bar.
2. Click **Set Context**. The Set Context dialog opens.
3. Type in the context to which you want to change. For example, if changing to [Root], type **[Root]** into the New context field in the Set Context dialog.
4. Click **OK** to close the Set Context dialog.

Enhancements to NetWare Administrator

There are two enhancements to NetWare Administrator which NetWare 5 provides. Through these enhancements you can now:

- copy or move trustee assignments when you copy or move directories or files
- choose whether to allow object and property rights of a container object to be inherited

This second option provides another means whereby the network administrator can distribute the workload. It is explained later in this chapter in the "Distributing the Workload with Role-based Administration" section.

Maintaining the Network's File System

Maintaining the network's file system requires that you manage the network's directories, files, and volume space. You can do this using utilities that ship with NetWare 5, as well as utilities that ship with Windows.

Because Windows and NetWare 5 are integrated at the workstation, including the administrator's workstation, you can use the following utilities:

- Rendir
- Ndir
- Ncopy
- Flag
- Filer
- NetWare Administrator

Of these utilities, NetWare Administrator is the one you will use most often. However, if you prefer a DOS menu-based text utility, you can user Filer for many file management tasks. The other four utilities are command-line utilities you use from a workstation. To take advantage of them, you must follow the specified syntax, as shown below.

- RENDIR path [TO] directory name [/? | /VER]
  Use to rename a directory, replacing path with the path leading to and including the directory you want to rename, and directory name with the new name of the directory.
- NDIR [path] [/option...] [/? | /VER]
  Use to view information about files, directories, and volumes, replacing [path] with the path leading to the file, directory, or volume whose information you want to view, and [/option] with any specific option you want to apply.
- NCOPY [source_path] filename target_path [filename] [/ option...] [/? | /VER]
  Use to copy files or directories from one location to another, replacing [source_path] filename with the path and name of file to be copied from, and target_path [filename] with the path to and new name of the copied file.
- FLAG path [[+ | -] attribute...] [/option...] [/? | /VER]
  Use to view or modify file and directory attributes or the search mode of executable files, and to change the owner of a file or directory.

Manage the File System with the Filer Utility

You can use Filer to expand and collapse the view of files and directories within a directory. To run the Filer utility:

1. Double-click **My Computer** to browse to the Public directory, or right-click **Start**, then click **Explore**, and browse to the Public directory.
2. Double-click the program file called **Filer.exe**. This action opens a DOS box and starts Filer, opening it to the Available Options menu (see Figure 10-6).
3. With **Manage files and directories** highlighted, press **Enter**. The Directory Contents view opens. You can now choose the double dots (..) to change the view to the parent directory of the current directory, choose the back slash (\) to change the view to the root of the file system, or choose one of the listed sub-directories to change to that directory.

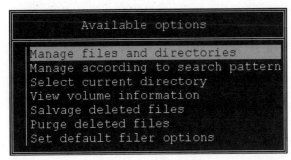

FIGURE 10-6 Example of the Filer utility's Available Options menu.

You can also view file and directory information using Filer, as well as perform various tasks using associated function keys such as **F3** to modify or **F5** to mark files and directories. (When you want to perform a task to multiple files or directories simultaneously, you must mark them all first.)

Manage the File System with the NetWare Administrator Utility

To access the file system from NetWare Administrator, you use the associated objects in the Directory tree. When a server is installed, the volumes created on that server, as well as the server itself are represented by objects in the Directory tree. Accessing the volume objects lets you see detailed information about the file system as well as the volumes themselves.

KEY CONCEPT

File system information you can view using NetWare Administrator includes:

- Directory information, such as the directory's name, any name spaces installed, the date it was created, the owner, and the directory's effective rights.
- File information, such as the file's name, size, date it was created, and date and time it was last modified or accessed, as well as the file's access rights, attributes, long name, and other details.

You can also manage various aspects of the file system and of volumes. For example, you can limit the amount of space a directory uses as well as the amount of space a user can have.

LIMIT THE SPACE A DIRECTORY USES

To limit the amount of space a directory uses, complete the following steps:

1. Expand the volume object (double-click the volume object to expand it) and subsequent directories until you can see the directory for which you want to limit space.
2. Right-click the directory, then click **Details**.
3. Click the **Facts** button. (See Figure 10-7.)
4. Click **Restrict size**.
5. In the Limit field, type in the number of kilobytes to which you want to restrict the size of this directory. For example, type **1024**.
6. Click **OK**.

LIMIT THE FILE STORAGE SPACE A USER HAS ACCESS TO

You can limit the amount of space any given user can have in the file system by following these steps:

1. Right-click the Volume object, then click **Details**.
2. Click the **User Space Limits** button.
3. Click the **Select Object** button next to the Search Context field.
4. Browse for the object to which you want to restrict access, then click it to select it.

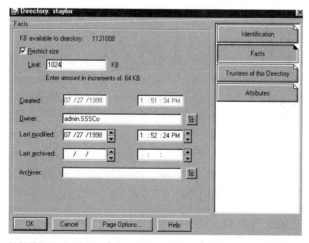

FIGURE 10-7 View of the page which provides you with facts related to the volume object.

5. Click **OK**.
6. Browse for then click the User object for whom you want to set the restrictions, then click the **Modify** button. (See Figure 10-8.)
7. Click **Limited volume space**.
8. Type in the maximum space you want this user to have, then click **OK**.
9. Click **OK** again.

VIEW AND CHANGE VOLUME INFORMATION

In addition to file system information, NetWare Administrator lets you view a wide range of volume information. Because each volume is represented in the Directory tree as an object, property pages associated with each volume provide a variety of information.

VIEW VOLUME INFORMATION

KEY CONCEPT

The following property pages are associated with Volume objects:

- Identification
- Statistics
- Dates and Times
- User Space Limits
- Trustees of the Root Directory
- Attributes
- See Also

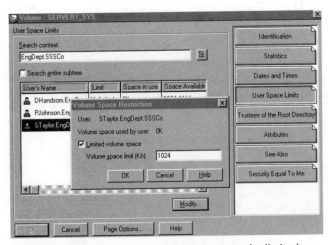

FIGURE 10-8 Displays how user volume space can be limited.

The Statistics property page provides some of the most basic volume information. It tells you how much disk space is available, whether there are deleted files available for recovery, how many directory entries exist, how much space on the volume the directory entries use, and other information. Figure 10-9 shows you the Statistics property page for the Sys volume on the server called Server1.

SET VOLUME OBJECT TRUSTEES

Besides being able to view volume information using NetWare Administrator, you can also assign volume trustees. Once you assign trustees to a volume, you then assign them specific rights. To assign a trustee to a volume, complete the following steps:

1. Right-click the volume object in the Directory tree.
2. Click **Trustees of this Object**. The Trustees of object_name dialog opens (see Figure 10-10).
3. Click **Add Trustee**.
4. Browse for the User object of the user you want to make a trustee of this volume.
5. Click the User object, then click **OK**.
6. Assign the needed rights. (For more information about rights, review Chapter 4, *Establishing Security on a NetWare 5 Network*, or reference the help associated with the rights page for the User object.)
7. Click **OK**.

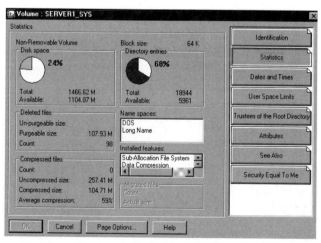

FIGURE 10-9 Sample Statistics property page.

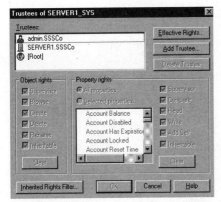

FIGURE 10-10 Graphic displaying trustees of a Volume object.

SET FILE COMPRESSION

You can also set compression on directories and files. To set compression, browse the file system inside NetWare Administrator until you locate the directory or file(s) for which you want to set compression. Then, follow these steps:

1. Right-click the directory or file, then click **Details**.

NOTE

If you want to set compression for multiple directories or files, you can select all of the directories or files you want to set compression for by holding down the **Ctrl** key, then clicking once on each file or directory.

2. Click **Attributes**.
3. Click the **Immediate Compress** check box to set these files to compress immediately after they have been closed, or click **Don't Compress** to prevent these files from ever being compressed (see Figure 10-11).
4. Click **OK**.

Using NetWare Administrator, you can also restrict the space a directory uses (which you can also do using Filer), change the ownership of a directory or file, or manage whether inactive data is automatically migrated to an optical disk storage device. Working with the NetWare Administrator utility and other utilities designed to help you manage the network and file system is a good way to learn about some of these and other tasks you can perform with NetWare.

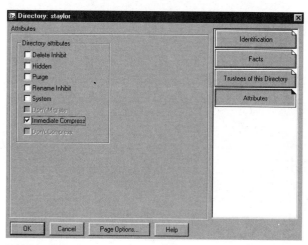

FIGURE 10-11 Example of how to set compression on a directory or file.

Manage the File System Using Windows

You are probably already familiar with using Windows to manage the file system on your computer's hard drive. You can also manage the file system on a NetWare file server using Windows. Using Network Neighborhood, you can map drives to point anywhere within the network file system for which you have rights.

To map a network drive using Windows, complete the following steps:

1. Right click **Network Neighborhood**.
2. Click **Novell Map Network Drive**. The Map Drive dialog opens (see Figure 10-12).
3. Provide the needed information, which includes the drive letter you want to assign (the next available one is supplied by default) and the path to the directory for which you want to map this drive. If needed, you can browse for the directory path by clicking the **Browse** button, or see a list of paths you have mapped in the past by clicking the **down arrow** next to the Path field.
4. If desired, click the available check boxes to identify this as a drive to be mapped as if it were pointing to the root of the directory (Map Root), as a drive to be reconnected automatically each time you log in, or as a search instead of a network drive. You can click all three if you choose.
5. Click **Map**.

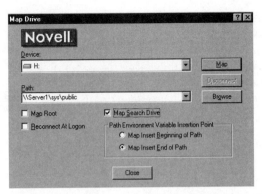

FIGURE 10-12 The Map Drive dialog which opens when you right-click **Network Neighborhood** and choose **Novell Map Network Drive.**

Distributing the Workload with Role-based Administration

There are two basic ways by which you can distribute the workload associated with administering your network:

- by allowing the object and property rights of a container to be inherited
- by creating an Organizational Role object, assigning users to it, and granting the Organizational Role object specific rights

Allow a Container's Object and Property Rights to Be Inherited

As indicated earlier in this chapter, you can take advantage of the NetWare Administrator feature which lets you choose whether to allow object and property rights of a container object to be inherited. By taking advantage of this feature, you can make one or more users responsible for managing individual properties. For example, you can make specific users responsible for administering login security, passwords, or any other specific properties you want them to be responsible for. By applying these rights to a container, they flow down the Directory tree to all levels below the container, thus giving the users in those containers the right and responsibility to administer those specific properties.

To establish this type of distributed administration, set specific NDS properties by completing the following steps:

1. In NetWare Administrator, click a User, Group, Organizational Role, Alias, or container object to be the administrator for one or more specific properties, and drag that object onto the highest-level container to which you want to assign the objects the responsibility for role-based administration.
2. Open the property page for this container, then click **Selected properties**.
3. Scroll through the list of selected properties until you find the one you want to grant. For example, if you want to grant rights for the container login script to this role-based administrator, scroll to the Login script property.
4. Click the **Inheritable** check box.
5. Click **OK**. The rights will now flow down the tree.

The role-based administrator receives the specific rights you granted from the container at which you granted the rights. They flow down through the Directory tree structure so that the role-based administrator has the same rights to lower levels of the Directory tree. While all users have the basic rights they need to view the Directory tree, assigning specific rights to the role-based administrator lets that user manage the tree.

For example, assume you want to give the Supervisor property right for all properties to one of your network users. You could grant that right by following the previous procedure. Then the role-based administrator would have the Supervisor property right for all properties of all of the objects in the Directory tree from the container at which you granted them. Now this user would be able to perform management tasks in that section of the Directory tree, such as changing a user's full name on the Identification page of a User's object.

Create and Implement Organizational Role Objects

To create an Organizational Role object:

1. Right click the container into which you want to create the Organizational Role object.
2. Click **Create**.
3. Click **Organizational Role**, then click **OK**. The Create Organizational Role dialog opens.
4. Type a name for the Organizational Role object into the Organizational Role Name field.
5. Click **Define Additional Properties**, then click **Create**. The Organizational Role Identification page opens.

6. Click the **Security Equal to Me** page button to open the associated page.

7. Click **Add**. The Select Object dialog opens.

8. Expand the directory tree view in the Browse Context area of the Select Object dialog until you find the object (such as a User object) you want to assign to this Organizational Role object (see Figure 10-13), then click that object.

9. Click **OK**. The object is added to the Security Equal to Me list, and thus to this Organizational Role object.

Now, you must make the Organizational Role object a trustee of other objects in the Directory, give that object specific rights, then the objects assigned to the Organizational Role will have those same rights. To accomplish that task, complete the following steps:

1. Assuming you just completed the steps in the previous procedure and that the Organizational Role object's details pages are still open, click the **Rights to Files and Directories** page tab for this Organizational Role object.

2. Click **Show** to locate the NetWare server on which the volume containing the files or directories to which you want to assign the Organizational Role object as a trustee is located.

3. Browse the tree until you find the file server in the Available Objects list, then click the server, and click **OK**.

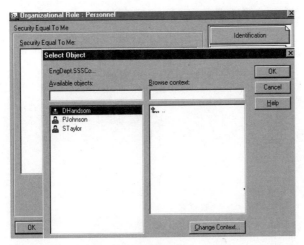

FIGURE 10-13 Select Object dialog from which you choose an object, such as User object DHandsom, to assign to this Organizational Role object.

4. With the file server's name and context displayed in the Volumes area on the Organizational Role object's Rights to Files and Directories page (see Figure 10-14), click **Add**. The Select Object dialog opens.

5. Locate the volume on the Browse context side of this dialog (the right side), then double-click it to expand it. The root of the volume, including the directories and files it contains, is displayed (see Figure 10-15).

6. On the Browse context side of the Select Object dialog, expand directories until you locate the directory or specific files you want to assign to this Organizational Role object. For example, you could expand Public, then expand Applications, so that you could assign this Organizational Role object as a trustee of the Human_ Resources sub-directory in the Server1_sys\public\Applications path (see Figure 10-16).

7. Modify the Organizational Role object's rights to this directory or file as needed. By default, Read and File Scan rights are granted. To modify any right, click the associated check box. A check mark in the box indicates the object has that right. No check mark indicates the object does not have that right.

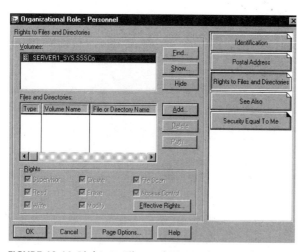

FIGURE 10-14 Rights to Files and Directories page for the Personnel
Organizational Role object. The server and volume object
(SERVER1_SYS) is listed in the Volumes area..

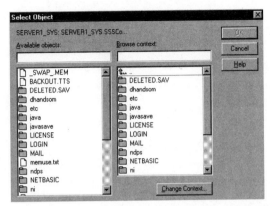

FIGURE 10-15 View of the SYS volume file system directory from root.

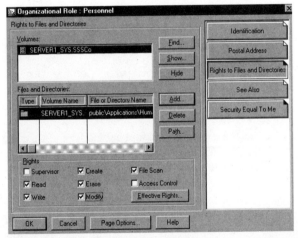

FIGURE 10-16 The Rights to Files and Directories dialog displaying the rights which this Organizational Role object has to the following directory: Server1_Sys\public\Applications\Human_Resources

In Figure 10-16 shown above, all rights except Access Control and Supervisor have been given to the Personnel Organizational Role object for the Human_Resources directory.

NOTE

8. Click OK.

You have now created an Organizational Role object, assigned that Organizational Role object as a trustee of a specific directory on the file server, granted the Organizational role object specific rights to that directory, and assigned one or more objects (user objects in this case) to the Organizational Role object. You have effectively assigned a user as administrator over that portion of the file system, and thus created a role-based administrative assignment.

Chapter Summary

This chapter described additional basic tasks you can perform using NetWare Administrator, including:

- Tasks associated with maintaining the network's file system
- Tasks associated with establishing role-based administration to help distribute some of the administrator's workload

You can also modify the presentation of NetWare Administrator by changing the appearance of the toolbar and the status bar, as well as by changing the order in which objects are displayed in the Directory tree, and how each object's property pages are displayed. To change the appearance of the toolbar and status bar, you specify whether to show, hide, or select items to be included. To show or hide either the toolbar or status bar, open the View menu from the menu bar, then click either **Show Toolbar** or **Show Status Bar**.

Using the View menu, you can also specify whether Hints or Quick Tips are displayed. To do so, click on either option to change its status (active if a checkmark appears next to it, inactive if there is no checkmark).

You can also change the order in which objects are displayed in the Directory tree. To do so, activate the window whose object view you want to change, click **View** on the menu bar, then click **Sort and Include**. You can either drag and drop an object class to move it, then choose **OK**, or use the **up** or **down arrow** button to move the class inside the list.

You can use NetWare Administrator to change your current context. Use the View menu, then click **Go Up a Level** or **Set Context**, depending on what you want to do. If you choose to set your context, the Select Object dialog opens, where you can browse through the tree to choose the context to which you want to set your workstation.

Maintaining the network's file system requires that you manage the network's directories, files, and volume space. You can do this using both Windows-based and DOS-based utilities that ship with NetWare 5, as well as utilities that ship with Windows, because Windows and NetWare

5 are integrated at the workstation, including the administrator's workstation. You can use NetWare Administrator, a Windows-based utility; Windows-specific utilities such as Network Neighborhood; or DOS-based utilities such as Rendir, Ndir, Ncopy, Flag, and Filer.

You can view file and directory information using Filer, as well as perform various tasks using associated function keys such as **F3** to modify or **F5** to mark files and directories. You can use Filer to expand and collapse the view of files and directories within a directory. Choosing the double dots (..) takes you to the parent directory of the current directory, and choosing the back slash (\) takes you to the root of the file system.

You can use Rendir to rename a directory. You can use Ndir to view information about files, directories, and volumes. You can use Ncopy to copy files or directories from one location to another. And you can use Flag to view or modify file and directory attributes, specify the search mode followed to locate executable files, or to change the owner of a file or directory. Of these six utilities, however, NetWare Administrator is the one you will use most often.

Using NetWare Administrator, you can:

- view directory information such as the directory's name, any name spaces installed, the date it was created, the owner, and the directory's effective rights.
- view file information such as the file's name, size, creation date, and the date and time it was last modified or accessed, as well as the file's access rights, attributes, long name, and other details.
- manage the network file system by performing tasks such as limiting the amount of space any given user or directory can have in the file system, view volume information to track the volume's usage and other relevant information, set compression on files and directories, and perform other management tasks both with NetWare utilities, and Windows utilities.

You can also use NetWare Administrator to set up role-based administration. To set up role-based administration, you can allow object and property rights of a container to be inherited. You can also create one or more Organizational Role objects, assign users to those objects, and then make the Organizational Role objects trustees of portions of the tree or of the file system, and give them the needed rights as well as the responsibility to administer what has been assigned to them.

Practice Test Questions

1. Of the following, which cannot be changed in NetWare Administrator?
   A. Toolbar
   B. Status bar
   C. Order of buttons
   D. Order in which objects are displayed in the file system
   E. How each object's property pages are displayed

2. To modify how Hints or Quick Tips are displayed, use which menu option?
   A. File
   B. Edit
   C. View
   D. Window

3. To modify how objects are displayed in the Directory tree, you can:
   A. Filter the tree view
   B. Filter the property page view
   C. Filter the information on the status bar
   D. Both A and B
   E. Both A and C

4. Which of the following statements is *not* true?
   A. You can change the order in which objects are displayed in the Directory tree using drag-and-drop in the Sort and Include by Object Class page.
   B. All object classes are displayed in the Directory tree, and you cannot prevent that.
   C. To see changes you have made to the order of object classes, you must collapse and then expand the Directory tree view.
   D. To view or change information about an object, you must open the object's details.

5. To change the current context to that of a lower level in the Directory tree:
   A. Expand the container object at that level.
   B. Click [**Root**] in the Set Context dialog.
   C. Use **View** > [**Root**] from the menu bar.
   D. None of the above.

6. Which two are NetWare 5 enhancements to NetWare Administrator?
   A. Copy or move trustee assignments when you copy or move directories or files
   B. Choose whether to allow object and property rights of a container object to be inherited
   C. Use drag-and-drop to change the order in which object classes display in NetWare Administrator
   D. Change the current context to [Root].

7. Which command-line utility would you use to rename a directory?
   A. Rendir
   B. Ndir
   C. Ncopy
   D. Flag
   E. Filer

8. Which command-line utility would you use to copy files from one location to another?
   A. Rendir
   B. Ndir
   C. Ncopy
   D. Flag
   E. Filer

9. If you want to change the attributes of a file, you can use which command-line utility?
   A. Rendir
   B. Ndir
   C. Ncopy
   D. Flag
   E. Filer

10. To simultaneously move multiple files using Filer, you must first mark them all using which function key?
   A. F1
   B. F3
   C. F5
   D. F7

11. By opening which button on the details for a directory can you limit the amount of space it uses?
   A. Fact
   B. View
   C. Modify
   D. Limit

12. Of the following, which property page is not generally associated with a Volume object?
   A. Identification
   B. Statistics
   C. Fact
   D. Attributes
   E. See also

13. The two compression options you can set are:
   A. Immediately compress
   B. Suspend compression
   C. Uncompress
   D. Don't compress
   E. Never compress

14. You use which option in Network Neighborhood to map a drive?
   A. Novell map network drive
   B. Map network drive
   C. Map Novell search drive
   D. Novell map search drive

15. To establish role-based administration, you can (choose two).
   A. Create an Admin object in each container, and associate a specific User object with each Admin object.
   B. Create and assign users to an Organizational Role object.
   C. Apply an Inherited Rights Mask to eliminate the Supervisor object right.
   D. Allow object and property rights of a container to be inherited.

Answers to Practice Test Questions

1. D	6. A,B	11. A
2. C	7. A	12. C
3. D	8. C	13. A,D
4. B	9. D	14. A
5. A	10. C	15. B,D

INDEX

access control list (ACL), 86, **86,** 102
Access control rights, 89
account restrictions, 97–99, **98**
addressing, 55
Admin User object, 52, 55
Alias object, 34, 40, 41, 64–66, **66,** 68
AOT file for Application objects, 164, 169, 174
application access, 14, 17
Application Launcher, 17, 136, 149, 155–178
  access rights for applications, 170, 175
  AOT file for Application objects, 164, 169, 174
  Application object creation, 163–166, **165**
  assigning rights to Application objects, 168–169, **169**
  associating objects with Application objects, 166–169, **167, 168,** 174
  benefits to user, 158, 174
  distributing Application Launcher, 171–173
  distributing network applications, 169–173, 175
  how it works, 156–158
  implementing Application Launcher, 157, 173
  installing applications with, 157
  login process/scripts use, 172–173
  managing/administering applications with, 157
  push-and-pull software distribution, 157
  setting up Application Launcher, 158–159, **160–163**
  Snapshot.exe to configure, 158–163, **160–163,** 173
  specifying where Application icon displays, 170–171, **171**
  updating applications with, 157
  workstation use, 171–172
application layer, 9
Application object, 34, 41, 64–66
  AOT file for Application objects, 164, 169, 174
  assigning rights to Application objects, 19, 22, 168–169, **169**
  associating other objects with, 166–169, **167, 168,** 174
  creation, within Application Launcher, 163–166, **165**
  specifying where Application icon displays, 170–171, **171**
applications access, 19, 22
attributes of directories and subdirectories, 89–91
auditing services, 20
authentication, 99, 141

Automatic Client Upgrade (ACU), 149, 136

backing up networks, 13, 17–18, 20
Backup/Restore NLMs, 50, 72
bindery gateways, 57
binding protocols, 54
block suballocation in custom volumes, 58
browsing & exploring the network, 147–149, 151
  Internet Explorer, 147, 151
  Java and browsers, 149
  Netscape Navigator, 147, 148, 151
  NetWare Directory Service (NDS), 147, 151
  Network Neighborhood, 147, 148, 151
  TCP/IP protocol support, 148–149
  Windows Explorer, 148

Capture utility, printing, 127
catalog services, 20
CD-ROM installation, 52, 53–56, 72
clients (see also Novell Client), 2, 5–11, 21, 22, 135–137, **137,** 149
coaxial cable connections, 5, 21
common (relative) distinguished name, 63
Common Name, 63
communications between client/server, 8–11, **11,** 22
compatibility mode, 20, 57
compression, file compression options, 58, 235, **236**
connections for network, 5, 21
console for file servers, 46–47
ConsoleOne, 18–19
Container login scripts, 142–144, **144,** 150
container objects, 30, 31, 33–34, 36, 40, 52, 60
  accessing resources, 64, 71–72
  Policy Package objects, 183
  role-based administration, 237–242
CONTEXT command, 61–63
contextless login, 20
Control Panel, customization using Policy Packages, 193–194, **194**
Country object, 33–34, 40, 166–167, 174
Create rights, 89
cryptography/keys, 19–20
current context, 39
  accessing resources, 64, 71–72
  common (relative) distinguished name, 63
  CONTEXT command, 61–63
  distinguised name, 62–63, 73
  naming conventions, 62–63, 73
  shared resources, 60–63, 73
  viewing directory tree, 227–229

Custom Hallway, 52
custom installation, 52, 53, 56–58, 72
CX utility in NetWare Administrator, 39

data migration options, 58
Default login scripts, 142–143, 150
default rights, 91
designing networks, 12, 45, 51–52
desktop/Control Panel customization,
    193–194, **194**
digital persona of Z.E.N.works, 182
directories (see also file management;
    NetWare directory service)
    attributes of directories and subdirectories,
        89–91
    file management system, 102, 83
    limiting directory space, 232
    limiting file storage space access, 232–233
Directory Map object, 34, 41, 68
directory tree (see NetWare Directory
    Service (NDS))
Disk Driver NLMs, 48, 49, 50, 72
distinguished names, 62–63, 73
distributed administration (see role-based
    administration), 237
documenting network, 13–14
domain name service (DNS), 18, 57
DOS partitioning, 52
drivers for printers, 110
dynamic host configuration protocol
    (DHCP), 18

effective rights, 84, 88–89, 91–93, 102
Erase rights, 89
Event Notification Service (ENS), printing, 115
exploring the network (see browsing &
    exploring the network)

file compression, 58, 235, **236**
file management, 3, 14, 15–16, 22
    Access control rights, 89
    attributes of directories and subdirectories,
        89–91
    components of file system, 83–84, **83**
    Create rights, 89
    default rights, 91
    directories, 102
    effective rights, 88–89, 91–93
    Erase rights, 89
    file compression, 58, 235, **236**
    File scan rights, 89
    Filer utility, 229, 230–231, **231**
    files, 83, 102
    Flag utility, 229, 230
    flow of rights, 88, **92**
    Hidden files, 89
    inheritance of rights, 92
    inherited rights filter (IRF), 88, 92
    inherited rights mask (IRM), 88, 103, 88
    limiting directory space, 232
    limiting file storage space access, 232–233
    Modify rights, 89
    Ncopy utility, 229, 230

Ndir utility, 229, 230
NetWare Administrator, 229–236
Network Neighborhood to manage files,
    236, **237**
Read rights, 89
Rendir utility, 229, 230
rights, 88–93, 92
root of file system, 82
security, 16, 81, 82–84, 101
servers, 83
spanning volumes, 84
subdirectories, 83, 102
Supervisor rights, 89
trusts/trustees, Volume object, 234, **235**
viewing file information, NetWare
    Administrator, 231
volume information, view and change,
    233–234, **233**
volumes, 83, 102
Windows to manage files, 236, **237**
Write rights, 89
File scan rights, 89
Filer utility, 229, 230–231, **231**
files (see file management)
filter how objects are displayed, 225–226, **226**
Flag utility, 229, 230
flow of rights, 88, **92**
full distinguished name, 63

Gateways, printing, 111, 114–115, 121–123, 128
global vs. network objects, 67–68
graphical user interface (GUI), 6–7, **7**, 20
Group object & groups, 35, 38, 41, 166–167,
    174
    rights assignment, 65
    trusts/trustees, 85–86, 93

hardware requirements (see also system
    requirements), 4–5, **5**, 21, 50–51
help desks
    Help Requester, 187–188, 201, 214–218
    policies, enable and configure, 215–217, **216**
    Remote Control, 180, 186–188, 208–214
Help Requester, 187–188, 201, 214–218
    distributing to workstations, 217
    help desk policy, enable and configure,
        215–217, **216**
    loading into workstation, 214–215
    minimum requirements, 215
    rights necessary to run, 215
    using, 217–218
Hidden files, 89
hierarchical order of directory elements (see
    directory tree)

I_2O support, 20
icons to represent objects in NDS, 34
inheritance of rights, 84, 92, 102, 229
    role-based administration, 237–242
inherited rights filter (IRF), 85, 88, 92, 102
inherited rights mask (IRM), 88, 103
installing & setting NetWare 5 networks, 45–79
    accessing resources, 64, 71–72

addressing, 55
Admin User object, 52, 55
Alias object, 64–66, **66,** 68
Application object, 64–66
bindery gateways, 57
binding protocols, 54
block suballocation in custom volumes, 58
CD-ROM installation, 52, 53–56, 72
common (relative) distinguished name, 63
Compatibility mode, 57
console for file servers, 46–47
container objects, 52
current context of directory tree, shared
   resource, 60–63, 73
Custom Hallway, 52, 11
custom installation, 52, 53, 56–58, 72
data migration options, 58
Directory Map object, 68
directory tree structures, 52, 55, 59, 66–68,
   73
Disk Driver NLMs, 48, 49
distinguished names, 62–63, 73
domain name service (DNS), 57
DOS partitioning, 52, 11
file compression options, 58
full distinguished name, 63
global vs. network objects, 67–68
hardware requirements, 50–51
Internet Protocol (IP), 52
IP addresses, 55
IPX, 52
Java Virtual Machine (JVM), 53
LAN driver NLMs, 48
licensing NetWare 5, 51, 55, 137, 150
memory, 49
modular design of NetWare 5, 49–50, 72
name contexts, 60–63, 73
name space NLMs, 48
naming conventions, 52, 55, 57, 62–63
NetWare Directory Service (NDS), 52, 55,
   57, 66–68, 59–60, 73
NetWare loadable modules (NLMs),
   47–49, 72
network board/network interface card, 51
network installation, 52
network operating systems (NOS), 47, 49,
   72
new installation, 51
Novell Client installation, 135–137, **137,** 149
operating systems, 56
partitioning, 53, 56, 57
passwords, 52, 55
Preferred server, 60
prerequisites to installation, 50–52
printing, 68
properties, 56, 60
protocols, 52, 54, 57
resources, 46, 58–68, 73
rights assignment, 67
router addresses, 55
Secondary Servers, 57
security, 67–68
servers, 46, 52, 54, 57

services, 52, 56
settings, 51
sharing resources, 46, 60
shortcuts to resources, 64–66
simple network management protocol
   (SNMP), 57
Single Reference, 57
software compatibility, 49–50
software requirements, 50–51
subnet masks, 55
system requirements, 50–51
Time Servers, 57
time zones, 52, 55, 57
trusts/trustees, 68
typeful and typeless distinguished names,
   62–63, 73
upgrade installation, 51
User Accounts, 68–71, 73
User objects, 60, 68–71, 73
Utilities NLMs, 48–49
volumes, 56–57
Z.E.N.works snap-in installation, 180
Internet access, 4, 19
Internet Explorer, browsing & exploring the
   network, 147, 151
Internet Protocol (IP), 4, 8, 18, 22, 52
intruder detection, 99–100
IP addresses, 55
IPX protocol, 4, 8, 18, 20, 22, 52, 149

Java, 4, 18, 149
Java Virtual Machine (JVM), 18, 53
Jet Direct boxes, 5, 17

kernel, 3, 18, 19
keys, public and private, 19–20

LAN driver NLM, 48, 50, 72
layers of network, 9, **10**
leaf objects, 30, 31, 34–36, 41
letter assignment for network drives,
   146–147
licensing NetWare 5, 51, 55, 137–140,
   138–141, 150
lightweight directory access protocol
   (LDAP), 20
limiting file storage space access, 232–233
logical printer (Printer Agent), 113–114
logical resources, 32
login process/scripts, 16, 20, 141–147, **142,** 150
   Application Launcher, 172–173
   authentication, 141
   commands for login scripts, 147
   Container login scripts, 142–143, 150,
      143–144, **144**
   creating login scripts, 143–147, 151
   current context setting, CONTEXT com-
      mand, 61–63
   Default login scripts, 142–143, 150
   MAP command, 145–146, 151
   modifying login scripts, 143–147, 151
   NetWare Directory Service (NDS) and,
      141, 150

Profile login scripts, 142–143, 145, 150
sample login scripts (template), 144–145
search drives vs. network drives, 146
User login scripts, 142–143, 145, 150
login security, 96–100
account restrictions, 97–99, **98**
authentication, 99
intruder detection, 99–100
login window, 6, **7**

managing networks, 12–13
MAP command, login process/scripts,
145–146, 151
mapping objects in NDS, 34, 41, 65
mapping to resources, static vs. dynamic, 32
memory, 19, 49
migration NLMs, 50, 72
migration, data migration options, 58
modems, 5, 21
Modify rights, 89
modular design of NetWare 5, 49–50, 72
Msbatch, 149, 136
multiprocessor support, 19

name contexts, 60–63, 73, 245
name space NLMs, 47, 48
naming conventions, 30, 32, 52, 55, 57, 62–63
common (relative) distinguished name, 63
distinguished names, 62–63
full distinguished name, 63
name contexts, 60–63, 73
typeful and typeless distinguished names,
62–63, 73
User Accounts, 68–71, 73
Ncopy utility, 229, 230
Ndir utility, 229, 230
NDPS Broker, 111, 115–116, **116,** 128
NDPS Manager, 111, 112–113, 118–119, **118,**
119, 128
Netscape FastTrack Server, 20
Netscape Navigator, browsing & exploring
the network, 147, 148, 151
NetWare Administrator (see also Zero Effort
Networking), 37–40, 41, **39,** 223–246
configuration, 223–227
current context to view directory tree,
227–229
distributing workload with role-based
administration, 237–242
enhancements, 229
file compression, 235, **236**
file management, 229–236
file system information, viewing, 231
Filer utility, 229, 230–231, **231**
filter how objects are displayed, 225–226,
226
Flag utility, 229, 230
limiting directory space, 232
limiting file storage space access, 232–233
Ncopy utility, 229, 230
Ndir utility, 229, 230
Network Neighborhood to manage files,
236, **237**

Policy Package objects, 180
public access printers, **111**
Rendir utility, 229, 230
role-based administration, 237–242
status bar appearance, 224–225, **225**
toolbar appearance, 224–225, **225**
trusts/trustee assignment, 229
trusts/trustees, Volume object, 234, **235**
User Agent applications, 209–210
User object creation, 69–70, **70**
view/change object information, 226–227
viewing directory tree, 227–229
volume information, view and change,
233–234, **233**
Windows for file management, 236, **237**
NetWare Directory Service (NDS), 3, 4, 14,
15, 16, 18, 22, 29–43, 52, 55, 57
access control list (ACL), 86, **86,** 102
accessing resources, 64, 71–72
Alias object, 34, 40, 41, 64–66, **66,** 68
AOT file for Application objects, 164, 169,
174
Application object, 34, 41, 64–66, 163–166,
165
associating objects with Application
objects, 166–169, **167, 168,** 174
associating objects with Policy Packages,
192, **193**
browsing & exploring the network, 147, 151
common (relative) distinguished name, 63
container objects, 30, 31, 33–34, 36, 40, 60
Country object, 33–34, 40, 166–167, 174
current context of directory tree, 39
current context of directory tree, shared
resources, 60–63, 73
CX utility in NetWare Administrator, 39
default rights, 91
design of directory tree structure, 36,
59–60, 66–68, 73
Directory Map object, 34, 41, 65, 68
directory tree, 29–30, **31,** 40, 59, 66–68, 73
distinguished names, 62–63, 73
effective rights, 84, 88–89, 91–93, 102
filter how objects are displayed, 225–226, **226**
flow of rights, 88, **92**
full distinguished name, 63
global vs. network objects, 67–68
Group object, 35, 38, 41, 65, 166–167, 174
hierarchical order of directory elements,
29, 30–31, 40
icons to represent objects in NDS, 34
inheritance of rights, 84, 92, 102, 229
inherited rights filter (IRF), 85, 88, 92, 102
inherited rights mask (IRM), 88, 103
leaf objects, 30, 31, 34–36, 41
License objects (see also licensing
NetWare 5), 137–140, 150
logical resources, 32
login process/scripts, 150, 141
managing NDS, 37–39
mapping objects, 34, 41
mapping to resources, static vs. dynamic, 32
moving through the directory tree, 39

name contexts, 60–63, 73
naming conventions, 30, 32
NDPS Manager creation, 112–113
NetWare Administrator, 37–40, **39,** 41,
    69–70, **70**
NetWare Server object, 35, 41
object names, NDS, 32
object rights, 86–88, 102
object trustees, 85–86
objects in NDS, 30–36, 40, 85, 102
Organization object, 33–34, 40, 166–167, 174
Organizational Role object, 34, 35, 41,
    238–242, **239–241**
Organizational Unit object, 33–34, 40,
    166–167, 174
partitioning of directory, 30, 40
physical resources, 32
Policy objects, 180, 181
Policy Package objects, 180, 181, 182, 183,
    185–186, 188–191, 202
Preferred server, 60
Print Queue object, 35, 41
Print Server (non–NDPS) object, 35, 41
Printer (non–NDPS), 35
Printer object, 41, 110–111
Profile object, 35, 41
properties, 37, **38,** 41, 60, 85, 102
property rights, 85, 88, 102
registering with Z.E.N.works, 204–207, **205**
replication of directory, 30, 40
resource design/organization, 31, 32, 66–68
rights, 38, 65
rights, 38, 65, 67, 84, 85–93, 102
role-based administration, 237–242
root object, 30, 31, 33, 36, 38, 40, 60
security, 67–68, 81, 82, 84–85, 93–95, **94,** 101
sharing resources, 60
shortcuts to resources, 64–66
single vs. multiple directory trees, 30
structure of directory, 30
Supervisor object, 85
trusts/trustees, 68, 84, 85, 93, 102
trusts/trustees, copy/move, 229
typeful and typeless distinguished names,
    62–63, 73
UIMPORT utility to create User objects,
    69, 70–71
User Accounts, 68–71, 73
User object, 35, 38, 41, 60, 68–71,
    166–167, 174
values, 37, **38,** 41
view/change object information, 226–227
viewing directory tree, 38, 227–229
viewing information associated with
    workstations, 207–208
Volume object, 35, 41, 84
Workstation Import Policy, 203–204, **203**
Workstation Inventory, 207–208
Workstation object, 35, 41, 180
workstations, making NDS aware of net-
    work workstations, 202–208
Zero Effort Networking (Z.E.N.works),
    182, 183–184, 202–208

NetWare loadable modules (NLMs), 20,
    47–49, 72
    Backup/Restore NLMs, 50, 72
    Disk Driver NLMs, 48, 49, 50, 72
    LAN driver NLM, 48, 50, 72
    migration NLMs, 50, 72
    name space NLMs, 47, 48
    Print Device Subsystem (PDS), 114
    Printing NLMs, 50, 72
    Server Monitoring NLMs, 50, 72
    storage management services (SMS), 50
    UPS services NLMs, 50, 72
    Utilities NLMs, 48–49
NetWare Server object, 35, 41
NetWare/network basics, 1–27
    application access, 14, 17, 19, 22
    Application Launcher, 17
    application layer, 9
    auditing services, 20
    backing up networks, 17–18, 20
    catalog services, 20
    clients, 2, 5–8, 21, 22
    coaxial cable connections, 5, 21
    communications between client/server,
        8–11, **11,** 22
    compatibility mode, 20
    connections for network, 5, 10, 21
    console for file servers, 46–47
    ConsoleOne, 18–19
    contextless login, 20
    cryptography/keys, 19–20
    current context of directory tree, shared
        resource, 60–63, 73
    distinguished names, 62–63, 73
    domain name system (DNS), 18
    dynamic host configuration protocol
        (DHCP), 18
    file management, 3, 14, 15–16, 22
    graphical user interface (GUI), 6–7, **7,** 20
    hardware components, 4–5, **5,** 21,
        50–51
    I$_2$O support, 20
    Internet access, 4, 19
    Internet Protocol (IP), 4, 8, 18, 22
    IPX protocol, 4, 8, 18, 20, 22, 149
    Java, 4, 18
    Java Virtual Machine (JVM), 18, 53
    Jet Direct boxes, 5, 17
    kernel, 3, 18, 19
    layers of network, 9, **10**
    licensing NetWare 5, 51
    lightweight directory access protocol
        (LDAP), 20
    login process/scriptss, 16, 20
    login window, 6, **7**
    memory, 19, 49
    modems, 5, 21
    modular design of NetWare 5, 49–50, 72
    multiprocessor support, 19
    naming conventions, 60–63, 73, 245
    Netscape FastTrack Server, 20
    NetWare Directory Service (NDS) (see
        NetWare Directory Service (NDS))

NetWare loadable modules (NLMs), 20,
47–49, 72
network administrator's
responsibilities/tasks, 12–14, **15,** 22
network boards/network interface cards
(NIC), 4–5, 21, 22
network operating systems (NOS), 2, 3, 6,
9, 19, 21, 47, 49, 72
"network"defined, 2
new and improved NetWare 5 features,
18–21
Novell Client, 6–7, 9, 10, 22
Novell distributed print services (NDPS),
4, 14, 17, 19
Novell storage services (NSS), 19
open system architecture (OSA), 2–3, 18
operating systems, 2–3, 4, 6, 7–8, 9, 18, 21,
22, 135–136
Oracle8 support, 20
peripherals, 2, 21
Preferred server, 60
printing, 4, 5, 14, 17, 19, 21, 22
properties, 60
protocols, 4, 8, 22
resources, 3, 14–18, 22, 46, 58–68, 73
restoring data, 17–18
search drives vs. network drives, 146
secure authentication services (SAS), 19
security, 4, 15, 16, 17–20, 22
servers, 2, 5–8, 18, 19, 21, 22, 46, 54
service location protocol (SLP), 19
services, network, 2, 3–4, 9, 14–18, 22
sharing resources, 46, 60
software components, 2, 6–11, 22, 49–51
Software Developer's Kit (SDK), 18–19
SPX protocol, 4, 20
storage management services (SMS), 4,
15, 17–18, 19, 22, 50
system requirements, 50–51
TCP/IP, 4, 8, 20, 22, 148–149
twisted-pair cable connections, 5, 21
WAN Traffic Manager NLM, 20
workstations, 2, 7–8, 22
X-Windows, 18
Zero Effort Networks (Z.E.N.works), 17,
20, 136, 149
network administrator's
responsibilities/tasks, 12–14, **15,** 22
network boards/network interface cards
(NIC), 4–5, 21, 22, 51
network drives
letter assignment, 146–147
search drives, 146
network interface cards (NIC) (see network
boards)
Network Neighborhood
browsing & exploring the network, 147,
148, 151
file management, 236, **237**
network operating systems (NOS), 2, 3, 6, 9,
19, 21, 47, 49, 72
"network" defined, 2
new and improved NetWare 5 features, 18–21

new installation, 51
non–NDPS printing, 110, 114–115
Novell Application Launcher (NAL)(see
Application Launcher)
Novell Client, 6–7, 9, 22
Automatic Client Upgrade (ACU), 136,
149
installation, 135–137, **137,** 149
Msbatch, 136, 149
TCP/IP support, 148–149
Zero Effort Network (Z.E.N.work)
Application Launcher, 136, 149
Novell distributed print services (NDPS) (see
also printing), 4, 14, 17, 19, 109–111, **112**
Novell Login (see login process/scripts)
Novell storage services (NSS), 19
Novell Workstation Manager, 180
Nprinter utility, printing, 127

object names, NDS, 32
objects in NDS, 30–31, 32–36, 40
access control list (ACL), 86, **86,** 102
associating objects with Policy Packages,
192, **193**
filter how objects are displayed, 225–226, **226**
global vs. network objects, 67–68
licensing, 139, **140**
object rights, 86–88, 102
object trustees, 85–86
printing, 117
role-based administration, 237–242
shortcuts to resources, 64–66
view/change object information, 226–227
open system architecture (OSA), 2–3, 18
operating systems, 2–3, 4, 6, 7–9, 10, 18, 21,
22, 56, 135–136
Oracle8 support, 20
Organization distinguished name, 63
Organization object, 33–34, 40, 166–167, 174
Organizational Role object, 34, 35, 41,
238–242, **239–241**
Organizational Unit distinguished name, 63
Organizational Unit object, 33–34, 40,
166–167, 174

partitioning directory, 30, 40, 53, 56, 57
passwords, 52, 55
Pconsole, printing, 127
peripherals, 2, 21
physical resources, 32
plug-and-print capability, 110
Policy objects, 180, 181, 182
Policy Package objects, 180, 181, 182, 183,
185–186, 188–191
associating objects with Policy Packages,
192, **193**
configuring policies/Policy Packages,
189–191
creating, 202
desktop/Control Panel customization,
193–194, **194**
enabling policies/Policy Packages, 189–191
printing policies, 195

Workstation Import Policy, 203–204, **203**
Port Handler, Gateway, printing, 114–115
Preferred server, 60
Print Device Subsystem (PDS), Gateway,
    printing, 114–115
Print Queue object, 35, 41
Print Server (non–NDPS) object, 35, 41
Printer (non–NDPS), 35
Printer Agent, 111, 113–114, **113,** 119–123,
    121, 128
Printer object, 41, 110–111
printing, 4, 5, 14, 17, 19, 21, 22, 35, 41,
    109–134, 127
    access for workstations, 124
    Capture utility, 127
    configuration using policies/Policy
        Packages, 186
    controlling print jobs, 124–127
    drivers for printers, 110
    Event Notification Service (ENS), 115
    Gateways, 111, 114–115, 121–123, 128
    installing printer software, 129
    loading NDPS Manager, 119, 129
    logical printer (Printer Agent), 113–114
    Managers, Operators, and Users, 125
    managing network printing, 123–127,
        129–130
    minimum requirements, 117, 128–129
    NDPS Broker, 111, 115–116, **116,** 128
    NDPS Manager, 111, 112–113, 118–119,
        118, 119, 128
    Ndpsm.nlm, 120
    non–NDPS printing, 110, 114–115
    Novell distributed print services (NDPS),
        17, 109–111, **112**
    Novell Workstation Manager, 180
    Nprinter utility, 127
    object creation, 119–123
    Pconsole, 127
    plug-and-print capability, 110
    policies, 195
    Port Handler, Gateway, 114–115
    Print Device Subsystem (PDS), Gateway,
        114–115
    Printer Agent, 111, 113–114, **113,**
        119–123, **121,** 128, 129
    printers, 127
    properties, additional, 122
    Pserver utility, 127
    public access vs. controlled access print-
        ers, 100–101, 110–111, 121–123, 128, 129
    public access vs. controlled access print-
        ers, converting, 123
    queues, 127
    Resource Management Service (RMS), 116
    rights, 117, 129
    Rprinter utility, 127
    scheduling print jobs, 110, 124–127,
        129–130
    security, 68, 100–101, 110
    servers, 127
    service advertising protocol (SAP) unnec-
        essary, 110

Service Registry Service (SRS), 115
    setting up print services, 116–123
    software installation, 117–118
    spoolers, 127
    Supervisor object, 117, 130
Printing NLMs, 50, 72, 50
Profile login scripts, 142–143, 150, 145
Profile object, 35, 41, 42
properties, 37, **38,** 41, 56
    access control list (ACL), 86, **86,** 102
    account restrictions, 97–99, **98**
    assigning properties, 60
    Preferred server, 60
    printing, 122
    property rights, 102, 88
property rights, 102, 88, 229
protecting networks, 13
protocols, 4, 8, 22, 52, 54, 57
Pserver utility, printing, 127
public access vs. controlled access printers,
    100–101, 110–111, 121–123, 128, 129
push-and-pull software distribution, 157

queues, printing, 127

Read rights, 89, 186–188, 208–214
Remote Control, 180, 201
    ending Remote Control session, 214
    minimum requirements, 209
    security, 211–212, **211**
    User Agent applications, 209–210
    workstation connection, 212–214
Rendir utility, 229, 230
replication of directory, 30, 40
Resource Management Service (RMS), print-
    ing, 116
resources, 3, 14–18, 22, 31, 32, 46, 58–68
    access control list (ACL), 86, **86,** 102
    accessing resources, 64, 71–72
    current context of directory tree, shared
        resources, 60–63, 73
    designing/organizing, 58–68, 73
    logical resources, 32
    NDS representation, 31
    physical resources, 32
    rights assignment, 65
    sharing resources, 46, 60
    shortcuts to resources, 64–66
restoring data, 17–18
rights, 38, 84, 85–93, 102
    Access control rights, 89
    assigning rights, 65, 67, 92
    assigning rights to Application objects,
        168–169, **169**
    Create rights, 89
    default rights, 91
    effective rights, 88–89, 91–93
    Erase rights, 89
    file management system rights, 88–93
    File scan rights, 89
    flow of rights, 88, **92**
    Help Requester, rights necessary to run, 215
    inheritance of rights, 92, 229

inherited rights filter (IRF), 88, 92
inherited rights mask (IRM), 88, 103, 88
inherited rights, role-based administration, 237–242
Modify rights, 89
object rights, 86–88, 102
object trustees, 85–86
Organizational Role objects, 238–242, 239–**241**
printing, 117, 129–130
property rights, 88, 102
Read rights, 89
role-based administration, 237–242
security equivalent rights, 96
Supervisor rights, 89
trusts/trustees, 85
Write rights, 89
role-based administration, 237–242
root object, 30, 31, 33, 36, 38, 40, 60
root of file system, 82
router addresses, 55
Rprinter utility, printing, 127

search drives vs. network drives, 146
Secondary Servers, 57
secure authentication services (SAS), 19
security, 4, 13, 15, 16, 17–18, 19–20, 22, 81–107
access control list (ACL), 86, **86,** 102
Access control rights, 89
account restrictions, 97–99, **98**
Alias object, 68
attributes of directories and subdirectories, 89–91
authentication, 99, 141
Create rights, 89
default rights, 91
designing for security, 67–68
Directory Map object, 68
effective rights, 84, 88–89, 91–93, 102
Erase rights, 89
file management rights, 88–93
file management security, 16, 81, 82–84, 101
File scan rights, 89
flow of rights, 88, **92**
global vs. network objects, 67–68
Hidden files, 89
implementing NDS security, 93–95, **94**
inheritance of rights, 84, 92, 102
inherited rights filter (IRF), 85, 88, 92, 102
inherited rights mask (IRM), 88, 103
intruder detection, 99–100
login security, 82, 96–100, 102
managing network security, 95–101
Modify rights, 89
NetWare Directory Service (NDS), 81, 82, 84–85, 101
object rights, 85, 86–88, 102
object trustees, 85–86
printing, 68, 82, 100, 102, 110
property rights, 85, 88, 102
Read rights, 89
Remote Control, 211–212, **211**
rights, 85–93, 92, 102

security equivalent rights, 96
server security, 82, 100, 102
Supervisor object, 85, 89
trusts/trustees, 68, 84, 85, 93, 102
Write rights, 89
security equivalent rights, 96
Server Monitoring NLMs, 50, 72, 50
servers, 2, 5, 6, 7–11, 18, 19, 21, 22, 35, 46, 52, 54, 57
console for file servers, 46–47
file management system, 83
Preferred server, 60
printing, 127
security, 100
volumes, 84
service advertising protocol (SAP) unnecessary, 110
service location protocol (SLP), 19
Service Registry Service (SRS), printing, 115
services, network, 2, 3–4, 9, 14–18, 22, 52, 56
setting up networks (see installing & setting up NetWare 5 networks)
settings, 51
shared resources, 46, 60
current context of directory tree, shared resources, 60–63, 73
shortcuts to resources, 64–66
simple network management protocol (SNMP), 57
Single Reference, 57
single vs. multiple directory trees, 30
snap-in installation, Z.E.N.works, 180
Snapshot.exe to configure Application Launcher, 158–163, **160–163,** 173
software components, 2, 6–11, 22, 49–51
Software Developer's Kit (SDK), 18–19
spanning volumes, 84
spoolers, printing, 127
SPX protocol, 4, 20
storage management services (SMS), 4, 15, 17–18, 19, 22, 50
structure of directory (see NetWare Directory Service (NDS), directory tree)
subdirectories (see directories; file management; NetWare Directory Service (NDS))
subnet masks, 55
Supervisor object, 85, 89, 117, 130
system requirements, 50–51
Help Requester, 215
printing, 117, 128–129
Remote Control, 209
Zero Effort Networking (Z.E.N.works), 182–183

TCP/IP, 4, 8, 20, 22, 148–149
Time Servers, 57
time zones, 52, 55, 57
tree, directory tree (see NetWare Directory Service (NDS))
trusts/trustees, 68, 85, 84, 93, 102
copy/move assignments, 229
object trustees, 85–86
Volume object, 234, **235**

twisted-pair cable connections, 5, 21
typeful and typeless distinguished names,
    62–63, 73

UIMPORT utility, User objects, 69, User
    objects, 70–71
upgrade installation, 51
UPS services NLMs, 50, 72
User Accounts, 68–71, 73
User Agent applications, 209–210
User login scripts, 142–143, 150, 145
User object, 35, 38, 41, 60, 68–71, 73,
    166–167, 174
    accessing resources, 64, 71–72
    account restrictions, 97–99, 98
    current context setting, 60, **61,** 73
    name contexts, 60–63, 73, 245
    NetWare Administrator to create, 69–70, **70**
    Policy Package objects, 183
    Preferred server, 60
    rights assignment, 65, 67
    trusts/trustees, 68, 93
    UIMPORT utility to create, 69, 70–71
    User Accounts, 68–71, 73
Utilities NLMs, 48–49

values, 37, **38,** 41
view/change object information, 226–227
Volume object, 35, 41, 84, 234, **235**
volumes, 35, 41, 42, 56–57
    block suballocation in custom volumes, 58
    file management system, 83, 102
    spanning volumes, 84
    trusts/trustees, 68, 234, **235**
    volume information, view and change,
        233–234, **233**

WAN Traffic Manager NLM, 20
Windows Explorer, browsing & exploring
    the network, 148
Workstation Import Policy, 203–204, **203**
Workstation Inventory, 207–208
Workstation object, 35, 41, 180
    Policy Package objects, 183
workstations, 2, 7–8, 22, 35, 41, 42
    Application Launcher, 171–172
    configuration using policies/Policy
        Packages, 186
    ending Remote Control session, 214
    Help Requester loading, 214–215
    importing for Z.E.N.works, 185, 201,
        205–207, **206**
    making NDS aware of network worksta-
        tions, 202–208
    managing using policies/Policy Packages,
        188
    Novell Workstation Manager, 180
    operating systems, 7–8, 135–136
    Policy Package objects, 202
    printer access, 124

registering with Z.E.N.works, 185, 201,
    204–207, **205**
Remote Control connection, 212–214
viewing information associated with
    workstations, 207–208
Workstation Import Policy, 203–204, **203**
Workstation Inventory, 207–208
wrapper files, Snappshot.exe, 159
Write rights, 89

X-Windows, 18

Zero Effort Networking (Z.E.N.works) (see
    also Application Launcher), 17, 20, 136, 149
    Application Launcher, 155–178
    associating objects with Policy Packages,
        192, **193**
    configuring policies/Policy Packages,
        189–191
    desktop/Control Panel customization,
        193–194, **194**
    digital persona created by, 182
    directory tree objects and, 184
    enabling policies/Policy Packages,
        189–191
    Full Pack, 181
    Help Requester, 187–188, 201, 214–218
    how it works, 182
    installing Z.E.N.works, 180
    managing network workstations using
        policies/Policy Packages, 188
    minimum requirements, 182–183
    NetWare Directory Service (NDS) and,
        182, 183–184, 202–208
    Novell Application Launcher (NAL) (see
        Application Launcher)
    Novell Workstation Manager, 180
    packages, version of Z.E.N.works, 181
    planning for Z.E.N.works and NDS use, 184
    policy actions/benefits, 185–186
    Policy objects, 180, 181, 182
    Policy Package objects, 180, 181, 182, 183,
        185–186, 188–191, 202
    printer configuration, 186, 195
    Remote Control, 180, 186–188, 201,
        208–214
    snap-in installation, 180
    Starter Pack, 181
    User Agent applications, 209–210
    viewing information associated with
        workstations, 207–208
    workstation configuration, 186
    Workstation Import Policy, 203–204, **203**
    workstation importing, 185, 201, 205–207,
        206
    Workstation Inventory, 207–208
    workstation numbers and, 184
    Workstation objects, 180
    workstation registration, 185, 201,
        204–207, **205**

ABOUT THE AUTHOR

DOROTHY CADY is fully Novell certified—CNA, CNE, MCNE, and CNI. She is the author of 12 books including *NetWare Training Guide: CNA Study Guide* (1994) and *CNE 4 Short Course* (1996). Dorothy is a Novell employee and has been working with NetWare since the development of version 2.2. She resides in Spanish Fork, Utah.